International Sports Volunteering

Sport volunteering is becoming an increasingly popular motive for international travel. Many tourism organizations now advertise sport volunteering projects, with colleges and universities also offering students the opportunity to participate in similar projects abroad. This is the first book to bring together diverse and interdisciplinary insights into the development of the contemporary sport volunteering phenomenon. It addresses conceptual uncertainties and challenges emerging from the growing international sport volunteering market, and offers insight into its future directions, impact and sustainability.

Drawing on both quantitative and qualitative methodologies, Part I examines volunteering in the context of international sporting events, while Part II evaluates volunteering initiatives related to sport development. Including case studies from Australia, Cameroon, Namibia, Norway, Russia, the UK, the US and Zambia, this substantial volume provides a truly international perspective on the changing roles of sport volunteering.

Showcasing the latest research from across the globe, *International Sports Volunteering* is a valuable resource for any course on sport studies, sport event management, sport development, sport tourism, sport geography, the sociology of sport or leisure studies.

Angela M. Benson is a Principal Lecturer at the University of Brighton, UK. She is the Founding Chair of the Volunteer Tourism Research Group on behalf of the Association for Tourism and Leisure Education (ATLAS); Adjunct Associate Professor of the University of Canberra, Australia; a Fellow of the Royal Geographical Society with IBG and a Fellow of the Higher Education Academy. Angela has recently been appointed by the International Standards Office (ISO) as the convener for the International Volunteer Tourism Standard that is currently being developed. She has published widely in the areas of volunteering, sustainability and research methods.

Nicholas Wise is a Senior Lecturer at Liverpool John Moores University, UK. His research interests traverse the subjects of sport, events and tourism, and human geography. Originally from Pennsylvania, Nicholas has been a sports volunteer in several countries, including Australia, the Dominican Republic and Scotland. He is a member of the Regional Studies Association and has served as co-secretary of the Sports Volunteering Research Network. Nicholas has published widely across several disciplines. His work has appeared in academic journals, book chapters, conference proceedings and encyclopaedias, and he recently co-edited books on sport and interdisciplinary perspectives.

Routledge Research in Sport, Culture and Society

68 **Embodying Brazil**
An Ethnography of Diasporic
Capoeira
*Sara Delamont, Neil Stephens and
Claudio Campos*

69 **Sport, Medicine and Health**
The Medicalization of Sport?
Dominic Malcolm

70 **The International Olympic
Committee, Law, and
Accountability**
Ryan Gauthier

71 **A Genealogy of Male Body
Building**
From Classical to Freaky
Dimitris Liokaftos

72 **Sport and Discrimination**
*Edited by Daniel Kilvington and
John Price*

73 **Seeking the Senses in
Physical Culture**
Sensual Scholarship in Action
Edited by Andrew C. Sparkes

74 **The Role of the Professional
Football Manager**
Seamus Kelly

75 **The Rugby World in the
Professional Era**
*Edited by John Nauright and
Tony Collins*

76 **Sport and English National
Identity in a 'Disunited
Kingdom'**
*Edited by Tom Gibbons and
Dominic Malcolm*

77 **Phenomenology and the
Extreme Sport Experience**
Eric Brymer and Robert Schweitzer

78 **Lifestyle Sports and Public
Policy**
*Edited by Daniel Turner and
Sandro Carnicelli*

79 **International Sports
Volunteering**
*Edited by Angela M. Benson and
Nicholas Wise*

80 **Football Fans, Rivalry and
Cooperation**
*Edited by Christian Brandt,
Fabian Hertel and
Sean Huddleston*

81 **The Feminization of Sports
Fandom**
A Sociological Study
Stacey Pope

International Sports Volunteering

Edited by Angela M. Benson and Nicholas Wise

Routledge
Taylor & Francis Group

LONDON AND NEW YORK

First published 2017 by Routledge

2 Park Square, Milton Park, Abingdon, Oxfordshire OX14 4RN
52 Vanderbilt Avenue, New York, NY 10017

Routledge is an imprint of the Taylor & Francis Group, an informa business

First issued in paperback 2019

British Library Cataloguing-in-Publication Data
A catalogue record for this book is available from the British Library

Library of Congress Cataloging in Publication Data
A catalog record for this book has been requested

ISBN: 978-1-138-69777-5 (hbk)
ISBN: 978-0-367-23137-8 (pbk)

Typeset in Sabon
by Wearset Ltd, Boldon, Tyne and Wear

Contents

List of figures   vii
List of tables   viii
Notes on contributors   ix

Introduction: directions and insight in international sport
volunteering research   1
ANGELA M. BENSON AND NICHOLAS WISE

PART I
International sport volunteering at sporting events   19

1   Co-creation in events: values of volunteers and volunteer
    tourists at Iditarod in Alaska and the Finnmark Race in
    Norway   21
    KARI JÆGER AND LINE MATHISEN

2   Creativity-based volunteering at the Winter Olympics in
    Sochi: beyond sport and borders   39
    VALERY GORDIN AND IRINA BOROVSKAIA

3   Living abroad and volunteering at the 2014
    Commonwealth Games in Glasgow   60
    NICHOLAS WISE

4   The transgressive potential of volunteering: issues and
    legacies at the 2014 Cleveland/Akron Gay Games   77
    NIGEL JARVIS

5 Pull factors for Perth: developing an International Golf
  Volunteer Engagement Strategy (iGoVolES) 98
  ALFRED OGLE AND DAVID LAMB

6 Indirect volunteers and application of the volunteer cube: a
  framework for international sport volunteering? 122
  BERIT SKIRSTAD AND ELSA KRISTIANSEN

PART II
International sport volunteering and sport and
development 143

7 International Development through Excellence and
  Leadership in Sport (IDEALS): the Namibia and Liverpool
  John Moores University programme 145
  TOM FLETCHER AND DANNY CULLINANE

8 International sport volunteering and social legacy: impact,
  development and health improvement in Lusaka, Zambia 165
  FIONA REID AND JENNIFER TATTERSALL

9 Learning about sport for development and peace through
  international volunteers 188
  MIKE BARTLE AND PETER CRAIG

10 The motives and social capital gains of sport for
  development and peace volunteers in Cameroon: a
  comparative analysis of international and national
  volunteers 212
  JOANNE CLARKE AND PAUL SALISBURY

11 Volunteer tourism and international sport volunteering 234
  ANGELA M. BENSON

  Concluding comments and future directions in
  international sport volunteering research 251
  NICHOLAS WISE AND ANGELA M. BENSON

  Index 255

Figures

2.1   Stage plan for 'From the Olympic spirit of friendship and
       peace' project   47
2.2   Project organization structure of IPP in Sochi 2014   50
2.3   Motives for participation in the project   53
5.1   Golf Tournament Attendee Push–Pull Factors Model   100
5.2   Golf Volunteer Engagement Strategy (GoVolES)
       framework   101
5.3   Understanding the volunteer market: the what, where,
       who and why of volunteering   108
5.4   International Golf Volunteer Engagement Strategy
       (iGoVolES) framework   115
6.1   The volunteer cube   126

Tables

I.1	UK volunteering in areas of sport from 2005 to 2016 (%)	3
I.2	Sport event typology	7
4.1	The growth of the Gay Games	83
5.1	Australia and the United States: volunteer motivations	104
5.2	Survey questions	109
5.3	Respondent demographic data	110
5.4	Respondents who love the game of golf	113
6.1	Indirect volunteer details	131
6.2	Motives on individual, sport club and community level in the nomination phase	132
6.3	Motives on individual, sport club and community level in the newcomer phase	132
6.4	Motives on individual, sport club and community level in the experienced phase	133
6.5	Motives on individual, sport club and community level in the established phase	135
8.1	IDEALS placement sites in Lusaka from 2006 to 2016	174
9.1	Research participants	193
11.1	Projects Abroad volunteer projects	238
11.2	Types of sport, country of project and volunteer stories	239

Contributors

Mike Bartle is Course Leader in Science & Sport at Dundee and Angus College. His academic praxis of informal learning within a sporting context, spiritual dimensions of challenging experiences and sustainable outdoor learning. His research interests stem from research with volunteers within contested societies, performativity within sport and the interdependence of trusting relationships and social growth.

Angela M. Benson is a Principal Lecturer at the University of Brighton, UK. She is the Founding Chair of the Volunteer Tourism Research Group on behalf of the Association for Tourism and Leisure Education (ATLAS); Adjunct Associate Professor of the University of Canberra, Australia; a Fellow of the Royal Geographical Society with IBG and a Fellow of the Higher Education Academy. Angela has recently been appointed by the International Standards Office (ISO) as the convener for the International Volunteer Tourism Standard that is currently being developed. She has published widely in the areas of volunteering, sustainability and research methods.

Irina Borovskaia is an associate professor at the National Research University Higher School of Economics and St. Petersburg State University of Economics, Russia. She has a number of publications in the areas of hospitality culture, creativity in hospitality industry, creative gastronomy and festival management.

Joanne Clarke is a third-year PhD candidate at Leeds Trinity University exploring the discourse of international sport for development NGOs operating in Cameroon, Central West Africa. A 15-year career working in sport development and coaching in the UK and New Zealand instigated her initial interest in the use of sport for development purposes. Subsequently Joanne has spent the past five years gaining experience as a practitioner and researcher in the sport-for-development sector in Sub-Saharan Africa, with particular interest to the local lived realities of volunteers from the Global North and the Global South delivering such programmes. In addition to her PhD research Joanne teaches at Leeds Trinity University in the areas of sport development, sports coaching and the sociology of sport.

Peter Craig is a principal lecturer in Sport Sociology in the School of Sport Science and Physical Activity, University of Bedfordshire. His scholarship draws extensively on critical analysis aligned to the development of applied practice relating to the role that sport practitioners play in the reproduction and transformation of everyday life. His current research interests are on: the social and cultural contradictions inherent in our current models of sport; behaviour change and the interconnections between lifestyle choices, health and well-being; the transformation of sport in respect to sustainability and a changing global climate.

Danny Cullinane is a senior lecturer and the Programme Leader for Sport Development at Liverpool John Moores University, UK. He has led the LJMU/Namibia section of the UK Sport 'International Development of Excellence and Leadership through Sport' (IDEALS) programme since its inception in 2007. His previous overseas work in this area includes co-ordinating and delivering a British Council sports volunteer programme in Jordan, and personal sports volunteering experience in Papua New Guinea. His research interests are in the development of sport development practice, in particular the processes involved in gaining expertise in the field.

Tom Fletcher is Programme Manager of Events Management and Tourism and Leisure Management programmes at Liverpool John Moores University, UK. He is also senior lecturer for the BA (Hons) and MA Events Management degree programmes. He was involved in the development of the LJMU/Namibia/UK Sport 'International Development of Excellence and Leadership through Sport' (IDEALS) programme and has led on the development of a sports volunteering programme in The Gambia. His research interests are in sports and events volunteering, graduate employability and entrepreneurship. His teaching interests mirror his research interests and he is involved in teaching modules related to human resource management, marketing and entrepreneurship on undergraduate and postgraduate events management programmes.

Valery Gordin is Professor and Head of Laboratory of Economics of Culture, National Research University Higher School of Economics, Russia. He has published material on creative tourism in large cities, personnel training for creative industries, gastronomic branding in destination promotion, informal entrepreneurship on the re-enactment of festivals and museum events in community development. He was the leading expert for a cultural heritage joint project supported by the World Bank and the Ministry of Culture, Russian Federation. He was also actively engaged in the funded project by the Ministry Council of Northern Countries regarding the creative industries in Saint Petersburg and Russian Northern West Regions of Russia.

Kari Jæger is Assistant Professor at UiT Arctic University of Norway, Department of Tourism and Northern Studies, in Alta, Norway. Prior to academia Kari worked for 15 years in the tourism and events industry. Kari has an MA in tourism from Finnmark University College. Her research is in event and tourism studies, with a focus on festivals, identity, volunteering, and the connection between tourism and events. Recent publications can be found in the *Scandinavian Journal of Hospitality and Tourism, Event Management,* and *Journal of Tourism and Cultural Change.* Kari's PhD will be submitted autumn 2016, titled: 'Tourist or resident in a rural festival meeting place: A mutually beneficial relationship'.

Nigel Jarvis completed his PhD in 2006 at the University of Brighton, which examined the meaning of sport in the lives of Canadian and British gay men. The research critically aids in understanding how the lived experiences of gay men taking part in sport relate to and inform relevant hegemonic and queer theoretical debates. Nigel undertook his MA in Leisure Management at the University of Sheffield (1996) and his BAA in Geography at Ryerson University in Toronto (1986). He has a keen interest in gender and sexuality issues in sport, leisure and tourism. He is currently working on a series of research papers related to the gay cruise sector as well as the potential legacies of the Gay Games sport movement.

Elsa Kristiansen is Associate Professor at the University College of Southeast Norway and the Norwegian School of Sport Sciences. She has published over 40 articles and book chapters, the majority of which are in the areas of sport psychology (e.g. motivation, coping with organizational issues and media stress, coping with youth competitions) and sport event management (e.g. volunteerism, Youth Olympic Games, stakeholders involved in talent development).

David Lamb is a senior lecturer and programme director at Edith Cowan University in Perth, Australia and lectures in the academic disciplines of sport, recreation and event management. His current research interest and publications span a number of academic disciplines, but are mostly concerned with event management and include: the nature and meaning of volunteering; volunteering motivation and decision making especially related to community based events; experiential learning and authentic learning in event management education; innovation in event management practice; professionalism in events sector; the theory–practice gap in event management; live sites as event venues; legacy in events and collaborative studies on unstructured play and independent forms of mobility.

Line Mathisen received her PhD in Tourism from University of Tromsø, the Arctic University in 2014, where she also completed her undergraduate studies in marketing and economics. Line has been employed by Norut (Northern Research Institute) since 2013, where she is a senior researcher currently working with projects in tourism, entrepreneurship and regional/organizational innovation. She has been involved in several tourism research programmes, e.g. Northern InSights, Winter: New Turns in Arctic Winter Tourism and VRI – a national programme for regional R&D and innovation. Her current research interests include nature and culture based tourism development and value creation, research on entrepreneurship and innovation in rural areas and service marketing and innovation.

Alfred Ogle is a researcher and academic specializing in Hospitality Management and Marketing. He has a research consultancy in Perth, Australia and is a sessional academic at Edith Cowan University and Edith Cowan College. A hotelier prior to his entry into academia, he enjoys boundary spanning applied research and hospitality industry collaboration. His current research interests include hospitality industry facilities management and environmentally friendly/sustainable design; service enterprise atmospherics; strategic marketing management; service innovation and service encounters; industry–academia symbiosis and theory–practice linkage; and curriculum design.

Fiona Reid is a lecturer in Sport and Event Management at Glasgow Caledonian University (Scotland, UK). Her research encompasses sports geography, sports development and sports events, and she is currently focusing on volunteers and the voluntary sector in sport. Fiona is the Secretary of the UK Sports Volunteering Research Network. Prior to joining academia Fiona worked for over 10 years in the sports industry. Fiona and co-author Jennifer Tattersall wrote 'Exploring some different perspectives within a sport project in Africa' in G. Reid and J. Lee (eds) (2013) *Social Justice in Sport Development* (London: Leisure Studies Association).

Paul Salisbury is a senior lecturer in Sport Management at Coventry University. He previously held management positions at Leeds Trinity University and within the sport and leisure industry. His research interests are in topics related to the politics of sport, specifically focusing on policy and mega events. His most recent research concerns national and local policy-making in host nations and cities.

Berit Skirstad is Associate Professor at the Norwegian School of Sport Sciences and responsible for the sport management study programme, which she founded in 1987. From 2005 to 2009 she was the president of the European Sport Management Association and is now honorary president. She is on the editorial board of *European Sport Management Quarterly*. Her research field is sports organizations, leadership and volunteers. She has experience from being on boards in sport organizations both nationally and internationally.

Jennifer Tattersall is the Sports Participation Officer in the Sports Development Service at the University of Stirling. Her background in sports coaching and sports development has led to her present, varied role within student, staff and community sports participation. Her current research interests are related to student volunteering in Africa. Jenny has a particular involvement with the UK Sport/Wallace Group of Universities 'IDEALS' Zambia project. She has been working with the project since its inception in 2006 and carried out research in Zambia during return visits from 2010 to 2015. She presented at the ICSEMIS and LSA conferences in July 2012, and attended the first Zambian National Sport Development Conference in Lusaka, during July 2015, which celebrated ten years of the IDEALS project.

Nicholas Wise is a Senior Lecturer at Liverpool John Moores University, UK. His research interests traverse the subjects of sport, events and tourism, and human geography. Originally from Pennsylvania, Nicholas has been a sports volunteer in several countries, including Australia, the Dominican Republic and Scotland. He is a member of the Regional Studies Association and has served as co-secretary of the Sports Volunteering Research Network. Nicholas has published widely across several disciplines. His work has appeared in academic journals, book chapters, conference proceedings and encyclopaedias, and he recently co-edited books on sport and interdisciplinary perspectives.

Introduction

Directions and insight in international sport volunteering research

Angela M. Benson and Nicholas Wise

Introduction

The concept of volunteering is well documented and is generally hailed as a valuable contribution to society, particularly within the western world, although it is clear that it is a phenomenon found across the globe and is a fundamental part of the most societies (United Nations Volunteers, 2011). Volunteering in western countries is generally around 20–25 per cent of the population, with occasional peaks and troughs. For example the percentage of Americans who volunteer fell from its peak of 28.8 per cent in 2005 to 25.4 per cent in 2013, and then in 2015 was around 24.9 per cent (Bureau of Labour Statistics, n.d.). In Australia these figures were 19.4 per cent in 2011, although the previous year (in 2010) it had been at 36.2 per cent (Volunteering Australia, 2015). In the United Kingdom (UK) the figures of people volunteering has stayed fairly static between 23.8 per cent in 2005–2006 to 25.9 per cent in 2012–2013, then slightly decreasing to 24.4 per cent in 2015–2016 (Taking Part, 2016). Whilst there clearly are statistics available for volunteering activity, what is less evident is the accuracy of data on the size, scope and dynamics, and the extent to which any of the data can be compared across boundaries.

What we can see is that not only is volunteering a global phenomenon, but that in particular, sport, is a key activity associated with volunteering. Volunteering is an activity in which an individual donates their time, efforts, skills and expertise. People volunteer to assist, for instance, those who are less fortunate, for the purpose of development, or to preserve the environment or ecosystems. Figures show that proportionate populations do engage in volunteerism and when we factor in mobility, much of the focus and voices come from those from developed countries. Volunteering has often been linked to altruism. While we do have tangible evidence in the form of statistics about volunteering, there are a number of intangible social impacts to consider. Today, it is argued we are moving beyond a focus on altruistic motivations of volunteering, to motivations and factors that are inevitably linked to new experiences or exposure. There is also the desire to work towards a sense of community togetherness or transfer skills to generate social and human capital that will give people new opportunities in the future. In recognizing this shift in meanings surrounding volunteerism, something that is evident is discourses around volunteering are influenced by western concepts and perspectives – and this clearly comes out in a number of the chapters.

This chapter will first introduce the concepts of sport volunteering that are in line with the title of this edited edition. This book is divided into two parts which link international sports volunteering with sporting events (Part I) and with sport and development (Part II); both of these concepts will be briefly examined in this opening chapter. The final section of this chapter then introduces the collection of 11 chapters.

Sport volunteering

Statistical data for sport volunteering is also available to some extent. In Australia, the sport and physical recreation sector attracted the largest number of volunteers (14 per cent of the adult population or 2.3 million people) in 2010 (Volunteering Australia, 2015). That same year in Canada, also the year Vancouver hosted the Olympic and Paralympic Games, it was reported that 47 per cent of Canadians volunteered in formal contexts (Vézina and Crompton, 2012). Looking at the United States, in 2014, the sport, hobby, cultural or arts segment of volunteering was 3.9 per cent, with volunteering associated with religion being by far the largest sector. In the UK, figures for sport volunteers were 20.7 per cent in 2010–2011, 20.9 per cent in 2014 and 19.3 per cent in 2015–2016 (see Table I.1 for more figures). If we examine the UK figures further (as they are annual and easily accessible) it can be seen that of the approximately 24 per cent per annum of UK citizens that volunteer, almost one-third are volunteers in the DCMS (Department of Culture, Media and Sport) areas, making sport the single biggest sector of volunteering in the UK (it is important to note the 2012–2013 figures were almost certainly influenced by the London 2012 Olympic and Paralympic Games).

What we can see is that sport volunteering is a popular activity for people in a global context to engage in. Therefore, it comes as no surprise that there is an extensive body of literature on sport volunteering which examines a host of concepts, for example: sports clubs (e.g. Lee *et al.*, 2016; Schlesinger *et al.*, 2015; Reid, 2012), training (e.g. Minnaert, 2012; Benson *et al.*, 2014), the role of governance (e.g. Shilbury *et al.*, 2013), and recruitment and retention (e.g. Lockstone and Baum, 2010). Furthermore, there is a literature pertaining to sport volunteers and social-psychological understandings specifically linked to motivation and satisfaction (see Allen and Shaw, 2009; Costa *et al.*, 2006; Hayton, 2016). This is very evident in the sport event volunteer motivations area, particularly when linked to

Table 1.1 UK volunteering in areas of sport from 2005 to 2016 (%)

	2005/ 2006	2006/ 2007	2007/ 2008	2008/ 2009	2009/ 2010	2010/ 2011	2011/ 2012	2012/ 2013	2013/ 2014	2014/ 2015	2015/ 2016
Volunteered in the last 12 months	23.8	24.0	24.0	25.0	N/A*	24.2	23.3	25.9	23.9	24.2	24.4
Volunteered in DCMS sectors (below) in last 12 months	7.0	6.9	7.2	7.8	N/A	7.7	7.1	9.3	7.4	7.9	7.9
Connected to the following areas:											
Arts	6.3	5.9	7.0	6.4	N/A	8.1	8.9	9.5	8.5	7.1	7.2
Museums/galleries	1.4	1.1	1.2	1.1	N/A	1.4	1.6	1.7	1.5	1.5	1.8
Heritage	4.9	4.2	4.0	4.7	N/A	4.2	5.6	5.3	4.4	5.4	5.7
Libraries	0.8	0.9	0.5	0.7	N/A	0.8	1.2	1.2	0.8	1.3	1.5
Archives	0.7	0.5	0.5	0.6	N/A	0.6	0.6	1.0	0.7	0.4	0.8
Sport	19.2	19.4	19.6	21.3	N/A	20.7	17.5	21.9	19.1	20.9	19.3
Any other sector	75.0	76.7	74.9	74.4	N/A	74.2	75.2	71.0	73.7	72.4	72.1

Source: Taking Part 2015/16 Quarter 4 Report: www.gov.uk/government/statistics/taking-part-201516-quarter-4-statistical-release.

Note

* Data unavailable for 2009–2010.

mega-events (Dickson *et al.*, 2013, 2014; Edwards *et al.*, 2009; Farrell *et al.*, 1998; Giannoulakis *et al.*, 2008; Hallmann and Harms, 2012; Khoo and Engelhorn, 2007, 2011; Love *et al.*, 2011; Strigas and Newton-Jackson Jr, 2003; Twynam *et al.*, 2002).

Another area of interest among sport volunteering researchers has been the making of community (see Cuskelly, 2008; Kristiansen *et al.*, 2015; Reid, 2012). Sport helps create a sense of cohesion, and bound people through shared emotional connections which lend to a sense of community (McMillan and Chavis, 1986; Wise, 2015). The role of sport in the community is also discussed around social capital (see Bradbury and Kay, 2008; Cuskelly, 2008; Cuskelly *et al.*, 2006; Darcy *et al.*, 2014). Similar to notions of community, social capital lends to a strong sense of belonging and mutual support among volunteers from members and employees of sport clubs and organizations (Darcy *et al.*, 2014) to youth sport programmes that place emphasis on involvement (Bradbury and Kay, 2008; Nichols *et al.*, 2014). Just as Chalip's (2006) work attempted to shift practical and conceptual perspectives by identifying how social outcomes were leveraged, for the individual as a sport volunteer, there exists a leveraging of individual skills contributing to human capital development (Darcy *et al.*, 2014) that relate to community outreach initiatives for individuals to gain experience or achieve new qualifications as sports coaches, mentors and leaders (Hayton, 2016).

In particular, Kristiansen *et al.* (2015) were concerned with community making among volunteers who make long-term commitments to get involved at local sporting events. There is a small literature on women, girls, ethnic/racial minorities and those with disabilities (however, generally their volunteer efforts often go unrecognized or unnoticed; see Chen, 2010; Darcy *et al.*, 2014; Hoeber, 2010; Lopiano, 2000). These groups were also observed as underrepresented in sports participation as well, showing the link between participation and volunteering in male-dominated sporting institutions.

More recently there has been a move to capture the economic value of volunteers,[1] in essence, valuing intangible assets. A recent report titled 'Hidden diamonds: Uncovering the true value of sport volunteers' (Join In, 2014) estimates that sport-based volunteering in the UK is worth £53 billion. David Andrew Haldane, Chief Economist at the Bank of England, states that 'volunteering is big business' (Join In, 2014, p. 26). This represents a substantial increase from the 2002 figures of £14,000 despite statistics being fairly static. It is also reported that 'We at Join In[2] believe that we've found the most valuable diamonds in the rough: volunteers in sport' (Join In, 2014, p. 26). However, there are others[3] who believe that measuring the economic value of volunteering (sport or other) can be misleading.

What we can see from this section is that the research into sport volunteering and its importance within national boundaries is reasonably well developed – but what of the research and *international* sport volunteering? The next section will now examine this.

International sport volunteering

While it is recognized that there are bodies of literature that concentrate on international volunteering, these discussions are much more closely linked to the literature on development aid (e.g. Dichter, 2003), social/community development (Carlton, 2015; Wise, 2011) disasters and relief efforts (e.g. Jobe, 2011), environmental preservation/conservation (e.g. Lorimer, 2010), and more recently to the closely related disciplines on tourism (Otoo and Amuquandoh, 2014; Wearing, 2001; see, in addition, Benson, Chapter 11, this volume) and, as referred to above, events (see, especially, Smith *et al.*, 2014). This section is going to focus on international volunteers in a sporting context. However, we would like to make it clear that we cannot ignore the focus on tourism, per se, as much of the international sport volunteering activity would be undertaken as part of the travel/tourism paradigm. This being said, the leading question for this section then must be to what extent has the sport volunteering literature been developed and expanded (or replicated) when examining international aspects of sport volunteering.

Linking volunteering and sport within an international (and therefore, tourism related) context is a more recent phenomenon with much of the research focusing on events. However, according to Baum and Lockstone (2007), even this area lacks a holistic approach and again is concentrated on predominantly national volunteers. We can see this in some of the literature where international volunteers are segmented as part of a larger data set but are not analysed independently (see Darcy *et al.*, 2014; Dickson *et al.*, 2013; Dickson and Benson, 2013; Nichols and Ralston, 2012). Nichols (2013) suggests that sport volunteering now plays a significant role in sports policy and the current demands and pressures placed on society are encouraging international volunteering.

The field of sport volunteering in an international context is clearly both dynamic and diverse with a range of opportunities. For instance, a growing number of volunteer tourism organizations are offering 'sport volunteer projects overseas'; colleges and universities are travelling with volunteer sport students to engage with communities in a sporting context; mobility of sport volunteers is occurring at events, with volunteers travelling both domestically and overseas to take part. To meet and manage the expectations of travellers, organizations are continually offering new opportunities to attract people to their programmes, and sport is an important part of encouraging people to travel and volunteer. Easton and Wise (2015) believe that to ensure that the needs of contemporary volunteers are adequately catered for, it is important to consider key factors contributing to both projected and perceived images of what an individual will do and experience abroad.

Consequently, we suggest that the literature on international sport volunteers, per se, is limited and this edited collection goes some way to address this.

Sport events

The events industry has rapidly expanded, and demand to volunteer at sport events has risen considerably in recent decades (see Costa *et al.*, 2006; Dickson *et al.*, 2014; Heggie, 2009; Kaplanidou *et al.*, 2016; Pappas, 2014). Cities and countries compete to host major and mega international spectacles, and as the scale of events increases, this results in more human capital to deliver events. Volunteers represent a major workforce of events around the world. As events attract competitors from around the world, this has resulted in increased interest to volunteer abroad at major and mega-events to be a part of the experience. We live in an increasingly mobile world, and those with disposable incomes are able to take advantage of visiting a new place, with the motive of experiencing a place or event as a volunteer. While the literature has focused much attention on international events as a global spectacle (Smith *et al.*, 2014), there are other small-scale events (see Table I.2) that attract competitors, and thus volunteers with a sincere interest in the sport the immediate region and neighbouring countries. The events in the forthcoming chapters (in Part I) are drawn from across the typology.

Volunteering at sport events is very diverse, and purposes and motivations arguably differ much more than when volunteering in sport for development. Demand is continually rising as the events are increasing in exposure and volunteers are playing a key role in supporting the delivery of events. Gallarza *et al.* (2013), for instance, discuss a range of value dimensions, in particular altruism, social value, play, efficiency and effort spent, that relate to value creation and co-creation, in what they refer to as 'give' and 'take' experiences. As noted previously, much of the value associated with volunteering is linked to the overall experience, and this may relate to an individual's interest in the sport at an event, to associate with a community, or to increase pride in place – these three points are explored in this book to various degrees in Part I. Alongside discussion of the motivation to volunteer at events is the satisfaction associated with volunteering (Allen and Shaw, 2009). Putting the element of satisfaction into a longitudinal framework there needs to also involve extended interest. Interest in a sport encourages people to commit to volunteering over time (Kristiansen *et al.*, 2015) and this helps recurring sport events to sustain year-on-year and helps to embed the event in the community. Community based events have established training support structures in place (see

Table 1.2 Sport event typology (adapted from Getz, 2005)

	Local or regional events	National events	International and/or hallmark events	Mega events
Multisport events	School sport event days or weeks (UK) Local and regional track and field meets (Canada)	National Special Olympics and Malaysian Paralympiad (Khoo and Englehorn, 2007, 2011)	Ara Fura Games (Australia) Indigenous Games (North America) Highland Games (Scotland) Paralympics Macabean Games (Israel)	Olympics (Bang, Alexandris et al., 2009; Giannoulakis et al., 2008) World Masters Games (Edwards et al., 2009)
Single sport events	Capital City Marathon (Strigas and Newton-Jackson, Jr, 2003) Life Time Fitness triathlon (Bang et al., 2009)	Canadian Curling Championships (Farrell et al., 1998)	Melbourne Cup Horse Racing Monaco Grand Prix Wimbledon Tennis Championships	FIFA World Cup (Bang and Chelladurai, 2003) Rugby World Cup IAAF World Championships

Source: Dickson et al. (2013, p. 16).

Costa *et al.*, 2006), but this can be more challenging for larger events where organizers need to logistically organize training for thousands of volunteers. Shaw (2009) looked further into training initiatives for volunteers at sport events and found that learning is necessary for the volunteering experience to have a lasting legacy. Learning to interact is a major factor for sport event volunteers. All volunteering involves social interaction, but for events, volunteers are not only interacting, but they are also seen as ambassadors of the event. Nicholas Wise (Chapter 3, this collection) discusses this point, and this is articulated during volunteer training, especially since we live in an era of social media and those organizing the event want to minimize negative publicity, but also maximize exchange and interaction among the volunteers.

Sport development

Defining and examining the concept of sport development is not without its problems as it is highly contested within the academic literature. This section seeks only to highlight key points in order to set the scene for Part II of the book.

The concept of sport development is not new and has been around since the 1970s. It is often publicly funded and, therefore, its aims, objectives and impacts are often linked to policy and policy-makers. Googling sport development jobs will highlight a number of opportunities at any given time and the National Careers Service[4] job profiles 'sport development officer'. Therefore, it is not uncommon to see sport development practitioners, which are often employed by the public sector or national sport organizations. There is a proliferation of Sports Development Degrees (for example at the Universities of Gloucester, Leeds, Cardiff in the UK, or Deakin and Griffith in Australia) on offer alongside reference material to support teaching[5] and a growing body of literature on sport development (see, for example, Hylton, 2013; Hylton and Bramham, 2008; Robson *et al.*, 2013).

Houlihan (2011, n.p.) states that 'one, perhaps wishfully simple, view of sport development is that is it about "getting more people to play more sport"'. Collins (1995, p. 21) suggests that sport development is

> a process whereby effective opportunities, processes, systems and structures are set up to enable and encourage people in all or particular groups and areas to take part in sport and recreation or to improve their performance to whatever level they desire.

More recently, Hylton and Bramham (2008, p. 2) believe that 'sport development is more accurately a term used to describe policies, processes and practices that form an integral feature of work involved in providing sporting opportunities and positive sporting experiences'. Houlihan (2011, n.p.) indicates that there are three orientations to sport development:

1 The first identifies the promotion of participation in sport as the central concern much along the lines of the *sport for all* policy of the Council of Europe launched in the mid 1970's (see, for example, Green, 2006).
2 The second prioritises talent identification and development (see, for example, Oakley and Green, 2001; Houlihan and Green, 2008).
3 And the third treats sport as an instrument to achieve a variety of non-sport objectives related to health, community development and education (see, for example, Giulianotti, 2011; Kidd, 2008).

It is to this third orientation that we now turn, as the chapters in Part II predominantly align with this. However, what we also see as part of this orientation is that sport development, per se, is used less and the terms of 'sport for development'[6] (SDP IWG, 2006), 'sport and development' (sportanddev.com) and 'sport-in-development' (Coalter, 2009) become more common. There is clearly a need to move the boundaries of the sport development concept to something more profound as sport becomes progressively part of humanitarian and development work. For the Part II section title we have used the term *sport and development* (however, this is not uniform across the chapters as authors have drawn their own emphasis of this term) As such, sportanddev.org[7] suggests that ' "Sport and development" refers to the use of sport as a tool for development and peace', which are the predominant focus of the chapters in Part II. Sport and development is still very contemporary and continues to progress largely due to major international policy developments. The timeline of major developments in sport and development can be found at sportanddev.org,[8] which highlights events from 1978 to 2014.

It is now evident that there are a number of volunteering programmes in developing countries that focus on sport and recreation. In North America and Western Europe, there are norms of sport and recreation teaching, and these may greatly differ from how sport is taught in developing countries. We accept that sport is well-organized and much time goes into developing the physical education curriculum. In the Global South, especially in more remote locals, sport and recreation is more organic in nature. Kids may not have structured programmes, but instead find enjoyment in what we might consider 'informal play and recreation'. Nonetheless, kids will play and find ways to engage in sport by making footballs, designating pitches out of any available space they can access, and will define marks as goal posts (see Alegi, 2010). Wearing (2001, p. 146) suggests that 'tourism in developing countries is often managed by people and companies physically external to the land area and communities in which operations occur', and this is still pertinent today. Consequently discourses around power relations, neo-colonialism and how we (are supposed to formally) participate in physical activity exist in sport for development programmes. Some of these issues are addressed in Part II of this book.

International sport volunteering: overviewing the chapters in this edited collection

This edited book takes a broad perspective on international sport volunteering. Consequently, this collection of 11 chapters from expert scholars and practitioners in the field on international sport volunteering takes an in-depth look at both the theory and application. This introduction, written by the editors, is an overview of a number of questions and critical points in the area of international sports volunteering. Furthermore, the chapter offers an insight into each of the following chapters. This edited book consists of two parts. Part I of the book focuses on international sport volunteers in the context of events and consists of six chapters (1–6). Chapter 1, by Kari Jaeger and Line Mathisen, examines two dogsledding events: the Iditarod in Alaska (United States) and the Finnmark Race in Norway. They focus on value co-creation and volunteering at rural sport events. Data were collected using a range of qualitative methods, spending time in the field at both events. The findings highlight that local, national and international volunteers work alongside each other for the common cause of the event. Chapter 2, by Valery Gordin and Irina Borovskaia, looks at the Cultural Olympiad. They conducted a survey questionnaire with international and domestic volunteers during the 2014 Winter Olympics in Sochi. Their focus is on an NGO, International Paint Pals (IPP), which is identified as an international volunteers' network partnership. Chapter 3 by Nicholas Wise offers a discussion on his experience as an international volunteer at the 2014 Commonwealth Games in Glasgow, United Kingdom. He presents a self-reflexive analysis of his motivations to volunteer in a city that he moved to for work. Drawing from a geographical perspective, Wise outlines notions of being in place and out of place throughout the process of training to become a volunteer and then ultimately his experiences during the event.

Chapters 4, 5 and 6 present a different perspective to the first three chapters in this section. Similar to a number of other chapters in this collection, all three chapters build on the role of community building among volunteers at sport events. Nigel Jarvis in Chapter 4 focuses on social legacies and community building at the 2014 Gay Games held in Akron and Cleveland. Sport events have played an integral role in community building among gay and lesbian communities. The chapter acknowledges that around 98 per cent of the volunteers were from the Akron/Cleveland areas and that there were very few international volunteers. While this study does include some focus on a very small sample of international volunteers, it sheds light on the need for a more informed international analysis of event volunteering at smaller events. Jarvis does note that those from outside the local area where the event was held (especially the few international volunteers that took part), allows for local volunteers to meet international attendees who travel to participate in the event. Alfred Ogle and David Lamb look at the Perth International golf event in Chapter 5. They use a push–pull framework to assess factors associated with volunteerism and engagement at professional international golf tournaments. The chapter addresses the point that outbound volunteering from Australia is more common than international inbound volunteering at golf events in Perth. To overcome the lack of international volunteers, Alfred Ogle and David Lamb have developed an International Golf Volunteer Engagement Strategy to assess motivations of current volunteers to increase the ability to attract international volunteers in the future. What can be seen here is that both Chapters 4 and 5 make reference to needing to improve upon the pull factors that influence attracting international volunteers for events regardless of their size and status. The final chapter in this first section (Chapter 6) is by Berit Skirstad and Elsa Kristiansen. They focus on a conceptual research framework (the volunteer cube framework) and offer a discussion around 'indirect volunteers' building on their work at Ski Flying events in Norway, an event that is attracting volunteers interested in this niche outdoor winter event. While their chapter does not focus on international volunteers directly, they believe that their framework is a useful potential tool in future international sport volunteering research.

The second part of this book, consisting of Chapters 7–11, is dedicated to international sport volunteering in the context of sport and development. The first two chapters in this section focus on the International Development through Excellence and Leadership in Sport (IDEALS) programme in Namibia and Zambia, and offer two different approaches in their analyses. Chapter 7, by Tom Fletcher and Danny Cullinane, investigates reactions and perspectives of student volunteers from United Kingdom who travel to Namibia to volunteer as sports coaches or assist a number of sport and social programmes. The chapter focuses on two key concepts that highlight the importance of international sport volunteering by university students, these being development of leadership skills and gaining cultural awareness in a setting abroad. The authors also suggest that long-term benefits are difficult to measure because the aim of international volunteering is to create a sustainable legacy, but the communities that students volunteer in are sensitive and fragile to outside influences and involvement – especially because groups regularly come and go. Shifting focus to look at the social impacts on how the local peer leaders gain from the presence of international sport volunteers, Chapter 8 by Fiona Reid and Jennifer Tattersall looks at a similar sports development programme in Zambia. They focused on the social impact of the IDEALS programme on the destination communities by examining insights from NGOs, peer leaders in Zambia and UK volunteers. Their findings led to interpretations of the social legacy aspects of the programme in Zambia.

The next two chapters focus on sports development and peace. Chapter 9 by Mike Bartle and Peter Craig seeks to understand the role of international volunteers who are involved in sport for development and peace (SDP) programmes and activities and the extent to which they transgress national boundaries. They raise a number of critical points, as do the other chapters in this section, in particular highlighting the lack of and limitations of assessment tools in that they fail to engage all stakeholders especially beyond the project outcomes and objectives. Their emphasis on social change is met by the role of internationals contributing to training programmes involving sport and peacebuilding – with a focus on Northern Ireland. The authors outline contact theory and how this relates to conflict resolution. They conclude by indicating that sport is used to shape experiences, but due to its commercialized devilment it only compounds the challenges of understanding the role of international volunteers. This chapter offers a wider context of sport and development and peace studies but also sets up the next chapter by Joanne Clarke and Paul Salisbury, which focuses on the case of Cameroon. While the previous chapter put emphasis on social change, Clarke and Salisbury focus on social capital and they compare perspectives of international and national volunteers who assist with sport development programmes surrounding the sport of cricket. The international volunteers come from an organization, Cricket Without Boundaries, while national volunteers are associated with the Cameroon Cricket Federation. The authors question whose interests are being serviced by the sport-for-development discourses and suggest that at a practical policy level the sport development programmes take a close look at the wider international volunteer sector criticisms but also draw from best practice initiatives that have emerged to deal with these growing concerns. Angela M. Benson, in Chapter 11, brings a number of the perspectives outlined in this section together. This final chapter of Part II, and of this edited collection, focuses on the role of volunteer tourism and addresses how sport is used as a vehicle for engaging in international development. Benson analysis 26 volunteer stories associated with a case organization (Projects Abroad). Whilst insight gained from the project website acknowledges how sport projects do impact the host community, the stories stress the personal benefits gained by the individual volunteers as a means of recruiting future participants and thus encouraging international (sport) volunteer tourism.

The book concludes with a short chapter by the editors that outlines some future directions in international sport volunteering research. This book brings together an important area of research which until now has been underdeveloped. We now turn to the chapters in this collection.

Notes

1 www.ivr.org.uk/ivr-volunteering-stats/196-what-is-the-economic-value-of-volunteering.
2 www.joininuk.org/.
3 www.scribd.com/document/241056892/New-Researchers-Session-Dostal-and-Vyskocil.
4 https://nationalcareersservice.direct.gov.uk/advice/planning/jobprofiles/Pages/sportsdevelopmentofficer.aspx.
5 www.sportdevelopment.org.uk/.
6 www.un.org/wcm/content/site/sport/home/sport.
7 www.sportanddev.org.
8 www.sportanddev.org/en/learn-more/history-sport-and-development/timeline-major-developments-sport-and-development.

References

Alegi, P. (2010). *African soccerscapes: How a continent changed the world's game.* Albany, NY: SUNY Press.

Allen, J.B. and Shaw, S. (2009). 'Everyone rolls up their sleeves and mucks in': Exploring volunteers' motivation and experiences of the motivational climate of a sporting event. *Sport Management Review* 12(2): 79–90.

Bang, H. and Chelladurai, P. (2003). *Motivation and satisfaction in volunteering for 2002 World Cup in Korea.* Paper presented at the conference of the North American Society for Sport Management.

Bang, H., Alexandris, K. and Ross, S.D. (2009). Validation of the revised volunteer motivations scale for international sporting events (VMS-ISE) at the Athens 2004 Olympic Games. *Event Management* 12(3–4): 119–131.

Baum, T. and Lockstone, L. (2007). Volunteers and mega sporting events: Developing a research framework. *International Journal of Event Management Research* 3(1): 29–41.

Benson, A.M., Dickson, T.J., Terwiel, A. and Blackman, D. (2014). Training of Vancouver 2010 volunteers: A legacy opportunity? *Contemporary Social Science: Journal of the Academy of Social Sciences* 9(2): 210–226.

Bradbury, S. and Kay, T. (2008). Stepping into community? The impact of youth sport volunteering on young people's social capital. In M. Nicholson and R. Hoye (eds) *Sport and social capital.* Oxford: Butterworth-Heinemann (pp. 285–315).

Bureau of Labor Statistics. (n.d.). Volunteering in the United States. www.bls.gov.

Carlton, S. (2015). Connecting, belonging: Volunteering, wellbeing and leadership among refugee youth. *International Journal of Disaster Risk Reduction* 14(2): 342–349.

Chalip, L. (2006). Towards social leverage of sport events. *Journal of Sport & Tourism* 11: 109–127.

Chen, P.-J. (2010). Differences between male and female sport event tourists: A qualitative study. *International Journal of Hospitality Management* 29(2): 277–290.

Coalter, F. (2009). Sport-in-development: Accountability or development? In R. Levermore and A. Beacom (eds) *Sport and international development: Theoretical frameworks.* Basingstoke: Palgrave Macmillan (pp. 55–75).

Collins, M. (1995). *Sport development locally and regionally*. Reading: Institute of Leisure and Amenity Management.

Costa, C.A., Chalip, L., Green, B.C. and Simes, C. (2006). Reconsidering the role of training in event volunteers' satisfaction. *Sport Management Review* 9(2): 165–182.

Cuskelly, G. (2008). Volunteering in community sport organizations: Implications for social capital. In M. Nicholson and R. Hoye (eds) *Sport and social capital*. Oxford: Butterworth-Heinemann (pp. 187–203).

Cuskelly, G., Hoye, R. and Auld, C. (2006). *Working with volunteers in sport: Theory and practice*. London: Routledge.

Darcy, S., Dickson, T.J. and Benson, A.M. (2014). London 2012 Olympic and Paralympic Games: Including volunteers with disabilities, a podium performance? *Event Management* 18: 431–446.

Darcy, S., Maxwell, H., Edwards, M., Onyx, J. and Sherker, S. (2014). More than a sport and volunteer organisation: Investigating social capital development in a sporting organisation. *Sport Management Review* 17(4): 395–406.

Dichter, T. (2003). *Despite good intentions: Why development assistance to the third world has failed*. Amherst: University of Massachusetts Press.

Dickson, T. and Benson, A.M. (2013). London 2012 Games makers: Towards redefining legacy (Meta-evaluation of the impacts and legacy of the London 2012 Olympic Games and Paralympic Games). London: Department for Culture, Media & Sport. www.gov.uk/government/publications/london-2012-games-maker-survey.

Dickson, T.J., Benson, A.M. and Terwiel, A. (2014). Mega-event volunteers, similar or different? Vancouver 2010 vs. London 2012. *International Journal of Event and Festival Management* 5(2): 164–179.

Dickson, T.J., Benson, A.M., Blackman, D.A. and Terwiel, F.A. (2013). It's all about the games! 2010 Vancouver Olympic and Paralympic Winter Games volunteers. *Event Management* 17(1): 77–92.

Easton, S. and Wise, N. (2015). Online portrayals of volunteer tourism in Nepal. *Worldwide Hospitality and Tourism Themes* 7(2): 141–158.

Edwards, D., Dickson, T.J. and Darcy, S. (2009). *Working paper no. 22: Sydney World Masters Games: Volunteer legacy outcomes*. Sydney: University of Technology Sydney.

Farrell, J.M., Johnston, M.E. and Twynam, G.D. (1998). Volunteer motivation, satisfaction, and management at an elite sporting competition. *Journal of Sport Management* 12(4): 288–300.

Gallarza, M.G., Arteaga, F. and Gil-Saura, I. (2013). The value of volunteering in special events: A longitudinal study. *Annals of Tourism Research* 40: 105–131.

Getz, D. (2005). *Event management and event tourism*. New York: Cognizant.

Giannoulakis, C., Wang, C.-H. and Gray, D. (2008). Measuring volunteer motivation in mega-sporting events. *Event Management* 11: 191–200.

Giulianotti, R. (2011). Sport, peacemaking and conflict resolution: A contextual analysis and modelling of the sport, development and peace sector. *Ethnic and Racial Studies* 34: 207–228.

Green, M. (2006). From 'sport for all' to not about 'sport' at all? Interrogating sport policy interventions in the United Kingdom. *European Sport Management Quarterly* 3: 217–238.

Hallmann, K. and Harms, G. (2012). Determinants of volunteer motivation and their impact on future voluntary engagement: A comparison of volunteer's motivation at sport events in equestrian and handball. *International Journal of Event and Festival Management* 3(3): 272–291.

Hayton, J.W. (2016). Plotting the motivation of student volunteers in sports-based outreach work in the North East of England. *Sport Management Review* DOI: http://dx.doi.org/10.1016/j.smr.2016.06.004.

Heggie, T.W. (2009). Traveling to Canada for the Vancouver 2010 Winter Olympic and Paralympic Games. *Travel Medicine and Infectious Disease* 7(4): 207–211.

Hoeber, L. (2010). Experiences of volunteering in sport: Views from Aboriginal individuals. *Sport Management Review* 13(4): 345–354.

Houlihan, B. (2011). Defining sport development. www.sportdevelopment.org.uk/index.php/rgsd/265-definition?catid=54%3Aintrosv.

Houlihan, B. and Green, M. (2008). *Comparative elite sport development: Systems, structures and public policy*. London: Butterworth-Heinemann.

Hylton, K. (2013). *Sport development: Policy, process and practice*. London: Routledge.

Hylton, K. and Bramham, P. (eds) (2008). *Sports development: Policy, process and practice*. London: Routledge.

Jobe, K. (2011). Disaster relief in post-earthquake Haiti: Unintended consequences of humanitarian volunteerism. *Travel Medicine and Infectious Disease* 9(1): 1–5.

Join In. (2014). *Hidden diamonds: Uncovering the true value of sport volunteers*. London: Join In Publication.

Kaplanidou, K., Emadi, A.A., Sagas, M., Diop, A. and Fritz, G. (2016). Business legacy planning for mega events: The case of the 2022 World Cup in Qatar. *Journal of Business Research* 69(10): 4103–4111.

Khoo, S. and Engelhorn, R. (2007). Volunteer motivations for the Malaysian Paralympiad. *Tourism and Hospitality Planning & Development* 4(3): 159–167.

Khoo, S. and Engelhorn, R. (2011). Volunteer motivations at a national Special Olympics event. *Adapted Physical Activity Quarterly* 28(1): 27–39.

Kidd, B. (2008). A new social movement: Sport for development and peace. *Sport in Society* 11(4): 370–380.

Kristiansen, E., Skirstad, B., Parent, M.M. and Waddington, I. (2015). 'We can do it': Community, resistance, social solidarity, and long-term volunteering at a sport event. *Sport Management Review* 18(2): 256–267.

Lee, Y., Kim, M. and Koo, J. (2016). The impact of social interaction and team member exchange on sport event volunteer management. *Sport Management Review* DOI: http://dx.doi.org/10.1016/j.smr.2016.04.005.

Lockstone, L. and Baum, T. (2010). 2006 Melbourne Commonwealth Games, Australia: Recruiting, training and managing a volunteer program at a sporting mega event. In K. Holmes and K. Smith (eds) *Managing volunteers in tourism*. Oxford: Butterworth-Heinemann (pp. 215–223).

Lopiano, D.A. (2000). Modern history of women in sports: Twenty-five years of Title IX. *Clinics in Sports Medicine* 19(2): 163–173.

Lorimer, J. (2010). International conservation 'volunteering' and the geographies of global environmental citizenship. *Political Geography* 29(6): 311–322.

Love, A., Hardin, R.L., Koo, G.-Y. and Morse, A. (2011). Effects of motives on satisfaction and behavioral intentions of volunteers at a PGA tour event. *International Journal of Sport Management* 12(1): 86–101.

McMillan, D.W. and Chavis, D.M. (1986). Sense of community: A definition and theory. *Journal of Community Psychology* 14(1): 6–23.

Minnaert, L. (2012). An Olympic legacy for all? The non-infrastructural outcomes of the Olympic Games for socially excluded groups (Atlanta 1996–Beijing 2008). *Tourism Management* 33(2): 361–370.

Nichols, G. (ed.) (2013). *Volunteers in sport: International perspectives*. London: Routledge.

Nichols, G. and Ralston, R. (2012). The rewards of individual engagement in volunteering: A missing dimension of the Big Society. *Environment and Planning A* 44(12): 2974–2987.

Nichols, G., Taylor, P., Barrett, D. and Jeanes, R. (2014). Youth sport volunteers in England: A paradox between reducing the state and promoting a Big Society. *Sport Management Review* 17(3): 337–346.

Oakley, B. and Green, M. (2001). The production of Olympic champions: International perspectives on elite sport development systems. *European Journal for Sports Management*: 83–105.

Otoo, F.E. and Amuquandoh, F.E. (2014). An exploration of the motivations for volunteering: A study of international volunteer tourists to Ghana. *Tourism Management Perspectives* 11: 51–57.

Pappas, N. (2014). Hosting mega events: Londoners' support of the 2012 Olympics. *Journal of Hospitality and Tourism Management* 21: 10–17.

Reid, F. (2012). Increasing sports participation in Scotland: Are voluntary sports clubs the answer? *International Journal of Sport Policy and Politics* 4(2): 221–241.

Robson, S., Simpson, K. and Tucker, L. (2013). *Strategic sport development*. London: Routledge.

Schlesinger, T., Klenk, C. and Nagel, S. (2015). How do sport clubs recruit volunteers? Analyzing and developing a typology of decision-making processes on recruiting volunteers in sport clubs. *Sport Management Review* 18(2): 193–206.

SDP IWG. (2006). *Sport for development and peace: Practice to policy*. Preliminary Report of the SDP IWG.

Shaw, S. (2009). 'It was all "smile for Dunedin!"': Event volunteer experiences at the 2006 New Zealand Masters Games. *Sport Management Review* 12(1): 26–33.

Shilbury, D., Ferkins, L. and Smythe, L. (2013). Sport governance encounters: Insights from lived experiences. *Sport Management Review* 16(3): 349–363.

Smith, K.A., Lockstone-Binney, L., Holmes, K. and Baum, T. (2014). *Event volunteering: International perspectives on the event volunteering experience*. London: Routledge.

Strigas, A.D. and Newton-Jackson Jr, E. (2003). Motivating volunteers to serve and succeed: Design and results of a pilot study that explores demographics and motivational factors in sport volunteerism. *International Sports Journal* 7(1): 111–123.

Taking Part (2016). Taking Part 2015/16 Quarter 4 Report. www.gov.uk/government/statistics/taking-part-201516-quarter-4-statistical-release.

Twynam, G.D., Farrell, J.M. and Johnston, M.E. (2002). Leisure and volunteer motivation at a special sporting event. *Leisure/Loisir: Journal of the Canadian Association for Leisure Studies* 27(3/4): 363–377.

United Nations Volunteers. (2011). *State of the world's volunteerism report: Universal values for global well-being*. Bonn: UNV Publication.

Vézina, M. and Crompton, S. (2012). *Volunteering in Canada*. Statistics Canada.

Volunteering Australia (2015). Key facts and statistics about volunteering in Australia. www.volunteeringaustralia.org/wp-content/uploads/VA-Key-statistics-about-Australian-volunteering-16-April-20151.pdf.

Wearing, S. (2001). *Volunteer tourism: Experiences that make a difference*. Wallingford: CABI Publishing.

Wise, N. (2011). Transcending imaginations through football participation and narratives of the *other*: Haitian national identity in the Dominican Republic. *Journal of Sport & Tourism* 16(3): 259–275.

Wise, N. (2015). Placing sense of community. *Journal of Community Psychology* 43(7): 920–929.

Part I

International sport volunteering at sporting events

Co-creation in events

Values of volunteers and volunteer tourists at Iditarod in Alaska and the Finnmark Race in Norway

Kari Jæger and Line Mathisen

Introduction

This chapter is about volunteers' value creation in events. Values created through co-creation among volunteer tourists that travel to events and work alongside local volunteers and others involved in the events. The chapter examines value creation for the volunteers themselves, both as a tourist volunteer or a local volunteer, and for the event.

Tourism is changing from being product-oriented to value-oriented, that is, tourists travel to pursue special interests and through this they seek to satisfy both ultimate and immediate goals. Furthermore, the boundaries between work and pleasure are becoming increasingly blurred, with work as play and play as work (Richards, 2011). This is particularly noticeable in special interest tourism activities such as volunteering to actively engage (work) at events. Events are co-created consumption spaces where the creation of value depends on those who participate. Typically in events, locals and visitors who participate create value through the consumption of the same services and products, blurring defined roles (Jæger and Olsen, 2016). Furthermore, the value created during an event can extend beyond the event itself when based on dimensions focusing on individual values and not only on salient desires and wants. This is particularly important from a sustainable and long-term perspective. For instance, Haanpää *et al.* (2016, p. 46) point out that these events 'clearly create meaning-based value for the people and places, but the monetary value created is often marginal'. Different dimensions of local value creation linked to events are the development of tourism products by lifestyle entrepreneurs, e.g. mushers and volunteers create tourism for those places (Viken and Jæger, 2012). Furthermore, events contribute to develop place stories, as event activities and happenings are being communicated via television during the event and online (website, social media, Twitter, Instagram) throughout the year (Jæger and Kvidal-Røvik, 2015). This type of value enhances the visibility and attractiveness of the events, which is important because these events totally depend on a volunteer workforce. The events are brought to life by the volunteers, who often travel long distances to participate, driven by a desire to learn, expand their networks and have fun (Wollebæk *et al.*, 2014, p. 30). The different desires illustrate different dimensions of value co-creation that, in events, might contribute to develop, improve and sustain the event in different/multiple ways while creating benefits for the volunteers, event participants and local society. Further, the value created depends on the quality or nature of the interaction between participants, which facilitates what Richards (2014) calls an 'active exchange'. A study on interaction in events conducted by Nordvall *et al.* (2014, p. 137) found that social interactions between event visitors were an important part of the event experience, and they identified three different types of interactions: known-group socialization, external socialization and audience socialization. While the literature discusses the values motivating volunteers to participate (Wollebæk *et al.*, 2014), it tells us less about what happens during the event. What exactly is co-created during the life of an event? What does this mean for the volunteers and the event? To answer these questions, this chapter takes a social constructivist approach to value creation to investigate what values volunteer locals and tourists, amateurs and semi-professionals create through working in events.

The research is based on the two dogsledding races, the Finnmark Race (Finnmarksløpet), arranged in Finnmark, Norway, and Iditarod, organized in Alaska, United States, with national and international participants. Both races are staged in rural areas, built from the bottom up on local premises and created by individuals with a genuine interest in both the area and dogsledding. The core activity of these sporting events is dogsledding, but at the same time it is a travel through nature, with many culture events arranged during the race period. The volunteers who participate have different nationalities, knowledge and skills. For example they can be: journalists, photographers, veterinarians, snowmobile drivers and pilots coming from different countries, and also other places inside the host countries (the United States and Norway). The nationalities differ every year, and those discussed in this chapter are representative of this study.

Thus, to understand the importance of co-creation in an event, this study investigates, analyses and discusses volunteers' value (co-)creation during their participation in events and identifies values that are important both for the volunteers and the events. The study recognizes the volunteer as guided by individual values shaping their experiences and, thus, value creation. Furthermore, it views the event as having the potential to access, shape and add benefit to and from volunteers' value creation. This chapter proceeds with a literature review followed by case descriptions of the events investigated in this study and a description of the methods used. The next sections of the chapter are divided into analysing and discussing the findings followed by the conclusion that offers advice for future research.

Value co-creation, events and volunteering

The concept of value co-creation posits that the creation of value emerges through processes of resource sharing that ultimately enhance the potential for participants to create value (Lusch and Vargo, 2014; Mathisen, 2012; Prebensen et al., 2014). The fuzziness of the value concept makes it difficult to define, but recent literature suggests that value emerges through use and entails enhanced imagined, perceived and/or evaluated feelings of being better off and/or enhanced wellbeing (Grönroos and Voima, 2013; Lusch and Vargo, 2014; Pera and Viglia, 2015). While value creation in tourism has focused on tourists' expression of meaning linked to participation in activities (as exciting or enjoyable), the service management literature goes beyond a focus on experiential value and includes value in use (Heinonen et al., 2013). Thus values are beliefs that shape and guide individuals' choices to create meaning (Rokeach, 1973; Sagiv and Schwartz, 2000; Schwartz, 2013). This means that while value can be subjectively defined in terms of what is, for example, enjoyable, values are multidimensional and socially/culturally shared universal priorities that can change through experiences, knowledge and skills (Schwartz and Bilsky, 1990).

Therefore, to have a value approach means to share and integrate knowledge and skills in ways that benefits both the volunteers and the event (Grönroos and Voima, 2013; Lusch and Vargo, 2014). While this view recognizes the volunteer as determining their own value creation, it also views the event as having the potential to access and shape volunteers' knowledge and skills while acknowledging the power the volunteers have to influence the events' value-creation processes. A volunteer participating in an event is driven by expectations of being better off based on what is considered to be valuable for the individual (Lusch and Vargo, 2014). What this entails is linked to feelings of wellbeing, e.g. social, economic and cultural wellbeing, and thus involves participating in activities they consider bring about benefits that increase this potential (Lusch and Vargo, 2014; Prebensen, 2012; Prebensen et al., 2014). From the vantage point of co-creation, viewing volunteers as co-creative resources entails analysing interactions to create awareness of all processes through which value can be co-created and shared. These processes can originate between volunteers and event management, but can implicate and affect knowledge creation and development beyond these interactions (Sfandla and Björk, 2013). From this perspective, volunteers and the event together hold a potential for event development that can be realized through a focus on knowledge and learning (Chandler and Vargo, 2011; Greer et al., 2016).

During an event, volunteers interact directly with their environment, including other volunteers, event employees, managers and locals. These processes are constantly evolving, where volunteers' and events' direct and indirect interactions follow non-linear patterns. This means that while volunteers' value co-creation is crucial for events, both volunteers and the event are part of a system where the creation of value at individual levels can expand beyond this level, thus holding the potential for increased value creation beyond the event (Binkhorst and Den Dekker, 2009; Lusch and Vargo, 2014). This highlights the importance for events to create and implement strategies for co-creation that facilitate interactions between and across volunteers, event employees and management team(s).

Events and festivals represent important social and cultural arenas, replacing the historic role of churches, village feasts and gatherings. According to Jepson and Clarke (2016, p. 3): 'Festivals and events are the lifeblood of society, they are inseparable and crucial to enhance and maintain community well-being or quality of life.' Put another way, events create unique settings where individuals from different cultures and social classes can meet, interact and sometimes find new friends. The number of events and festivals has increased (de Brito and Terzieva, 2016), indicating their social importance. Furthermore, the event's role in a community as a temporary place in a physical place means that events are venues for value co-creation – that is, both the tourists and the local people can use events as value-creating areas (Haanpää *et al.*, 2016).

Co-creation takes place during the various interactions between local volunteers, the volunteer tourists and the members of the event team. The type of value co-created during these interactions depends on the participants' willingness to share, for example, knowledge and interaction dynamics. When the volunteers get time to reflect on what they have shared and on what has happened during the life of the event, they know whether their efforts have resulted in any personal or social changes, e.g. have they met old 'volunteer friends', made new friends or gained new skills? Therefore, the value (co-)created can also result in an increased motivation to maybe volunteer next time. Zátori (2016, p. 14) describes a three-step co-creation process in her study on guided tours where a service provider aims to: '(1) provoke attention, (2) engage and involve, and (3) make consumers discover'. Zátori's study emphasizes the consumer's perspective, which means that:

> co-creation can be realized only if the intention of the provider and the value co-creation steps meet an optimal response from consumer side. In case the consumer has no attention, interest or willingness to get involved and participate, the co-creation will not take place.

Similarly, volunteer tourists in events are offered work tasks during the event, but unlike ordinary tourists they have to facilitate the experiences themselves. Moreover, a critical part of the co-creation takes place between the volunteers, thus not facilitated by the event management. For example, value is co-created when knowledge is shared and developed during interactions between, for example, members in a veterinarian team in the Finnmark Race or Iditarod. The team members then use what they learnt during the races when they treat dogs in their own clinics, thus the value co-created during the events extends beyond the event. Many of the local and international volunteers also start to plan the next year's event during this phase. Understanding events holistically facilitates insights into events' extended value creation – that is, the gaining of knowledge of the value created also after the event is arranged. Moreover, this gives a frame for understanding the parallel lifecycle/parallel value creation processes for the people involved in the events, such as the volunteer tourists' value creation studied in this chapter. The core of event value creation depends on direct and indirect interactions, which can result in the creation of relationships that give value throughout the year, outside the time period of the actual event.

Many events are totally reliant on the involvement of volunteers (Monga, 2006). This is also true for the Finnmark Race and Iditarod cases investigated here. The term 'volunteer' is derived from the word meaning 'to willingly give' (Cnaan et al., 1996, p. 366), and one definition of volunteering is 'any activity in which time is given freely to benefit another person, group, or organization' (Wilson, 2000, p. 215). The nature of volunteering can also be understood in terms of what Cater (2006) describes in connection to adventure tourism and leisure. He underpins that it is important that the activities are freely chosen so as to achieve what Csikszentimihalyi (1975, p. 36) describes as flow and defines as a feeling of 'complete involvement of the actor with his activity'. To achieve flow is attractive, because it gives a feeling of total immersion. This kind of involvement might be compared with the volunteers' activities in an event, where people, after working day and night for a week with little sleep and food, are still feeling happy, and are already longing and planning for the next year.

While volunteering can increase the feeling of flow, it seldom results in economic gain for the volunteers. For instant, in some events and also in the Finnmark Race and the Iditarod, the volunteers generally work for free, but can have parts of their costs covered. Stebbins (2013) examines whether volunteering is unpaid work or if it is leisure. He suggests a definition of volunteering based on the understanding that volunteering is both unpaid work and attractive leisure:

> It is an un-coerced, intentionally productive, altruistic activity framed in a distinctive context and engaged in during free time. It is also an altruistic activity people want to do and, using their abilities and resources, actually do in either a satisfying or a fulfilling way (or both). If people are compensated, the payment in cash or in kind is significantly less than market value.
>
> (Stebbins, 2013, p. 342)

The compensation mentioned by Stebbins (2013) might relate to how volunteer professionals such as veterinarians, pilots and the media, who work as volunteers in the Finnmark Race and Iditarod, are rewarded. Although some costs are covered, it is much less than they would have earned in their regular jobs. Volunteering is changing. For example, previously in Norway, volunteerism was characterized by great popular movements with labour unions, the Red Cross, health, sport and missionary organizations, linked to personal identity, moral and social fellowship. Today, this is for some volunteers replaced with a selective and time-framed volunteerism based on 'what is in it for me?' logic – that is, individual needs and what each person finds interesting here and now (Aagedal *et al.*, 2009; Lorentzen and Hustinx, 2007). This change is also discussed by Wollebæk *et al.* (2014), who describe sporting events as meeting places between the traditional volunteer culture and a late modern volunteer culture. What they found to be characteristic of the late modern volunteers was 'The effort required is limited in time, the purpose is specific, and the activity can prove beneficial for volunteers with regard to building their human and social capital' (Wollebæk *et al.*, 2014, p. 23). The authors further argue that:

> these sporting events depend on the experience and commitment of core volunteer groups, whose reasons for participating are to a greater extent related to the values intrinsic to the activity itself. The motivation is expressive rather than instrumental and not nearly as reflexive as 'late modern'.
>
> (Wollebæk *et al.*, 2014, p. 23)

The values related to the commitment from the core volunteers are especially identified in our study, pointed out by the veterinarians, pilots and media workers. In addition, having fun, friendships and helping others are reasons to return to help out at events, thus events that do not satisfy this can find it difficult to recruit volunteers (Wollebæk *et al.*, 2014). This is also supported by Allen and Bartle (2014, p. 46), who point out that volunteers who were both intrinsically motivated and felt they received managerial support were more likely to report greater engagement whilst volunteering. The change in focus for some to the purpose of volunteering might underpin the growth in volunteer tourism at events.

The focus in our chapter is taking the volunteer role related to tourism a bit further, investigating the volunteer tourists that work for free at events, where they are living out their special interests and are mostly arranging their own travel and stay. The way the volunteer tourists book their travel and the reasons that they participate as volunteers at festivals differ from the traditional way of understanding volunteer tourism. This is compared with how volunteering has been described and researched traditionally, exemplified by Wearing and McGehee (2013), with, for example, a focus on alternative tourism, new tourism and goodwill. In volunteer event tourism, the travel is often not a pre-booked package where a tour operator or a local tourism company has promised to give them a certain experience, but a 'package' that the volunteer tourists have to create themselves. There are some examples of volunteer tourist packages related to dogsled races, however, for example, in 2014 the Bayfield Chamber of Commerce and Visitor Bureau offered packages to experience the Midwest's largest sled dog race as a 'voluntarist'.

The two events: the Finnmark Race and Iditarod

The Finnmark Race is Europe's longest dogsledding race at 1,000 km, arranged in Finnmark, the northernmost county in Norway, bordering Russia and Finland. It starts in the beginning of March every year in Alta, goes through the whole county to Kirkenes, and then back again to Alta, taking the dog teams around five to seven days. The race was initiated locally in 1981 with three dog teams. Through the years, it has developed from including mostly local participants to become an international sporting event, with around 150 mushers participating in three different distances. The mushers (dogsled drivers) always bring at least two handlers that will help the mushers. Handlers are not volunteers, but are part of the support team. Different nationalities participate every year, and in 2016 the mushers were from Norway, Finland, Scotland, Sweden, England, Germany, Spain, Poland, Belgium and Hungary. The dogsledding race is a journey through a whole county for the mushers: the race is staged in an event venue, a trail, which goes through a vast and wild natural landscape, interspersed with meetings with local cultures and societies at different checkpoints located in villages and cabins along the trail. Handlers – those who help the mushers at the checkpoints throughout the race – together with veterinarians, media and race managers, follow the race by car. All checkpoints except for two are located by the road. The Finnmark Race is totally dependent on volunteers, with only four employees and around 650 volunteers. Whilst the majority of the volunteers come from Finnmark, volunteer tourists also come from other places in Norway and other countries. Where the volunteer tourists come from differs every year, and those investigated in this study related to the Finnmark Race came from England, Spain and Norway.

The Iditarod is the world's longest dogsledding race at 1,600 km, and is held in Alaska. It starts in Anchorage each year on the first Saturday in March, and it ends when the last musher reaches Nome, usually 9–12 days. Iditarod was also initiated locally and was started in 1973, where 32 dog teams participated. Today, an average of 65 teams start the race each year, with mushers mostly resident in Alaska, but also from other states, as well as from Canada and Europe. In 2016 they came from the United States, Switzerland, Norway, Czech Republic, Germany, France, Sweden, New Zealand, England and Hungary. Iditarod is a journey through a whole state, where most of the trail passes through wild natural landscapes with no access by road. Participants pass through small villages with native people, where the mushers and dogs have their checkpoints for resting. Veterinarians, media and race managers follow the race by plane or snowmobile. The handlers mainly have access to the mushers at the start and restart, and also at the finish line in Nome. Iditarod is also dependent on volunteers, having around six employees and 1,200 volunteers participating each year. Many of the volunteers are from Alaska, but once again, volunteer tourists also come from other states in the United States and some from other countries. The volunteers who worked during Iditarod and took part in this study came from Alaska and other states.

Method

This study is part of an international research project titled *Winter: New turns in Arctic winter tourism: Adventuring, romanticising and exoticising, and demasculinising nature?* The research has been conducted through case studies on two rural sports events. In exploring the questions guiding our research, the study builds upon a qualitative approach involving interviews, participating observations and field conversations. The research was conducted during Iditarod in 2014, and at the Finnmark Race in 2013, 2015 and 2016. The data were collected by first author, Jæger, a former musher and manager, and also a long-time volunteer at the Finnmark Race. The chapter is based on interviews with 14 volunteers, 9 men and 5 women. The informants from the two events presented in this study were chosen against a background of broadness related to both races, their volunteer role, experience, gender, age and nationality. They are between 18 and 70 years old and are chosen from a larger sample representing the main findings related to volunteer tourism and values. The informants are volunteers who can be divided into two main volunteer categories. The first category is the volunteer professionals, such as veterinarians, media workers and pilots. The second category is the volunteers in general who have different occupations in their daily lives other than the race, and therefore, they might get random jobs with different tasks from year to year. Most volunteers are local and/or from the event's home country. The international volunteers are in both races mainly represented by the veterinarians, but also by volunteers in general. The volunteers in Iditarod investigated in this study included three from Alaska and five from other states in the United States – five were volunteer professionals and three general volunteers. The respondents in the Finnmark Race included two from Finnmark, two from other places in Norway and two from other parts of

Europe (Spain and England) – two were volunteer professionals and the other four were general volunteers. The names used in the findings are pseudonyms.

Value creation: findings and discussion

This section splits the analysis into three key themes: volunteers' value creation; value created for the event; and value co-created in events.

Volunteers' value creation

Events like the Finnmark Race and Iditarod might work with the volunteers in ways that resonate with what the volunteers seek to accomplish as a result of participating as a volunteer. For example, professional volunteers such as pilots, veterinarians and media workers are motivated to participate in events by the potential to learn. Anne, a veterinary student from Norway who volunteers in the Finnmark Race, emphasizes the aspect of learning in saying that 'the race is an arena where I can practice sport medicine on more than a thousand dogs and I can work together with many experienced veterinary experts'. The opportunity to learn is also highlighted by Miguel, an experienced veterinarian from Spain who points out that he always learns something new in the races, both from other veterinarians but also from working with a diversity of dogs, often in harsh weather conditions. The fact that gaining skills and knowledge gives credit can also enhance the volunteer's value creation. Like the pilots in Iditarod that come from all walks of life, including cardiologists, Supreme Court judges and commercial pilots. Jeff, who co-ordinates the pilots in the Iditarod Air Force, has been a volunteer at Iditarod since 1984. He was introduced to the race by his father, who was a dog musher when he was young.

> Well, I've been flying all of my life up here in Alaska. I was born and raised in Anchorage, and I just was interested. It was kind of fun to follow the race, and one of my buddies just called me up and said 'We need some help flying some stuff up for this dog race, can you help me?' and then I've been here ever since. All of us use our own aircraft and we have 30 pilots right now. Our longest flier, Danny, he's been here since '81. So, we have a lot of longevity here. Most of our guys come back, so we have a tremendous amount of experience here also, just doing this flying.

Jeff also points out that they gain skills volunteering for the Iditarod:

> It is assumed that pilots in the Iditarod Air Force is better than the average guy, because, well, basically, you put them through our

training, and the most important thing about our guys, I would say, is that they are current, they're up to date, they haven't been sitting around for months.

The social aspect of volunteering, for instance creating friendships and communities, is important. Jeff says that one reason for this is that:

Everybody works together, we're here because we want to fly, and we're here for the Iditarod. We all volunteer and nobody gets paid, so it's kind of very cohesive ... or a draw that keeps us all in, and it's a lot of fun, and we've got to the point now where I would trust any of my pilots to fly any of my family anywhere. And everybody here, I'm sure, feels the same, and if they do not, we attempt to remedy this situation.

The social aspect is also important for other types of volunteers. Hugh, who is a return volunteer from England to the Finnmark Race, has no specialization and has been assigned different tasks during the six years that he has been a volunteer. He outlines that

there is a tremendous number of people who know me, recognize me and speak to me. The musher Harald Tunheim (a well-known musher in Norway) came and shook my hand and I visited him in his house. You go back and they recognize you.

He also emphasizes that: 'One of the attractions for me is the slightly amateurish nature, because it is run by volunteers; you can't do it otherwise – 600 volunteers and you cannot run it with paid people.'

Similarly, Max from Pennsylvania, who works at a checkpoint, describes how you learn about togetherness in the 'Iditarod family', and he stated:

It is a family, and you keep getting closer year after year, as you make new acquaintances. That family just keeps growing, and it is an Iditarod family. And when you're in contact with somebody for six or seven days, 24 hours a day in the same room basically, you learn how to get along with people.

In addition to friendships and feelings of togetherness, volunteers are attracted by unpredictability – for example, living a non-routine bubble life, and working in the wild. Kevin from New York works for three weeks at Iditarod, and has done so for eight years. He stated that:

To work with Iditarod is different from what I am working with in my ordinary job in media. It is interesting, challenging, frustrating and sucks you in. It is about the people you work with, and the freedom to develop technology and marketing new ideas. You must have the right people. I am from New York. There is some novelty to it – the volunteering life, and Alaska with its myths.

Jack also has a media company in New York which films the Super Bowl. He has worked at Iditarod for eight years and works for two weeks every time: 'Alaska is not like any other place I have been … you get addicted.' This is for some a flow-like way of living, where the volunteers are immersed in the moment. This makes them feel more alive.

The different aspects of the value created are strongly interwoven, which influences the perceived attractiveness of the events. For instant, part of the attraction is that the volunteers feel in control but at the same time they know they depend on the other volunteers, the presence of the dogs and the wild nature conditions. John, who has his own veterinarian clinic in another state in the United States, worked as a volunteer at Iditarod for three years before taking a year off, but he had to come back because he missed being a part of the team, an important reason for him to volunteer:

> When you have worked one time, you are hooked…. It is nice to meet the other veterinarians again, and to work with healthy dogs. I am a surgeon, so I just see dogs from the inside in my ordinary job at the clinic.

He also highlights 'being out in the nature, in the wilderness, seeing wild nature and animals'. The natural environment fascinates many of the volunteers. Olga is a volunteer tourist from south Norway who worked at a checkpoint in the Finnmark Race for the first time this season (she has been following the race on television for many years).

> I love to stay out in the nature, and to go on holidays where you can experience something, and meet people and dogs that are out in nature. The arctic winter and the mountain plateau is fascinating. Here you can get a real storm – but people and dogs are managing these challenges. It is interesting to follow different mushers, and that some are participating not with the goal to win, but to have a good time…. It is most important to be a part of the race.

Hugh, from England, who worked at the Finnmark Race, also highlights the natural environment and phenomena as important reasons for volunteering:

> People back home ask me, why do you go in the middle of the winter? Rural, open, vast country, open spaces, landscape, real weather. We

got a mixed weather at home, with snow for a few days.... When I was driving outside checkpoint Levajok, we stopped; there was no light or sound pollution. There were the stars and the Northern Lights. I have seen the Northern Lights every year. It is a rare event, to hear nothing.

The volunteers' interactions are dynamic and varied, e.g. new tasks emerge, they meet new volunteers and the weather changes. This creates a type of unpredictability that many find exciting because they have to learn to adapt. Further, to meet people they do not know from different cultures and societies is a part of this excitement.

Value created for the event

The value created is based on the events, that is, on a 'time out of time' and a 'special place' (Getz, 2012); but most of all the events influence the volunteers by proposing a holiday where the volunteers' activities increased their feelings of being in the moment. Or as Aina, a volunteer from Finnmark at a checkpoint, describes her feelings related to the Finnmark Race:

> It is amazing that you can gather so many people in one place, just this week, with the same interests. It is much the same from year to year, but it is new people and always changes. Most people that are here are positive. If you are a negative person, you are not here. There is a lot of positive energy.

The events' attractiveness means that they gain access to different people, where volunteers who return possess valuable knowledge about the event that they can share with those who are new.

The value of volunteers for the event can be illustrated through Mike, a volunteer tourist from another state in the United States who has been volunteering as a pilot in the Iditarod Air Force for 12 years. He tells us that because Iditarod means a lot to many of the pilots in this air force, they return. He exemplifies this by describing what Iditarod means for one of the volunteer pilots who works as a doctor in his ordinary job.

> He makes probably half a million dollars a year or something like that. He said to me, 'You could not pay me enough to do this job, but as a volunteer for free, I'll do it any day of the week'. Just ... it's that kind of camaraderie, you just want to be part of it, the excitement of the race, especially when you get to the coast and you start to see things get competitive, you're a part of it, so, you know, from bringing the food out to the dogs, to bringing the sick dogs back, and, you know ... there's two kinds of Iditarod pilots: the ones that say 'I'm

not going to do this again, this is my last year', and they're back again, doing it, and the other ones say, 'I can't wait for next year' ... anyway it's what we do, I've done it for 12 years, so ... yeah, maybe 12 years more.

This camaraderie is enabled by the event, which has become 'the special place' where pilots from different walks in life interact to make the event happen. This is illustrated by several volunteers, amongst them Jeff, Jenny, Brad and Alice. Jeff, a pilot, indicates that: 'The Mushers are all our favourites. Because without them, we wouldn't be there.' Mike adds:

> You know, some mushers set themselves apart by coming up person-ally and thanking us. We had one the other day that we rescued off one of the lakes near the Rhone and he went to every pilot he saw and said, 'Are you an Iditarod pilot? I want to thank you so much for doing this.' So ... he was literally, you know, he had to be brought back to town, he was dying in there, kind of beaten up ... it's been a rough year for some of the mushers.

Jenny is a local volunteer and has worked as one of the leaders in the Finnmark Race since 1988 in many different jobs, but especially with the media. She comments on the fascination with the co-operation between animals and people, noting that it is a competition out in the wild and in nature. This creates a lot of passion and feelings, especially because it is out in the wilderness. Jenny thinks that establishing a connection with the volunteers is essential for value creation. She states:

> I think that working with the Finnmark Race is about the connection to people. [She continues] It is a big difference to being a leader in a company, where you can force people to do particular tasks because it is part of their job. However, you cannot do that in the Finnmark Race: you can't influence them whatsoever. You must get people to do their job because they are motivated and feel they are having a good time.... We are talking about a Google generation where we get the answers immediately, immediately. Instead of being bemused, this I'm really wondering about. This is an event that is arranged by volunteers with a very few people working full time. And then, to be able to maintain the soul in the race, people must feel ownership of the race. This is a precondition to be able to conduct good reputation building, and because you need a story to tell.

What Jenny indicates is that the event also brings life to the local society through the event stories and reputation. This can have a positive influence on other types of industry, e.g. the tourism industry.

Brad, from the United States, and Alice, from Alaska, also point this out (Brad is a former musher and has been a volunteer at Iditarod for many years while Alice has volunteered as a race official):

> I have an attachment to the Iditarod, many friends, and like watching the event. Just the excursion by airplane of 1,000 miles of trail is incredible. I never get tired of seeing Alaska.
> The Iditarod is an unusual sporting event because the action is continuous for ten days. It is not like a stadium sport, which lasts only two or three hours. Iditarod is a unique opportunity to tell a story – particularly if you already know something about the event, the people living along the trail, and Alaska.

Alice is both fascinated about the race and what it does for the rural communities:

> I'm just a race official. I'm a flunky, right? I've been helping on the Iditarod since '86, and I think I've been a judge for, I don't know, ten, 15 years.

Further, Alice describes the importance of the Iditarod:

> In actuality, Iditarod brings the whole state together. This is the closest the state is together, there. They're all sharing Iditarod, concerned about the community. It's hard to get Alaskans to agree on something that they do ... I think Iditarod is great. I think it does a lot for the rural communities. That's one reason I work on it.

Value co-creation in the events

The findings show that what drives volunteers to enrol in events can strengthen or change during the multiple interactions the volunteers engage in throughout the life of the event. In particular, knowledge, skills and the social aspects are highlighted by both the Finnmark Race and Iditarod volunteers as reasons to return. These benefits illustrate that volunteers' creation of value goes beyond the event itself and that can grow, given that the events create possibilities for co-creation, e.g. organization of space, time and people to allow for deeper interactions in which participants can share knowledge and experiences (Heinonen *et al.*, 2013; Lusch and Vargo, 2014). It is crucial for the events to be aware of and facilitate volunteers' value realization – that is, the events must map and analyse points of interaction to ensure that they have the right team composition, and perhaps introducing a type of mentorship for new volunteers to facilitate and strengthen feelings of community and knowledge acquisition. Moreover, volunteers' skills and knowledge development are at the core of the event. New skills brought in by experienced volunteer tourists, especially among veterinarians and media workers, brings in new knowledge to the event. Hence, events that fail to co-create value with the volunteers risk that volunteers decide not to return, which will influence the event's knowledge repository. For events like the Finnmark Race and Iditarod, which are arranged in rural areas, gaining knowledgeable and skilled national and international volunteers is critical, as these events depend on new knowledge to develop and strengthen their position as events.

The value of knowledge and skills are closely interlinked with friendship, community and the creation of cohesive groups. This increases the feeling of meaning for the volunteers – a feeling that is shared across individuals and cultures (Sagiv and Schwartz, 2000; Schwartz and Bilsky, 1990). Feelings of community depend on the nature of the group and the events can facilitate teamwork. For instance, working together in teams over time means that the volunteers get the opportunity to know each other better (Wollebæk et al., 2014). Many volunteers decide to return for this reason only, to 'meet their once-in-a-year family'. The 'once-in-a-year family' shows that co-created value really can extend beyond the point of interaction and facilitates future recruitment of skilled volunteers.

This means that volunteers' core values can serve as cornerstones for future development of the events, which, when compromised, can result in lower event quality. The flipside is that a strong focus on values can limit the events' operational freedom, as a strong adherence to core values can influence which volunteers are preferred, how they are treated, and what possibilities they will have to pursue their own values. At the same time, knowing what is motivating the volunteers and what values are created for whom will enhance the capacity for the event to facilitate co-creation between the event management and the volunteers, and thus event value creation and volunteers' value creation (Grönroos and Voima, 2013).

Furthermore, interacting with what is considered by the volunteers as 'the wild' (i.e. in a sparsely populated arctic landscape with changing weather conditions, snowstorms and cold temperatures) adds an extra dimension to the volunteers' experiences. As Lund (2013, p. 169) describes: 'Nature is not a passive being on which cultural meanings is ascribed. Rather it emerges when we enmesh with it through physical encounter, on our journey with it.' The nature promises the volunteers both beauty and safe adventures.

Conclusion

The aim of this chapter has been to examine the extent to which value creation has been achieved through the co-creation of the actual event and the volunteers themselves, regardless of whether the volunteer was international (a tourist volunteer) or local. We have in this chapter presented a small sample of the volunteers working in the two races. The findings demonstrate that value creation in events is an individual responsibility, but that value can be proposed. This means that the event organizers, by being aware of what values the volunteers cherish, can help facilitate value creation (Zàtori, 2016). The events management teams can propose certain activities that can be used as a 'platform for co-creation' to match what volunteers seek (e.g. increased knowledge) and how volunteering creates feelings of community. Thus, as Zàtori (2016) highlights, important enablers of co-creation are to: provoke attention, engage and involve the volunteers and make them discover what working together can bring. However, the volunteers do have expectations linked to experiential value creation; they want to have fun and feel excited, much like on a normal holiday. In addition, they seek to learn about something they are passionate about or that will make them better professionals. Further, friendships that emerged during the events are considered very valuable by the volunteers as they create a form of togetherness that is long lasting. By adopting a value co-creation approach, events management teams can propose activities that facilitate interactions where knowledge sharing and friendships can occur. This can enhance the possibility for mutual value creation, that is, the events become more attractive for the volunteer, thus securing future volunteers, and the volunteers know that by participating they can gain knowledge, skills and friendships.

Future research could include a larger sample to compare the two races, and further identify values created through co-creation, both outside for the local society and also inside the races. This with an emphasis on what dimensions the international and national volunteer tourists bring to the events, focusing upon the differences between the local, national and international volunteers, related to expectations, experiences and values created for themselves, the events and the local society. In addition, future research could include the event management team to identify and elaborate on the impact of volunteers' value co-creation for the event.

References

Aagedal, O., Egeland, H. and Villa, M. (2009). *Lokalt kulturliv i endring*. Norsk kulturråd: Fagbokforlaget.

Allen, J.B. and Bartle, M. (2014). Sport event volunteers' engagement: Management matters. *Managing Leisure* 19(1): 36–50.

Binkhorst, E. and Den Dekker, T. (2009). Agenda for co-creation tourism experience research. *Journal of Hospitality Marketing & Management* 18(2–3): 311–327.

Cater, C.I. (2006). Playing with risk? Participant perceptions of risk and management implications in adventure tourism. *Tourism Management* 27: 317–325.

Chandler, J.D. and Vargo, S.L. (2011). Contextualization and value-in-context: How context frames exchange. *Marketing Theory* 11(1): 35–49.

Cnaan, R.A., Handy, F. and Wadsworth, M. (1996). Defining who is a volunteer: Conceptual and empirical considerations. *Nonprofit and Voluntary Sector Quarterly* 25(3): 364–383.

Csikszentmihalyi, M. (1975). *Beyond boredom and anxiety*. San Francisco: Jossey-Bass.

de Brito, M.P. and Terzieva, L. (2016). Key elements for designing a strategy to generate social and environmental value: A comparative study of festivals. *Research in Hospitality Management* 6(1): 51–59.

Getz, D. (2012). *Event studies: Theory, research and policy for planned events*. London: Routledge.

Greer, C.R., Lusch, R.F. and Vargo, S.L. (2016). A service perspective: Key managerial insights from service-dominant (SD) logic. *Organizational Dynamics* DOI: 10.1016/j.orgdyn.2015.12.004.

Grönroos, C. and Voima, P. (2013). Critical service logic: Making sense of value creation and co-creation. *Journal of the Academy of Marketing Science* 41(2): 133–150.

Haanpää, M., García-Rosell, J.C. and Tuulentie, S. (2016). Co-creating places through events: The case of a tourism community event in Finnish Lapland. In A. Clarke and A. Jepson (eds) *Managing and developing communities, festivals and events*. Basingstoke: Palgrave Macmillan (pp. 34–50).

Heinonen, K., Strandvik, T. and Voima, P. (2013). Customer dominant value formation in service. *European Business Review* 25(2): 104–123.

Jæger, K. and Kvidal-Røvik, T. (2015). 'Du får som fortjent': Destinasjonsmarkedsføring, eventer og sosiale medier. In K.A. Ellingsen and T. Blindheim (eds) *Regional merkevarebygging*. Bergen: Fagbokforlaget (pp. 135–150).

Jæger, K. and Olsen, K. (2016). On commodification: Volunteer experiences in festivals. *Journal of Tourism and Cultural Change* DOI: 10.1080/14766825. 2016.1168827.

Jepson, J. and Clarke, A. (2016). An introduction to planning and managing communities, festivals and events. In A. Clarke and A. Jepson (eds) *Managing and developing communities, festivals and events*. Basingstoke: Palgrave Macmillan (pp. 3–15).

Lorentzen, H. and Hustinx, L. (2007). Civic involvement and modernization. *Journal of Civil Society* 3(2): 101–118.

Lund, K.A. (2013). Experiencing nature in nature-based tourism. *Tourist Studies* 13(2): 156–171.

Lusch, R.F. and Vargo, S.L. (2014). *Service-dominant logic: Premises, perspective, possibilities*. Cambridge: Cambridge University Press.

Mathisen, L. (2012). The exploration of the memorable tourist experience. In J.S. Chen (ed.) *Advances in hospitality and leisure (Advances in hospitality and leisure, volume 8)*. Bingley: Emerald Group Publishing Limited (pp. 21–41).

Monga, M. (2006). Measuring motivation to volunteer for special events. *Event Management* 10(1): 47–61.

Nordvall, A., Pettersson, R., Svensson, B. and Brown, S. (2014). Designing events for social interaction. *Event Management* 18(2): 127–140.

Pera, R. and Viglia, G. (2015). Turning ideas into products: Subjective well-being in co-creation. *The Service Industries Journal* 35(7–8): 388–402.

Prebensen, N.K. (2012). *Value creation in experience-based networks: A case study of sport events in Europe*. In M. Kasimoglu (ed.) *Strategies for tourism industry: Micro and macro perspectives*. Rijeka, Croatia: InTech Europe. INTECH Open Access Publisher (pp. 185–200).

Prebensen, N.K., Chen, J.S. and Uysal, M. (2014). *Creating experience value in tourism*. Boston: CAB International.

Richards, G. (2011). Creativity and tourism: The state of the art. *Annals of Tourism Research* 38(4): 1225–1253.

Richards, G. (2014). The new geographies of tourism: Space, place and locality. Paper presented at the Wageningen Geography Lectures, January, Wageningen, Netherlands.

Rokeach, M. (1973). *The nature of human values*. New York: Free Press.

Sagiv, L. and Schwartz, S. (2000). Value priorities and subjective well-being: Direct relations and congruity effects. *European Journal of Social Psychology* 30(2): 177–198.

Schwartz, S. (2013). Value priorities and behavior: Applying a theory of integrated value systems. Paper presented at the The Psychology of Values: The Ontario Symposium.

Schwartz, S. and Bilsky, W. (1990). Toward a theory of the universal content and structure of values: Extensions and cross-cultural replications. *Journal of Personality and Social Psychology* 58(5): 878.

Sfandla, C. and Björk, P. (2013). Tourism experience network: Co-creation of experiences in interactive processes. *International Journal of Tourism Research* 15(5): 495–506.

Stebbins, R. (2013). Unpaid work of love: Defining the work–leisure axis of volunteering. *Leisure Studies* 32(3): 339–345.

Viken, A. and Jæger, K. (2012). Festivalisering av Bygde-Norge – lokalsamfunnsutvikling ispedd turisme. In M. Forbord, G.-T. Kvam and Rønningen (eds) *Turisme i distriktene*. Trondheim: Tapir Akademisk Forlag (pp. 131–150).

Wearing, S. and McGehee, N.G. (2013). Volunteer tourism: A review. *Tourism Management* 38: 120–130.

Wilson, J. (2000). Volunteering. *Annual Review of Sociology* 26: 215–240.

Wollebæk, D., Skirstad, B. and Hanstad, D.V. (2014). Between two volunteer cultures: Social composition and motivation among volunteers at the 2010 test event for the FIS Nordic World Ski Championships. *International Review for the Sociology of Sport* 49(1): 22–41.

Zàtori, A. (2016). Exploring the value co-creation process on guided tours (the 'AIM-model') and the experience-centric management approach. *International Journal of Culture, Tourism and Hospitality Research* 10(4): DOI: /pdfplus/ 10.1108/IJCTHR-09–2015–0098.

Chapter 2

Creativity-based volunteering at the Winter Olympics in Sochi

Beyond sport and borders

Valery Gordin and Irina Borovskaia

Introduction

Sporting mega-events have long ago expanded beyond the border of merely 'sport events' with various cultural events often being held in parallel. Today, events (in addition to festivals, exhibitions, film shows) are aimed at promoting humanistic messages that create added value and additional benefits for a range of stakeholders. For example, the Olympic Games is not just a sporting event, but also a cultural phenomenon. The Cultural Olympiad hosted by Olympic capitals has become an integral part of the Olympic Games with a significant potential impact on the image of the host city and the host country at local, national and international levels (García, 2002, 2017; Gilmore, 2014; Lander and Crowe, 2010).

Traditionally the research of volunteer practices focused on the sporting aspect of the Olympic Games. Volunteering was considered a form of public support of the Olympics, its recognition by the local community, a technology to reduce costs for organization of the Olympic Games and to improve the quality of sporting events. More recently volunteers have become an integral part of all Olympic Games, undertaking a number of functions on welcoming guests and participants of the Olympics. However, starting with the Olympic Games in Barcelona in 1992, the Cultural Olympiads have become an integral part of the Olympic Games. Their characteristic feature is that the events of the Cultural Olympiad are held throughout the four years of the Olympic cycle. The Cultural Olympiads in Athens (Greece), London (Great Britain) and Sochi (Russia) were organized according to this pattern. As part of the Cultural Olympics, there is a wide volunteer movement which spreads out with some significant features resulting from the creative nature of the events. Due to this, a significant portion of the volunteer functions at the cultural events has shifted to creativity, exchange of creative ideas and artistic products. Volunteers at the Cultural Olympiads have a special motivation for co-operation and channels for involvement in volunteer activities which are different from those used at the sports Olympic Games. Study of the characteristics of volunteer activities at the Cultural Olympiad and review of a specific case study at the Cultural Olympiad in Sochi has become the subject of consideration in this chapter.

A review of the features of volunteer activities at the Cultural Olympiad is highly important, as the volunteer motivations include both pride in participation in the sports mega-event and promotion of certain creative ideas incorporated in the works of arts and crafts and acting skills. Participation of youth volunteers as creative entities actively engaged in the participation and organization of cultural programmes is very significant. In this chapter, in terms of such an interesting experience, we consider the case of International Paint Pals (IPP) – a well-known non-governmental organization (NGO), which could be identified as an international volunteers' network partnership, organizing many international art and educational events at the Olympic Games and global venues. In this chapter we also examine the concept of creativity-based volunteering by analogy with the skill-based volunteering concept, and explore it with the case of a youth art exhibition, organized by IPP over the last 20 years.

This chapter[1] is organized in the following way: the next section outlines literature which focuses on the use of volunteers within the cultural component of sporting mega-events and in particular outlines creativity-based volunteers. The study design is then outlined, which includes an introduction of the IPP NGO that implement projects at the Cultural Olympiad. This section also discusses the research method, which is based on a survey of 'Peace and Friendship through the Olympic Spirit' Youth Art Exhibition volunteers in Sochi, 2014. The findings detail the volunteers' profile and descriptive statistics regarding their motivation to participate in the project. The final section of the chapter summarizes the results obtained and proposals for further research arising on their basis.

The use of volunteers for cultural programmes

The idea of a special cultural programme carried out concurrently with sporting competitions was a part of the original vision of the modern Olympic Games as a synthesis of sport, culture and education. The history of the Cultural Olympiads originates in 1912, when during the Olympic Games in Stockholm awards were given in such categories as: Architecture, Music, Painting, Sculpture and Literature. Preceding the 1948 Olympics in London, arts competitions were held with various changes associated with the complexities of their implementation (García, 2002). After 1948 it was decided to replace the contests with exhibitions and festivals, which at first just accompanied sports events for two weeks, but then developed into more ambitious projects, continuing for several months or even over a year in some cases. The most striking example from this point of view was the 1968 Summer Olympics in Mexico City, which were highlighted with the first annual national and international Cultural Olympiad. 'Cultural Olympiad' as a phrase was widely spread already at the Games in Mexico City, but came into official use only during the 1992 Barcelona Olympics, when the actual four-year Olympics of cultural events took place connecting the end of one Olympic Games and the beginning of the next one. Since the Games of 1992 in Barcelona, the Cultural Olympiad has become a separate event, combining under this title a series of events supposed to introduce the cultural heritage of the host country of the Games to the whole world. This format has remained since then at all Summer Olympic Games but was first used as part of the Winter Olympics in Vancouver 2010. Sochi 2014 then became the second Winter Games offering a full four-year cultural programme.

The International Olympic Committee (IOC) currently declares the mandatory implementation of the cultural programme in parallel with the competitions (thus according to Rule 39 of the Olympic Charter) (International Olympic Committee, 2015), although the IOC do not clearly specify the programme (and its assessment). On the one hand, this gives organizers complete freedom of action, and on the other, it could potentially restrict the cultural component as a low priority. Further, it affects the efficient management and financing of these events. One of the solutions to these difficulties may be the use of different categories of volunteers in the realization of cultural events.

As such, volunteer activities under events organization can provide a number of advantages to the different stakeholders. First and foremost, volunteers can supply the event with additional or enhanced capabilities, thus helping organizers to save resources. Visitors can enjoy the event, which otherwise could not take place due to the lack of human or financial resources (Holmes and Smith, 2009). When involving volunteers, the organizers have the opportunity to create additional services at the event to work with a large number of visitors. Second, the enthusiasm, interest and responsibility of volunteers contribute to the formation of relationships with the public and local communities, and a broad range of diverse skills, experience and knowledge brought by volunteers can enhance the value of the festival or event (Nichols and Ojala, 2009). Third, volunteering contributes to local social and public involvement and cohesion (Smith, 2012). Fourth, when examining the case of volunteers from disadvantaged sections of society, they have the opportunity to develop new skills through involvement in a variety of organizational work during an event (Moscardo, 2008). Further, involvement of volunteers contributes to the rising status of the project, helping to create an image of the event as more open, socially oriented and close to the society. Fifth and finally, the volunteering expands and strengthens the international links of organizations involved in the Cultural Olympiad. To enhance the effectiveness of cultural events that are part of sporting mega-events it is necessary to implement a differentiated approach to volunteers and to understand current differences between them.

There are several basic types of volunteering activities in cultural projects. Organizers execute work packages and they lead on any variety of projects for an event, such as development, training, fundraising or investing funds for their implementation. Fundraisers work on attracting various resources (foremost the financial resources). Co-ordinators control the work of various groups of performers. Social groups and event website administrators manage various Internet resources to promote the event. The performer deals with implementing parts of the event and works directly in the field. Indeed, according to the scale of event conducted and to the features of the project, it is possible to combine different roles and to get the job done by one person. It is evident that there are various forms of volunteer activities.

Two basic forms of organization of events with volunteering could be identified. The first case refers to the involvement of volunteers for the large project as performers (for example, the work of volunteers at the Olympic Games directly at the competition venues, athletes' accommodation facilities, in many functional zones), which are characterized by clear instructions for the preparation and specific action within a specific function for the volunteer performers, a specific role in the event or project limited by delegated powers and rather strict internal hierarchy. That means, in this case, that the project by its nature is not a volunteer one, but the organizers, due to certain reasons (resources saving, formation of emotional perception of events by the population, training personnel for future large projects), attract additional manpower represented by volunteer performers. In the second case, the event/project are initially volunteer projects and are performed by volunteer organizers who in the case of project development build the institutional structure of the project, differentiate the roles of, for instance, volunteer organizers, volunteer supervisors/co-ordinators, volunteer performers. In this case, the creation of such an organizational structure is a necessary condition for the existence of the project, vital to the implementation of large-scale projects involving multiple network partners and supervisors/co-ordinators from different countries.

Analysing the role and value of volunteering in cultural events and cultural projects carried out as part of sport mega-events, it is essential to note that an important aspect in the organization of volunteers' work is the motivational factor of their involvement. Volunteering is based on a support or assistance without any financial remuneration, and therefore the motives for volunteering are not financially rewarded, but are dependent on social, philanthropic and spiritual interests. The analysis of volunteer work motivation served as a subject for many scientific studies. As a rule, volunteers do their volunteer work under the influence of two or more factors (Treuren, 2014). For example, it is possible to divide all the volunteers into two groups: (1) input-oriented volunteers are those who are more focused on helping others and the knowledge they can pass on to others, and those who are primarily interested in receiving certain benefits through the volunteering; and (2) output-oriented, who can be distinguished based on the experiences the volunteer seeks. The motives of input-oriented volunteering are connected with re-socialization, altruistic attitudes of giving, family traditions and belonging to a community. The motivations of output-oriented volunteers could include gaining new/necessary experiences, professional development, self-knowledge, useful leisure time and awareness of the benefits of volunteer work (see Csordas, 2011).

Of special importance is the personal sense of satisfaction of volunteers who undertake the performed work. Dwyer *et al.* (2013) have studied the influence of this factor on the productivity of the volunteers, but there is another challenging question concerning the role of the relationship between volunteers and their mentors and the presence of a strong leader in the volunteer team. It is known that, as a rule, large international projects involve volunteers from different countries and sometimes it is hard to come to terms with each other and with organizational structures. A more positive approach and support contribute to the achievement of better results and further quality development of relations between team members (Hede and Rentschler, 2007). The process of volunteer recruiting and further work with them requires a greater extent of customization, and it is therefore necessary to consider not only the fact of a multicultural community of volunteers, but also to take into account the peculiarities of volunteers' activity in different countries and regions, focusing on the benefits that potential volunteers can provide to the project (Randle and Dolnicar, 2009).

Volunteering is currently rising to a new level. The daily life of modern volunteers in the projects in the sphere of culture does not consist only of 'rough' work (meaning 'hands-on' volunteering). The volunteers often create a project 'face'. This involves communicating with the media and visitors; accompanying the invited guests; helping in the direct organization of events, lectures, concerts and master classes; and promoting organization profiles in social networks. While working as a volunteer in project teams of cultural institutions, it is possible to acquire valuable experience in various fields, to obtain authoritative guidance and a promising job.

Thus, volunteering has now becoming an indispensable resource for a variety of projects in the sphere of culture and art. Volunteer work has certainly taken its place in the sector of labor resources as part of numerous events of all sizes. Motivation, and methods of its stimulation, plays an important role in the nature and effectiveness of volunteer work. Proper management of volunteer work, understanding of its characteristics, strengths and weaknesses, allows the volunteer work to be not only a worthy substitute for the lack of resources, but also to be more efficient and even bring additional dividends to the organizers.

Volunteering at cultural events in the sphere of culture and art is a recognized phenomenon and in recent years has become increasingly popular (Lockstone and Smith, 2009). The growing popularity of active involvement of volunteers in events and festivals organization is connected with the tendency of more non-traditional forms of volunteering (Barron and Rihova, 2011). One should pay attention to a significant role of volunteers in the online promotion of cultural events, the formation of the flexible image of cultural events, attractive to different target groups, and in the prolonged volunteering, which is carried out in the period before, during and after the event.

Some authors (e.g. Barron and Rihova, 2011; Stebbins, 2000) tend to describe volunteer activity through a leisure model of volunteering. According to this model, the volunteers and volunteer activities can be classified according to the nature of activities in three main forms: serious leisure, casual leisure and project-based leisure. Serious leisure is characterized by systematic, regular volunteer work during the events, which is distinguished by a serious attitude to work, required training, obtaining specific skills, knowledge and experience and even the opportunity to build a career in the chosen direction. Casual leisure is a relatively non-durable pleasurable activity requiring little additional preparation or no preparation at all. Project-based leisure is represented as short-term, often one-time, or repeating volunteer activities during spare time. Activities are characterized by relatively easy tasks and do not require training due to the time limitations.

Developing this classification, it is possible to propose two more categories of volunteers based on variety of their activities. One part of the volunteer activities can be characterized as routine-based volunteering, including implementation of relatively simple, regularly repeated actions that reduce the burden on staff. The other part is characterized as a creativity-based volunteering and represents the functions that have a creative nature and require high professional training that allows for the implementation of knowledge and experience gained in the public and commercial sectors, in the specific conditions of the organizations of the third sector, such as organizing cultural events. In other words, creativity-based volunteering is the work of a creative professional in non-profit organizations with a special humanitarian message and based on the relevant motivations.

Creativity-based volunteering can be compared with the approach of skill-based volunteering, which is defined as a 'service to nonprofit organizations by individuals or groups that capitalize on personal talents or core business or professional skills, experience or education, often for the purpose of building organizational strength and increasing capacity' (Maranta and Sladowski, 2010, p. 8). But skill-based volunteering 'typically involves applying or transferring individual or organizational skills – for instance, strategic planning, property management, marketing or information technology management – to a community organization or entity, such as a NGO, non-profit group, school, hospital or cause' (Allen Consulting Group, 2007, p. 2). This activity in the creative cultural projects is complicated, as it implies a certain regulation, explicit goals, but not necessarily the use of creative skills. Creativity-based volunteering might turn out to be more appropriate for special kinds of events, having creativity as the most valuable component. In our opinion cultural programmes as part of the Olympic Games could be considered to be this type of event. Creativity-based volunteering has significant features that distinguish it from other volunteering types and, in particular, from sports volunteering which is in demand at the Olympics.

There is an established base of research looking at volunteering at sporting mega-events and cultural events. However, for works dedicated to the Cultural Olympiads, there is a gap in the research, especially concerning international volunteering at the Cultural Olympiads. In particular, as discussed in this chapter, there is a need to focus on features of the engaged volunteers and their motivations.

Research methods

The research included two parts: a case study of the research subject (IPP), and a quantitative survey of its volunteers using a questionnaire. This case method was based on the review of the internal documents of the organization, materials on the organization activities published in the Internet and completion of the questionnaire by Linden Longino (Head of IPP).

A total of 40 self-administered questionnaires were delivered to project volunteers (participating in the preparation of the exhibition in 2014) by email; 25 of them were completed and returned, indicating a rate of response of 62.5 per cent (see also Panova, 2014). The development of the questionnaire was based on surveys used in other research relevant to the topic (Barron and Rihova, 2011; Christauskas *et al.*, 2012; Waikayi *et al.*, 2012). The questionnaire consists of five blocks including 18 open, rank, alternative questions:

- Demographics (personal information concerning gender, age, citizenship, level of educational qualification and current occupation).
- Volunteering experience (previous work for Cultural Olympiads and similar projects).
- Current IPP project experience (making decision to take part; features of project as reasons and the most important motivational factors; resources invested; level of satisfaction by various aspects of project and work; success score of the project).

- Future intentions (continuation of participation in the projects; recommendation for improvement).
- Open question concerning inspiration to take part in the project with possibility to describe personal experience, work, motivation, that have not been considered in previous questions.

All collected data was carefully processed and analysed; however, the motivational aspects are of primary interest for the purposes of this chapter.

The case of International Paint Pals

In order to illustrate the activities of creativity-based volunteers, we should look at the project initiated and implemented entirely on a voluntary basis, from ideas and organization to the project execution. In that regard, as an object of our research the international 'Peace and Friendship through the Olympic Spirit' Youth Art Exhibition, organized by the NGO, IPP, was chosen. It was a single project in the series of projects implemented as part of the Cultural Olympic Games in Sochi 2014, initiated and carried out from a bottom-up approach (i.e. by a volunteer organization completely on a volunteer basis). All other projects were included in the approved list of events organized from top-down, and were, as a rule, funded by the budget.

This exhibition is especially unique as it has been implemented as part of the Cultural Olympics since 1996, and for many years it brings together people from different countries and different nationalities united by the desire to promote the Olympic values through children's art. Figure 2.1 introduces the main project stages, as they were realized in Sochi.

IPP is an independently incorporated NGO, headquartered in Atlanta, United States, formed in 1995 with the support of the Atlanta Project of the Carter Presidential Center to organize a creative forum for young people as a platform for them to express their personal views on global issues through the universal language of art. Related to the success of the first IPP Olympic project in 1995–1996 in co-operation with the Atlanta Committee for the Olympic Games, a temporary project turned into an ongoing developing organization that implements large-scale projects.

In 2013, the IPP has teamed up with Friendship Force International (FFI), an organization that is responsible for more than 400 international exchange programmes every year in more than 60 countries. This partnership was initiated as part of the preparation for the Sochi Olympics, and was then enforced with an agreement for FFI to acquire the IPP programme. Linden Longino, the founder of IPP, stayed on with the FFI and serve as the organization's newly established Advisor for Youth Cultural Programs. One specific feature of the IPP operation is a self-financing system at the expense of private investments made by project participants

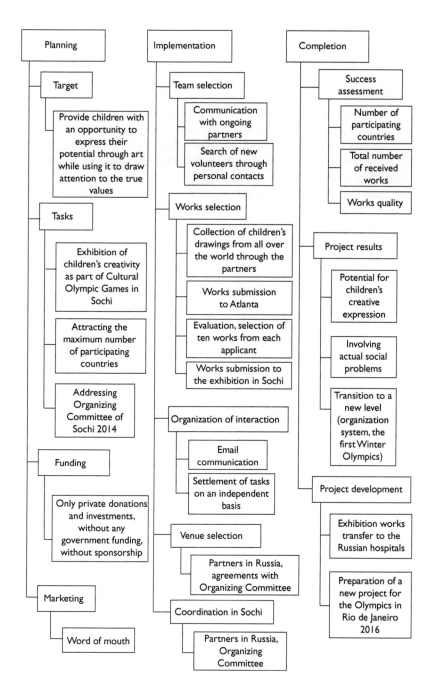

Figure 2.1 Stage plan for 'From the Olympic spirit of friendship and peace' project.

and its organizing partners (without any state assistance and regular sponsors).

The main idea of the IPP project for the Cultural Olympiads – exhibitions of youth and children's art – was as follows: IPP is responsible for collecting paintings by local volunteer co-ordinators from as many countries as possible. A committee of artists and art teachers evaluates the paintings, received at headquarters in Atlanta. Selected works are then sent to the Olympic Games destinations for the exhibition. Olympic Organizing Committees and local IPP partners arrange exhibitions before and during the Games. These exhibits are very popular with the athletes as well as with thousands of spectators.

More than 200,000 young artists aged 6–18 from over 100 countries have participated in the activity of the organization. IPP has organized many international art and educational events for the United Nations, the most famous of which represents the exhibitions for the Summer Olympic Games in Atlanta, USA (1996), Athens, Greece (2004), Beijing, China (2008), the Winter Olympic Games in Sochi, Russia (2014) and for the World Summit of Nobel Peace Laureates in Barcelona, Spain (2015).

The number of participating countries has grown gradually, and the absolute maximum was registered at the Olympic Games in Beijing (China) in 2008 – with 75 countries involved in the project. In 2014, there were 54 countries in Sochi, though such a decline shall not be considered an indication of some problems or deficiencies on the part of the organizers, as there have been many changes in the level of the works, as well as preparation and implementation procedures at the project in the past. There is a significant fact that the actions of the organizing volunteers have become more scheduled and co-ordinated, thus contributing to the more effective work on the project.

The project keeps up to its concept, however, regarding the project organization, for the last 20 years, certain changes have been introduced. These changes were considered through a comparative analysis of the organizational structure of projects implemented in Atlanta, Athens and Sochi. It can be seen how an increase in the project scale results in complications in terms of the structure, processes alteration, formation of a stable network.

Linden Longino, IPP's founder, is the main leader and inspiration of the project. He is responsible for all the co-ordination work, from the choice of the main exhibition topic to the final selection of children's works and their delivery as a part of direct exhibition activity. In the early years of project implementation of the Cultural Olympiads Linden Longino provided most of the work on an independent basis. During the first project he came into contact with the Organizing Committee of the Olympic Games in Atlanta and directly agreed with them on the exhibition issues, then searched for various organizations in different countries, addressed their leaders and made direct agreements to collect works for the exhibition.

The participants were originally recruited as volunteers as there were no monetary rewards for the performed work – they had to cover all the costs for creating, collecting, sending and submitting their works. Thanks to its non-profit nature, the project was appreciated by a large number of people, then recognized and successfully implemented.

Over the years there have been introduced important amendments to the project work principles. An exhibition project titled 'Children Paint the Olympic Games' was organized at the 2004 Olympic Games in Athens; it was characterized by the fact that Linden Longino ceased to work directly with the organizing committees of the Olympic Games in the host countries. The new approach used the search for a reliable partner in the host country of the Games that could take on the national part of the project, such as working in co-operation with the Organizing Committee of the Games, the media, various administrative institutions and organize work on collecting exhibits for the exhibition. In many ways this change in the organization of work was due to the very significant need to consider the specifics of work in general and the work on volunteer non-profit projects in each country hosting such exhibition, and it is easier to co-operate with a partner residing in this country. In Athens, the local private Museum of Greek Children's Art became such a partner, undertaking all the work on the national part of the project. The second important innovation in the work on the project was represented by the country co-ordinators. Linden Longino directly addressed different secondary and special schools, art studios and NGOs. From 2004 he sought a partner in each country that would undertake the co-ordinator's functions for the promotion and collection of children's works in the correspondent country. This is a very important aspect, indicating the improvement of system of work on the project, developing it to a new extent.

Figure 2.2 shows the organizational structure of the project in Sochi. Its implementation was marked with significant differences when compared with all previous years: there was one new level in the structure, specifically, the network partners, and there was added a mediator between the main organizer and Sochi Institute of Fashion, Business and Law (SIMBiP), the partner in the host country. SIMBiP provided all the practical work on co-operation with the Olympic Organizing Committee in Sochi 2014 and covered the major costs as the main partner of the project on the territory of Russia while being responsible for the Russian part of project implementation.

However, unlike previous years, in Sochi the co-ordination of international and national components of the project was not carried out between the organizers/partners (as was the case in Athens in 2004). This was done through the facilitation (or mediation) activity of the Institute for

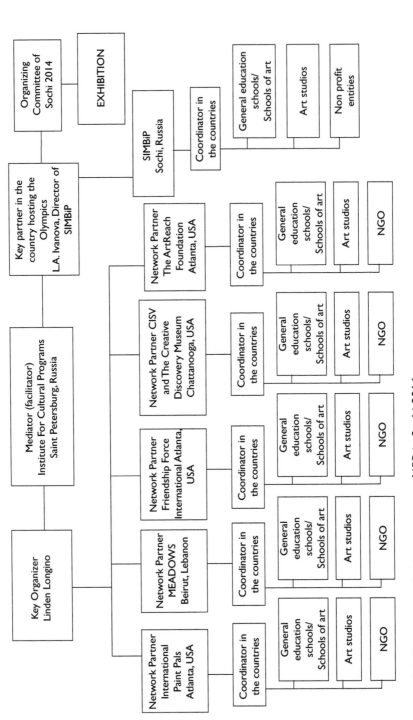

Figure 2.2 Project organization structure of IPP in Sochi 2014.

Cultural Programs in St. Petersburg. The Institute works in the sphere of information, continuous education and scientific research in the cultural sphere, and participates in the preparation and execution of local, regional, national and international projects. The Institute for Cultural Programs has been co-operating with the IPP organization since 1995, and it has become the first international partner of the project.

Further, an important characteristic of the project implementation in Sochi was the organization of interaction between IPP and its ongoing partners – large international NGO and cultural organizations: FFI (Atlanta, United States), the ArtReach Foundation (also Atlanta), MEADOWS – Mediterranean Endeavors Advancing Development of Widespread Sustainability (Beirut, Lebanon), CISV and the Creative Discovery Museum (Chattanooga, United States). All these institutions acted not as project volunteer co-ordinators in certain countries, but as major network partners. A certain feature of the network partners which distinguishes them from the country co-ordinators is primarily the transition from the national to the cross-country level. All of them assisted Linden Longino not only within their countries, though they spread information and acted as project representatives in the whole region. All of these organizations actively addressed their partners, colleagues and friends in different countries, the latter, in their turn, directly approached different schools, studios, non-profit organizations and undertook responsibility for the collection of children's works. Thus, the institutionalization of the project emerges, there are stable forms of interaction between all participants and the formation of a network partnership is taking place.

Such institutionalization of the project occurred due to the fact that employees, those that had previously participated in IPP projects, could attract to their organizations. On the basis of personal connections the inter-organizational relations appeared, as is often the case in the networking formation under informal relationships and trust. Individual creativity-based volunteering promoted the expansion of corporate creativity-based volunteering. This enabled the project being increased in scale as organizations' resources were involved. All organizers, partners and artists have worked to bring their ideas to life as volunteers on an unpaid basis. Both partners and their organizations have invested their own money. Some organizers bought the materials for children's works at their own expense, while others provided their lecturers or facilities so that everyone invested some form of private resource.

Co-ordination of partners' and colleagues' work was organized only through Internet communication. Discussion and settlement of all issues was performed via email. It is important to understand that all participants had absolute freedom in their decisions on task performance, there was no control or instructions to follow, the organizers were delegated to consider the best ways to fulfil their part of the project. This suggests that complete trust between the organizers was an important aspect of the project, contributing to its final success.

Findings

This section presents the results of processing and analysing the collected data: descriptive statistics based on data collected through the questionnaires – respondents' profile and their motivation to participate in the project.

The majority of respondents were women (between the ages of 18 and 25). The age of survey participants varied – the youngest were under 25 and the oldest were over 60 years old. Most of the respondents belong to the older age categories; this may indicate that managers, masterminds and active participants of the reviewed volunteer project are people with rich life experience, who have fulfilled their career potential. They demonstrate rich life experiences, lots of contacts, all aspects which are so important for specific volunteer activities. Volunteer work sometimes gives them an opportunity to fulfil their potential in a new sphere, offering the possibility to work and to open new horizons. The majority of respondents were from the United States (eight volunteers) and Russia (four volunteers). We also received project participant questionnaires from Canada, Spain, South Africa, Ghana, Afghanistan, Lebanon and New Zealand. It is natural that most of the organizing partners are accounted for by such countries as the United States and Russia. As the organization of the IPP has its headquarters in Atlanta, the project management tried to involve its ongoing partners in the United States and Canada with whom they had already settled some kind of co-operation. They actively searched for partners in Russia as well, as it was necessary to interest and promote the idea of the project in the country of project implementation. When it comes to the area of professional activity, there is a large diversity of sampled information. Survey participants included students, with their participation in the project associated with the specifics of their studies. Respondents cited the following activity areas: painting tutor, teacher, actor, high administrative officials, director and manager. Further, many of the respondents are currently retired, though they intensively follow their social activities in the form of participation in volunteer projects. The majority of respondents had no or little experience in organizing and conducting cultural volunteer projects. This suggests that people are not afraid to risk their funds (including financial) to invest various resources for the project, even without any available experience of volunteer projects.

Figure 2.3 shows that the largest number of respondents chose the explanation about the cultural significance of the project and the motive of personal desire to do something to promote peace and friendship. Many

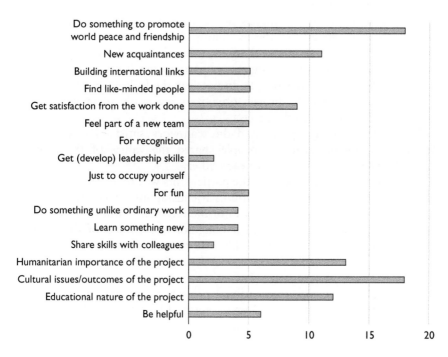

Figure 2.3 Motives for participation in the project.

also noted the humanitarian and educational nature of the project. Important motivational factors include the desire to obtain satisfaction through the performed work and to acquire new professional contacts and acquaintances. This means that the main motives of the project participants are primarily altruistic ones. Pleasure derived from performed work, as well as personal growth, are rather significant factors. The results reveal that the main motive of the organizers is a pure desire to draw attention to the important issues of today, to show the extreme importance of art, children's creativity, its ability to overcome many barriers and produce benefits. In addition, the identified motives of volunteering either refer to input-oriented volunteering or to output-oriented volunteering.

Resources that project participants invested in the project often resulted in responses such as 'own time' (seven out of 25 responses), 'one's skills and experience' (five out of 25), as well as 'contacts and personal acquaintances' (four out of 25). From here we can draw a conclusion on the specific features of the work on this project, including personal contacts, acquaintances and personal communication of its members. The organizers have actively involved their colleagues and friends in co-operation with IPP. Finances do not play a critical role for the project; the top priority is to search for interested people, enthusiasts who, in turn, can also attract new partners. It should be emphasized that some respondents did not actively participate directly in the exhibition, but they managed to attract organizations and funds they belong to, using their professional relations. A significant number of the organizers participated in this event for the first time. This means that people do not fear the lack of experience, and we can conclude that the project organizers are ready to take a risk in attracting new recruits to the project.

Respondents highly appreciated the teamwork satisfaction and interaction with the organizers – people shared the values of the project, worked well in co-operation with each other.

Naturally, the main motive of the participants was represented as a pure desire 'to convey a children's vision of friendship and freedom to a large number of people through the prism of the Olympic Games' (male volunteer, age 30). According to Linden Longino, mastermind of this project and its key manager, 'helping children is the highest form of volunteer work':

> participation in such international projects as the exhibition of children's paintings 'From the Olympic spirit of friendship and peace' does not only give sponsors and partners a large opportunity for creative fulfillment, but rather allows one to join the activities of a deep humanitarian significance.

Ten of the 12 organizers actually are artists, initiators of various exhibitions in their home countries – they also participate in social organizations. Participation in the project offered them an opportunity to involve the children they are working with, to give them a chance to express themselves through art, as 'teaching kids peace through art and cultural activity is an important part of their education and formation as an individual' according to Linden Longino. A few volunteer organizers are supporters of the art therapy promotion among children who have suffered serious trials in their lives, such as violence, poverty and natural disasters.

Also project participants marked a new opportunity to co-operate with IPP as an important motive, as they are ongoing participants of various projects launched by this organization and are familiar with its founder. In general, it was revealed that personal sympathy, acquaintances, contacts and friendly relations play a very important role in the implementation of such projects as the exhibition 'From the Olympic spirit of friendship and peace'. Respondents repeatedly stressed that they were personally familiar with the project manager, and that they had worked with him several times and they were always enthusiastic about his goals. Probably, the project success can be largely contributed to this friendly, family atmosphere that was created by the organizers. Communications aspect, renewal of old contacts and desire to establish new international contacts was an important motive for participation in the project for many volunteers, identified as 'to meet people worldwide who share our common values, believe in the same things as me – all this is another reason in favor of this project', according to Linden Longino. Additionally, an important factor for the volunteer organizers was this feeling of being involved in such a project as part of world-class events. One respondent noted: 'during preparation and activities in the project context there was a continuous feeling of being a part of a large international event, a feeling of grandeur, historical, significance of the current proceedings' (female volunteer, 41).

The study revealed that there are certain differences in the motivation of the international volunteers and Russian volunteers; for example, it is necessary to highlight that international volunteering is a tradition (for people from the United States and across Europe). This work is perceived as a normal activity and not as something exceptional. The Russian national character also has some traits that demonstrate characteristics for volunteer work, but in essence there is no tradition of this. Therefore, in Russia volunteering is mainly developed by institutions. While the international volunteer organizations primarily appeal to people, they often rely on an individual contributor; here in Russia one basically addresses corporations, governments or specialized funds for volunteer requests. A distinctive feature of volunteering in Russia is the influence of a strong leader in order to involve other people – this may be a media or authoritative person. Of course, such practice is used as well in other countries, but it is more accentuated in Russia – unheard and invisible volunteer activities, as a rule, do not resonate with the people. Further, in Russia it is important for people to know that the project is successful, it is very important for a volunteer project to be associated with major events. Thus, the projects associated with the Olympic Games were so successful – as everything that is somehow connected with this large-scale project cannot go unnoticed, and people are more willing to participate in such projects. It is easy to see that large projects with international appeal such as the Olympic Games act as a powerful stimulus for the development of the volunteerism movement in Russia.

It is important to recognize the differences in motivation of volunteers participating in the project and operating at different levels. The higher the level, the more engaged and motivated participants are. Motivation of volunteer organizers acting as network partners and country co-ordinators is high, much higher than motivation of volunteers of national organizations working with children; each answer here contained satisfaction with the performed work and some pride in the project. They really believe in the project and are proud to have been able to attract their organizations to the project implementation on a voluntary basis, they are actively involved in project promotion, lobbying, going to regions and addressing individual organizations to engage in the project and taking the implementation to a supra-national level. That is to say that the motivation of the project participants from this point of view has two levels: national (local) and global (international).

Concluding remarks

The phenomenon of volunteering at the Cultural Olympiads, described in this chapter, has confirmed a theory of creativity-based volunteering as developed by the authors. Creativity-based volunteers have done more than express themselves through the presentation of their works at the exhibition. This was the way for them to fulfil a set of motives, desires and wishes. The survey identified the main motives of volunteer activities in terms of this project, which allowed us to make a conclusion about the deep humanitarian principle of the entire project. Project characteristics define not only creative abilities, but talents are the main resource of the project, as well as contacts and relationships. Invested resources have paid off, volunteers acquire new friends, and they open up opportunities for their personal professional development and, therefore, have the ability to work on new projects. This happens also as a result of the homogeneity of the professional environment. The majority of volunteers are somehow connected with culture, art, painting, art therapy and non-commercial projects for children.

All participants are given freedom of expression, project promotion, children involvement, probably their training, master classes and local exhibitions – everything depends on the capabilities and desires of the volunteer. The lack of strict rules has contributed to the common good and international involvement in the project. The project also offers a supportive and inspiring environment with varied activities for the creative person. Such a trustful atmosphere is based on the fact that the volunteers know each other and have experience in professional interaction. Given the scale of the project, not all volunteers are familiar with each other, of course, but the involvement of new volunteers occurs on the basis of personal acquaintance and/or through contacts with the participating organizations.

This type of volunteering has a larger focus on personality. Network partners and co-ordinators attract these already known and recognized creative individuals, and it is easier for them to come to terms with organizations that are working with children. Moreover, it is easier to convince the organization where they are employed to participate in the project and to provide some assistance. Creativity, professional recognition and opportunities derived from their social networks were the resources of volunteers, enabling them to implement the project. Such a flexible partnership network allows IPP to scale the experience and to transfer it to new locations, and to attract new cities and countries. The evolution of this partnership and its measurable growth (and change in the structure) are an indication of its existing potential. In order to achieve their goals, such project development would be difficult if it was not for creative volunteers and unpaid professionals.

In turn, it is not only the humanistic orientation of the project, but the scale of a sporting mega-event that makes the project attractive to creative volunteers. While the volunteers are not necessarily sport volunteers, such an initiative would not exist if it were not for the Olympic Games. Its periodic repeatability allows to use the accumulated experience, adjusting the tactics and entire strategy, if necessary, to expand the scale, to provide innovations, while enjoying the opportunities for creativity. Therefore, the analysed case shows the great potential of attracting creativity-based volunteers for sports events, the cultural component of which currently tends to become more and more important. There are tasks for scholars and practitioners to further investigate when it comes to motivation and this type of volunteering, in addition to work on engagement and best practices of already implemented projects.

The review of the IPP case – the analysis of the IPP's organizational structure and development, and the participants' interactions (and their motivation factors) – allows us to define what characteristics of the events (or project) make it possible, and offers a perspective on creative-volunteering practices. Such common event/project features could be described as follows:

- there is a large number of independent participants engaged in the project;
- project realization is assumed to be partially or entirely done on a voluntary basis;
- voluntary labour is used at all organizational levels;
- there is only a basic event/project concept, but ways of its realization are independently chosen by participants;
- the project gives the participants creative freedom;
- organizers have no resources to provide the voluntary work;
- all participants could significantly impact on the outcomes.

This research can be further developed in two directions. First, we have to better understand specific features of creativity-based volunteering as a special type of volunteer activities by combining both skill-based volunteering and the unique abilities of engaged people to express themselves through creativity. Second, it is important to continue the study of various aspects of the cultural programmes associated with sporting mega-events. Such cultural programmes, as well as the Cultural Olympiads, are able to support a more humanistic nature of sport competitions and to make a real contribution to strengthening friendship between local and international volunteers.

Acknowledgements

The authors would like to thank Dr L. Longino, Head of International Paint Pals, for the openness and all the information given. We also offer our special thanks to our colleagues Dr I. Kizilova and A. Panova for the access to the material and results of their research of IPP and intellectual-creative volunteers.

Note

1 The study was implemented in the framework of the Basic Research Program at the National Research University Higher School of Economics (HSE) in 2016.

References

Allen Consulting Group. (2007). *Global trends in skill-based volunteering.* Melbourne: Allen Consulting Group.

Barron, P. and Rihova, I. (2011). Motivation to volunteer: A case study of the Edinburgh International Magic Festival. *International Journal of Event and Festival Management* 2(3): 202–217.

Christauskas, C., Petrauskiene, R. and Marcinkeviciute, L. (2012). Theoretical and practical aspects of volunteer organisation members (volunteers) motivation. *Inzinerine Ekonomika-Engineering Economics* 23: 517–524.

Csordas, I. (2011). Volunteer management in cultural institutions. Notes for the participants of the Volunteer Management in Cultural Institutions: Practical issues and hints. In-Service Training Museum of Fine Arts Budapest 6–10 November. www.ne-mo.org/fileadmin/Dateien/public/topics/Volonteering/Volunteer Managementin_CulturalInstitutions.pdf.

Dwyer, P.C., Bono, J.E., Snyder, M., Nov, O. and Berson, Y. (2013). Sources of volunteer motivation. *Nonprofit Management & Leadership* 24(2): 180–205.

García, B. (2002). *The concept of Olympic cultural programs: Origins, evolutions and projections: University lecture on the Olympics.* Barcelona: Centre d'Estudis Olímpics.

García, B. (2017). The Cultural Olympiads. In J.R. Gold and M.M. Gold (eds) *Olympic cities: City agendas, planning, and the world's games, 1896–2020.* New York: Routledge (pp. 90–113).

Gilmore A. (2014). Evaluating legacies: Research, evidence and the regional impact of the Cultural Olympiad. *Cultural Trends* 23(1): 29–41.

Hede, A.M. and Rentschler, R. (2007). Mentoring volunteer festival managers: Evaluation of a pilot scheme in regional Australia. *Managing Leisure* 12: 157–170.

Holmes, K. and Smith, K.A. (2009). *Managing volunteers in tourism: Attractions, destinations and events.* Amsterdam: Elsevier Butterworth-Heinemann.

International Olympic Committee. (2015). Olympic Charter, Lausanne, Switzerland. https://stillmed.olympic.org/media/Document%20Library/OlympicOrg/General/ EN-Olympic-Charter.pdf#_ga=1.227432660.811267502.1469493864.

Lander, D. and Crowe, R. (2010). Delivering a Cultural Olympiad: Vancouver 2010 meets London 2012. *Culture @ the Olympics* 12(7): 35–46.

Lockstone, L. and Smith, K.A. (2009). Episodic experiences: Volunteering flexibility in the events sector. In T. Baum, M. Deery, C. Hanlon, L. Lockstone and K. Smith (eds) *People and work in events and conventions: A research perspective*. Wallingford: CABI (pp. 108–127).

Maranta, A. and Sladowski, P.S. (2010). *The changing culture of volunteering: A skills-based approach to volunteer involvement*. A discussion paper by Volunteer Benevolves, Canada.

Moscardo, G. (2008). Sustainable tourism innovation: Challenging basic assumptions. *International Journal of Culture, Tourism and Hospitality Research* 8(1): 4–13.

Nichols, C.D. and Ojala, E. (2009). *Annual volunteer survey: Global report*. http://files.peacecorps.gov/multimedia/pdf/policies/2009_Annual_Volunteer_Survey.pdf.

Panova, A. (2014). Managing volunteer services at cultural mega events (unpublished master's thesis). Research University Higher School of Economics, St. Petersburg, Russia.

Randle, M.J. and Dolnicar, S. (2009). Does cultural background affect volunteering behavior? *Journal of Nonprofit & Public Sector Marketing* 21: 225–247.

Smith, A. (2012). *Events and urban regeneration: The strategic use of events to revitalize cities*. New York: Routledge.

Stebbins, R.A. (2000). Optimal leisure lifestyle: Combining serious and casual leisure for personal well-being. In M.C. Cabeza (ed.) *Proposals for the 6th World Leisure Congress*. Bilbao: University of Deusto (pp. 101–107).

Treuren, G.J.M. (2014). Enthusiasts, conscripts or instrumentalists? The motivational profiles of event volunteers. *Managing Leisure* 19(1): 51–70.

Waikayi, L., Fearon, C., Morris, L. and McLaughlin, H. (2012). Volunteer management: An exploratory study within the British Red Cross. *Management Decision* 50(3): 349–367.

Chapter 3

Living abroad and volunteering at the 2014 Commonwealth Games in Glasgow

Nicholas Wise

Introduction

International sport volunteering has seen increased interest in the past decade. While much research has focused on those who leave their home countries to volunteer as part of short-term stays abroad, far less work has considered the role of transnational migrants volunteering in the place where they now reside abroad. Places are becoming synonymous with sporting events (Cornelissen, 2010; Dashper *et al.*, 2014; Hall and Page, 2012). Today, major international sporting events increasingly rely on volunteers to assist everyday operations and a successful delivery (Allen and Bartle, 2014; Doherty, 2006; Farrell *et al.*, 1998; Smith *et al.*, 2014). While many volunteers are sourced locally, the people who assist as volunteers often do so to fulfil social benefits to reinforce a sense of community or place. In this era of fluid global movements and multicultural societies, people who move to new places are also seeking opportunities to get involved and create a new sense of belonging when living abroad.

Major events represent an opportunity to connect people, may it be the host city residents, the spectators or the international guests. We now live in an interdependent world where identities are no longer fixed, but fluid. Transnationalism has resulted in a global workforce where mobility has never been greater and opportunities exceed national borders. There exists a range of literature concerning sport and transnational migration (Carter, 2007; Darby and Solberg, 2010; Grainger, 2006; Mangan, 1996; Wong and Trumper, 2002), but this chapter moves beyond a focus on transnationalism, theoretically, per se, and focuses on my own personal perspectives as critically linked to volunteering at a major international sporting event. People who lead mobile lifestyles are referred to as global citizens. While people often identify with a particular home (i.e. where an individual was born and grew up), such traditional understandings of home are now challenged, because where someone belongs can be multi-faceted. In the United States there is very little recognition, if any coverage, or mention of the Commonwealth Games in the media. Although the event may not be exposed in non-Commonwealth countries, someone working and/or living in Glasgow from outside the Commonwealth might question the rationale behind such a major (not mega) event. In total 71 countries competed in the 2014 Commonwealth Games comprising of 17 sports. I argue more research that includes the voice of an international volunteer is needed.

This chapter is a self-reflexive piece addressing my role as an international volunteer after moving to Glasgow, UK ahead of the 2014 Commonwealth Games. While living in Glasgow I took the opportunity to be a volunteer at the Commonwealth Games. Coming from the United States, I am from outside the Commonwealth, and as such, I outline new feelings of belonging to a new community as a Clydesider.[1] As a volunteer, I was assigned to work at the Emirates Area during the Commonwealth Games as a member of the spectator services team. Each day I would rotate jobs to interact with attendees inside and outside the stadium, or assist with entry clearance to certain areas in or out of the venue. I reflect on community and identity below, as volunteers we were easily recognized by our red polo shirts and grey trousers. Taking a self-reflexive autoethnographic approach, this chapter examines differing notions of identity and sense of belonging based on my role as a spectator services volunteer at the 2014 Commonwealth Games. Before moving to the United Kingdom, I did not have any formal ties to Glasgow or Scotland. Similarly, the Commonwealth Games is not an event featured in my country of origin. The focus of this work is to offer insight into relocation and volunteering in a place and at an event that I did not have an immediate connection to – with the intension to discuss how volunteering helps individuals develop a sense of belonging in a new place. This work will incorporate geographical notions of in place/out of place to reinforce discussions of transnationalism and self-identity.

In this chapter I will overview my reactions and perspectives as an international sport event volunteer whilst linking my narratives to pertinent conceptual social geographical understandings of sense of place and sense of belonging. Next this chapter turns to the academic literature addressing volunteer motivations and sense of place and belonging. A brief overview of my method precedes my accounts, self-reflections and experiences as a 2014 Commonwealth Games Clydesider (or volunteer).

Motivations to volunteer

Given the growing popularity and interest in both local and international sport volunteering, we have seen much development in this specific area of research (Allen and Bartle, 2014; Østerlund, 2013; Ralston *et al.*, 2004; Wise, 2011). However, there is still a need for more research in order to understand the significance of volunteering (Ringuet-Riot *et al.*, 2013;

Taylor *et al.*, 2012). There exists a strong base of sport volunteering literature but a more defined international focus is needed as people are becoming more mobile. Events rely on volunteers, and we have seen this in the cases of London and Vancouver, where these events involved 70,000 and 25,000 volunteers, respectively (Dickson *et al.*, 2013). An accepted definition of volunteering is 'any activity in which time is given freely to benefit another person, group or organisation' (Wilson, 2000, p. 215). While the quote includes the word *benefit*, it is argued that the public are increasingly volunteering for *personal benefits* (Raymond and Hall, 2008), but with the intension to play a role in benefiting the wider group or place. While focusing on the benefits of volunteering is crucial, this work is more concerned with motivations for volunteering.

My own motivation to volunteer was to make a new and stronger connection with Glasgow. There are numerous reasons that motivate people to volunteer – with many reasons commonly linked to altruism or social-psychology (see Yeoman, 2008; Wilson, 2000). Specifically, work by Clary *et al.* (1998) sought to inventory personal volunteer motivations, and the authors suggest six dimensions: values, understanding, enhancement, career, social and protective. This chapter addresses the social dimension, by offering an understanding that includes conceptualizations of place brought in from the geography literature to discuss notions of transnational migrations in relation to understanding how volunteering links to creating a new sense of belonging in a new place. It is widely accepted that people who volunteer for one-off major events have different motivations because they are part of a wider celebration that involves their city, region or country. Major sporting events are in the international spotlight, making them unique opportunities for people to be a part of. This was true with my motivation as I wanted to be part of the event experience. Socially and psychologically, this is linked to a sense of belonging (in my case to a new place). People who have grown up in Glasgow have a certain connection to Glasgow – it is the place they call home. For transnational migrants such as myself, the attachment and sense of belonging is different. Volunteering allows us new ways to integrate ourselves to seek that newfound attachment to a new place. Smith (2012) argued just this by mentioning that volunteering is an important social benefit and helps people increase their pride in a place.

Sense of place and sense of belonging

Research focusing on migration and sport has seen much development (Bale and Maguire, 1994; Elliott and Harris, 2014; Wise and Harris, 2016). However, there has been little consideration addressing personal reflections of an individual migrant as an international sports volunteer. The literature focusing on place and community is necessary to frame conceptual links to the experience of migrants and international volunteers. People strive to achieve a sense of community; may this be where they live or when they join a group of people with similar interests – or volunteer. McMillan and Chavis (1986) suggest that a sense of community is based on four conditions: membership, influence, shared emotional connections and integration/fulfilment of needs. *Membership* is an essential component and communities are often defined or recognized by boundaries, whether local, regional or national. When we consider social roles, we are dealing with the condition of *influence* (Castells, 1997; Delanty, 2010; Jenkins, 2008), which can be structured upon certain biases pertinent to political, social or cultural norms/ideals (Delanty, 2010). Additionally, García *et al.* expand on the influences of community politics, which greatly impact shared emotional connections and the fulfilment of needs (García *et al.*, 1999). *Integration and the fulfilment of needs* are addressed in case studies that assess togetherness relative to recreation or other various community activities or associations. Moreover, García *et al.* (1999, p. 731) recommend acknowledging that there are a 'series of processes established that make personal satisfactions possible while collective needs can also be fulfilled'. Social collectiveness and belonging to a community also depends on *shared emotional connections*, referring to a location (place) and associated history (Poplin 1979). García *et al.* (1999) further build upon these conceptualizations, suggesting that time and place are significant, especially when people celebrate milestones or embark on something new. Anderson's (1991) conceptual approach, which is further outlined below, links to shared associations and *horizontal comradeship*, as emotions are always shared among members of a particular community (García *et al.*, 1999).

The existing literature is extensive when considering transnational migrants and attempting to understand how people create a new sense of belonging in a new place (Borer, 2006; Elliott and Harris, 2014; Larsen and Johnson, 2012; Manzo and Devine-Wright, 2014; Wise, 2011, 2015). To develop a geographical understanding, the notion of sense of place has been commonly used along with notions of in place/out of place to help guide critical interpretations. Sense of place, according to Rose (1995, p. 88), is:

> the phrase used by many geographers when they want to emphasize that places are significant because they are the focus of personal feelings ... to refer to the significance of particular places for people. These feelings for 'place' are not seen as trivial; geographers argue that senses of place develop from every aspect of individuals' life experience and the senses of place pervade everyday life and experience.

Linking this quote to the paragraph directly above, these is a link to sense of community and belonging (further outlined in Wise, 2015). Cresswell's

(2004) understanding and approach adds subsequent critical thought to integrate discussions of transgression into understandings of place, and when considering the role of individual migrants in attempting to establish a sense of place this is worth considering. To Cresswell (2004), transgression is envisioned through where people fit and interact, and this idea was used by Wise (2011) and is outlined later in this chapter. The points briefly outlined here in this review of the literature speak to the conceptual discussions incorporated below alongside my self-reflexive narrative as an international sports volunteer at a major event. The next section offers a note on the autoethnographic approach used in this self-reflexive research.

Method: autoethnographic self-reflective narrative

An autoethnographic, self-reflexive, approach, is used to offer insight on my perspectives and experiences volunteering at the 2014 Glasgow Commonwealth Games. This chapter represents a form of ethnography looking critically at the process of volunteering. It offers meaningful geographical insight pertinent to place and belonging. Since the volunteering took place at an international sporting event, several scholars have conducted sport ethnographies. Ethnographic research is about describing and writing about how people create and influence places, cultures, interactions and experiences specific to a group of people (Watson and Till, 2010). Pertinent to the direction of this work, self-reflexive autoethnographies aim to produce new knowledge about a group or community of people by placing the researcher's experiences and interactions at the centre of the study (see Chang, 2008; Sands, 2002; Wise, 2011). Qualitative research methods are best explained as gathering data inductively, and attempting to understand social or cultural phenomena. Harris (2006, p. 156) states: research is best learnt by 'doing' – becoming familiar with the site, and subjects of the inquiry. This becomes especially important in social scientific studies of sport and tourism, where the aim is usually discovery – to find out more about how and why a particular social world is as it is. Being a reflexive ethnography, Harris (2006, p. 165) argues self-reflection is important because researchers 'bring [their] own individuality and personality into the text', placing the researcher within the study (Chang, 2008; Sparkes, 2000, 2002; Sugden, 2007; Weed, 2006).

This chapter's methodological and epistemological rationale reflects upon the individual *self* and individual *experiences* gained through volunteering at an international sporting event. Such reflexive approaches put *self* and *experience* at the centre of research inquiry to critically frame an individual's position, role and any points of contestation (Chang, 2008). Equally important is reflexivity where the researcher evaluates their own truths relative to the research findings (Harris, 2006; Smith and Weed, 2007; Weed, 2006) to address how this has changed their perspective or outlook. Autoethnographies construct and narrate explored productions of knowledge (Smith and Weed, 2007; Sparkes, 2000; Sugden, 2007). Sport ethnography has emerged over the past several decades and present insight into lived experiences, and 'such experiences have been an under-investigated area' (Smith and Weed, 2007, p. 253), especially autoethnographies. The main criticism of autoethnography is the very focus of the approach itself, and that is the emphasis on self (Holt, 2003). While the focus on oneself in this case is at the centre of the research, the researcher needs to critically support their observations, interactions and experiences, so they are not just describing a story, but engaging with theory to produce new cultural and social knowledge.

Reflecting on my time as an international volunteer, I relate critical points to place, identity and belonging from the time of training through to volunteering at the Emirates Arena in Glasgow. Participating and observing surroundings are both common procedures in ethnography (Sands, 2002; Sparkes, 2002; Weed, 2006). Existing ethnographic studies in the field of sport, especially, have focused on a range of areas, including surfing (Sands, 2002), marathon running (Sugden, 2007) to viewing major sporting event matches in public settings (Weed, 2006) or the role of football in rural communities (Wise, 2011). Wise's (2011) study was based on international volunteering with Haitians and Dominicans in a rural community. Given the different focus in each of the studies just noted, they each attempted to achieve similar goals of qualitative analysis. According to Wise (2011), sport ethnography aims to inquire specific knowledge through direct immersion to extract cultural knowledge and the production of case-specific sporting identities. Ultimately, ethnographies and autoethnographies are a snapshot of a community's everyday cultural practices – or in this case the ongoing happenings at an international event. Regardless, the researcher takes on some proximate role in order to immerse themselves within a group's everyday setting (Chang, 2008; Harris, 2006; Sugden, 2007). This study is based on my daily field notes that I recorded from the time of my application through to volunteering. I wanted to evaluate my role and interactions (and conversations) with other volunteers, training staff, fans and public officials during the volunteering process and experience. The data collected details my direct immersion, involvement, and observations as a Clydesider.

The foreign feeling

Volunteering at an international sporting event as a foreign volunteer was a unique opportunity. In 2012 I moved to Glasgow from the United States. Before my move, a lot of contacts from Scotland were always talking about the 2014 Commonwealth Games and what this will do for Glasgow. I noticed a sense of excitement and pride among Glaswegians[2] as they prepared for the largest event the city would likely ever host. When I arrived I took notice of all the murals and banners around the city. I could tell that people in the city were eager to host and meet people from fellow Commonwealth countries. Being from the United States, the Commonwealth Games gets very little, if any, media attention or publicity. However, I did have prior knowledge of the Commonwealth Games. In 2006 I was studying abroad in Melbourne, Australia and that ironically happened to be at the same time as the Commonwealth Games. As a sport enthusiast I was eager to see what the event was like and see who participated so I bought tickets to the athletics finals. My second connection with the games, given the purpose of this chapter, was again timely – having moved to Glasgow two years prior to the event. The next two sections outline my motivations to volunteer and becoming part of a new community, putting emphasis on the notion of sense of place and a new sense of belonging, respectively.

My motivation to volunteer: finding a sense of place

In the above section I mentioned all the murals and Glasgow 2014 banners up around the city and the positive morale across the city as people anticipated the arrival of the games. In my first year in Glasgow many people asked me if I was aware of the Commonwealth Games – and mentioned that there was probably not much coverage of the event in the United States. Since I was exposed to the event from my time in Melbourne, people were happy to hear that I had some prior knowledge. I did add that since I was back in the United States working on my graduate studies from 2007 to 2012, I was unaware of the 2010 event that took place in Delhi. People in Glasgow whom I interacted with were excited about the opportunity to host the Commonwealth Games. This is what motivated me to get involved, so when I found out about the opportunity and process to become a volunteer, I did not hesitate. Such an opportunity to volunteer at an international event does not come around that often, so the timing of me being in Glasgow was an ideal opportunity.

After I applied, a few weeks later I received an email saying that I had been selected for an interview. In total, over 50,000 people applied, around 25,000 were interviewed, but only 15,000 were selected to be Clydesiders (BBC, 2013). When I arrived for my interview, I signed in and when people heard my accent they immediately asked 'oh, where are you from?' This was consistent each time I checked in to a training session. Perhaps people did not expect to hear a foreign (American) accent in Glasgow, but the constant questioning each time implied I was not from Scotland. Being foreign to Glasgow, my accent implies that I am different – and made people want to know where I was from. As a geographer interested in international sporting events and socio-cultural relations, there is a lot of geographical insight tied to such questionings of where someone is from. This is linked to behavioural geographies, because people interact differently in different places and with people from different places, which can be determined by accents or even appearance. All volunteers were asked to write on a card what our motivations to volunteer were. Given the complexities of people consistently asking where I was from, and that I was living in a new place, I wrote on my card: 'To become a part of the place where I now live.' The geographical insight that I added here put emphasis on my current residence, and the desire to connect with a new place. Cresswell (2004) stresses that interactions help reinforce new connections. Being a lecturer in sport, events and tourism management at this time, volunteering provided me with an opportunity to create a sense of place in Glasgow as I was eager to be a part of the Clydesider community.

During the interview I was also asked if I had a preference of venue. To increase my chances of being selected I said that 'I am flexible and could volunteer at any of the venues'. Since I was still relatively new to Glasgow at the time, I did not have a particular preference and not had an immediate connection with a particular area of the city, and I felt by being open to whatever opportunity would present itself, this would be a chance to learn more about and get to know a different area of the city. In January 2014 I was informed that my application and interview were both successful. I was thrilled by the result as I was going to be part of an international spectacle and one of the faces of the games. What was important to me was having the opportunity that I did. As I went through the process and training, I got more involved, and I got to meet and get to know other Clydesiders, so that feeling of being part of a new community increased – creating a greater sense of belonging to a new city.

Becoming part of a new community: towards a sense of belonging

The purpose of this section is to discuss how the volunteer training and picking up my uniform overcomes differences of place. I focus on becoming part of a new community and creating a new shared sense of belonging. I was by far not the only person from outside Glasgow, Scotland, or even the UK to volunteer. I met people originally from other places in continental Europe and across the UK who had to travel to Glasgow for their interview – and then again for orientation, training and to collect uniforms. To me they were making more of a sacrifice of time and finances to be a part of the games than myself, I simply had a different accent and just had to make a ten-minute train journey to attend orientations and training meetings. So the complexities of place were again at play, people from across the UK were still connected as this was their country, and their

Commonwealth Games. My identity, from a different nationality, was still different since I am not British.

Moving beyond discussions of place and transnational identities, a shared sense of belonging links to a conceptual framework outlined by McMillan and Chavis (1986). People are continually looking to strengthen community bonds and shared associations. Moreover, Anderson (1991) discussed the notion of imagined communities, where he addresses the idea that people are bound through *horizontal comradeship*. Wise (2011) borrowed this notion to address how this comradery extends beyond national borders, by using Anderson's (1991) work that focused on nationalism and national identity. This chapter is not necessarily linked specifically to national identity, but to a common shared identity. Therefore, Anderson's (1991) perspective of *horizontal comradeship* connects people through shared associations such as volunteering.

To put this notion of a sense of belonging and being part of an imagined community of volunteers into perspective, one evening after an orientation I was walking back from the Emirates Arena to Glasgow's city centre. As I walked up Buchanan Street I saw other volunteers. At this point we were not wearing our uniforms, but there was another way to tell who fellow volunteers were. At the orientation we were all provided with a very distinctive red Glasgow 2014 paper bag, which included all of our important materials about how to act and respond as a volunteer in different situations. As I walked up Buchanan Street I reunited and spoke with fellow volunteers carrying the same red bag, which reinforced that sense that we belonged to the same imagined community. This was the first point I acknowledged that this sense of connectedness no longer needed verbal explanation. Because people would signify I was different based on my accent, carrying volunteer materials represented a recognition that created that shared sense of belonging with other volunteers.

On another occasion when I arrived to collect my uniform, I verified my identity and right to volunteer by showing my passport and visa. Because they needed to check foreign nationals to confirm our eligibility to volunteer, the people at the check-in counter were interested to speak further to people with different passports – and again I was asked why I was volunteering. Again, I mentioned that I now lived and worked in Glasgow. Collecting the uniform added some material semblance to sense of place, with the Glasgow 2014 Commonwealth Games brand on each item provided. Sociologically this reinforced that sense of community and connection with everyone I interacted with from that point on who also wore volunteering gear. Materialism helped enhance shared identities and experiences, and the connection with other volunteers. No longer would I have to say I am interested in volunteering or I will be volunteering only to have my accent questioned to signify that I was different. Wearing the uniform acted as an imaginary façade that I now must be Glaswegian and a part of Glasgow solely based on my new appearance. Such materialism to this regard suggests connectedness to a community. If you are a volunteer, you are now connected to Glasgow. Being a part of a new imagined community, whether carrying my branded bag through the streets or wearing the distinctly red Clydesider polo shirt. I did not know any of these people personally – but we were bound through our shared association as Glasgow 2014 volunteers. My difference (based on my nationality or accent) was often addressed during training, and once the curiosity of my difference wore off once, the games had started. The next section moves on to address experiences and reactions.

Experiences and reflections from volunteering at the Commonwealth Games

Hall and Page (2012) note that events are seeing increased numbers of spectators and consumer demands, which result in organizers increasingly relying on volunteers. With increased demand, consumerism and expectations, this can take a burdensome toll on those who decide to volunteer. Volunteering is often one's desire to assist, or be a part of, an event in a very unique way. It is the desire and dedication to be a part of something that I feel can often be overlooked as the wider operations of an event take over. To reinforce the importance of volunteers at events, organizers kept repeating that volunteers make events happen – the volunteers were 'the friendly faces of the [Commonwealth] games' (BBC, 2013). Each volunteer was expected to dedicate at least eight days. I was fortunate to have five days on then a day off before completing my last three shifts. My day off allowed me to attend other events that were in the elimination stages so I had the opportunity to enjoy the event as a spectator as well.

My first day volunteering was the most memorable, although I did receive some mild harassment. I was positioned in the area between the entrance to the Velodrome and the badminton courts. I had to control access to the elevators and only people who had obtained certain access identification codes (appropriate entry clearance) were allowed to enter the elevators. On the day there seemed to be much misunderstanding as well as miscommunication. A number of people who were employed to work full-time in the Emirates Arena did not have passes and therefore (technically) could not access the elevator (or even the staircase) to get to their offices – their access was meant to be prearranged but this had not been completed. Given that I was in charge of allowing people entry into the elevators it came as a surprise to those employed there that some American guy was not allowing them to get to work. I also had to turn down police and media personnel in addition to other volunteers, athletes and referees/judges who did not have appropriate entry clearance. I was a bit concerned by the wider operations due to the lack of joined-up thinking and lack of communication. Another problem was there was supposed to a volunteer with the same instructions checking identification and entry clearance to the elevator on each floor – which was not the case. Disagreements turned to arguments over she said/he said, so the process at the start suffered from miscommunication and poor organization across the different operational groups. This was especially frustrating for volunteers because people became verbally abusive towards the people who were there to assist. Despite denying people based on entry clearance, people would go on and on, 'I used this lift yesterday', 'I should have access', 'I am [so and so]', in an attempt to state their authority. Speaking with fellow volunteers, there was a lot of disrespect for volunteers at the start given the operational pressures people were under. Some people found it difficult to hold back frustrations if something did not go right or they could not access part of the venue. On a few occasions I had to stand to block or hold my hand in front of the elevator door to stop the lift from moving. It turned out that access to the elevator on the floor beneath where I was standing was not secured, so people who wanted to use the elevator gained access from the floor below.

The operations issues on the first day resulted in a few people using profanities at me and other volunteers, releasing their frustration. I found myself having to hold back from laughing when one man got angry and started using coarse language. By the time I started volunteering I was familiar with Glaswegians, so I knew how to control the situation if a problem arose. However, if another international volunteer who was not familiar with Glasgow was there, they may not have been very impressed by how people interacted with volunteers. Another problem was that it was difficult to manage two simultaneous events in one building. Despite the criticisms I identified, these operational struggles experienced at the start were then fixed in the days thereafter. Later in the morning on my first day of volunteering I saw one of the headpersons from the police. He asked if 'all was ok?' I said 'I am enjoying it, but people are getting frustrated!' I continued to discuss that I had to deny access to some of his uniformed police. His response was, 'well I hope you do not get punched'. To which I responded (and to his amusement): 'I have been in Glasgow now for almost two years and have yet to receive a Glasgow Kiss' (which is a head-butt). While I did enjoy the volunteering experience, and although sometimes I was frustrated, we were trained as volunteers to keep our composure and maintain a positive attitude (and smile) as we were the 'friendly faces of the games' (BBC, 2013).

Despite some of the wider geographical and sociological connections I address in this chapter, I found the operations examples that I recorded in my field notes to be useful in my teaching. I often felt there were too many volunteers at the venues. In several instances this actually created a sense of disconnectedness from actually being a volunteer. For instance, when I volunteered inside, I noticed spectators got a bit tired of all the volunteers greeting them as they made their way to the spectating areas. However, when I was positioned outside people would pass me and I would say 'hello'. Oftentimes, by this point spectators who were entering the venue would have already been greeted by probably five or six Clydesiders. Overall, I felt the spectators were perhaps overwhelmed by the number of volunteers and it seemed they just wanted to avoid any further interaction – and so began racing past us to get to their seats. When I was positioned inside the Emirates Arena I took on a similar role to that of an usher by greeting people as they made their way to their seats. People were thankful if I was able to find them a good seat (because badminton matches had open seating), but a lot of times people would bypass me to ask the steward who was also standing nearby. Inside the venue, volunteers were placed around the staircase entrances next to the seating areas, but a steward was also there with us and there was usually another steward close by as well. Normally, when I attend a sporting event in a much larger venue than that of the Emirates Arena I am greeted by one usher at each seating area. In my experience volunteering inside the Emirates Arena at the Commonwealth Games people often had three people greeting them as they found their way to the open seating. This was perhaps another operational issue to help organize spectators when there is open seating to avoid any issues or potential conflict among spectators. However, it was when positioned in the seating area that I felt I was not needed as a volunteer because paid stewards were approached much more often. I was inside the venue taking on this role on two occasions, and both times I felt we were rotated inside just to have the opportunity to spectate and experience the competitions rather than undertaking a volunteering role.

I personally found volunteering outside to be more enjoyable because I could meet the spectators sooner as they made their way to the venue. I found that spectators were much more pleasant towards us as volunteers. When positioned outside on the last mile, this was the first point of welcome for many people using public transport to get to the Emirates Arena. When I would greet people many seemed a bit confused when they heard a different accent. Again, I was often asked where I was from, and I replied 'Pennsylvania, but I am now living in Glasgow'. People always seemed shocked when I would say the United States, but then it made more sense once I added that 'I am now working and living in Glasgow'. They realized I had no connection with the Commonwealth and some people seemed to be perplexed and sometimes I noticed confused looks on people's faces, but generally, people were friendly and welcomed me to Glasgow.

Another challenge was the location of the Emirates Arena and interactions with local residents. The venue is located in Glasgow's East End adjacent to a residential area. While most people out walking were spectators heading to the venue, there were still local residents passing by. Local residents seemed to take little interest and did not want to be bothered – because events can be a disruption of their everyday life. At no other time would local residents typically be greeted just walking down the street. The vast majority of people passing had Glasgow 2014 memorabilia or a national flag. The spectators attended to support either their country or the overall *Friendly Games* message.[3] One couple from Cameroon stopped and wanted to take a picture with me. They gave me a Cameroon hat and called me an honorary supporter. Given my nation is not competing in these games I find myself lost in terms of who to support in such an international competition – so I mainly just maintained my neutral stance. Therefore my sense of identity was not lost, but fulfilled by interactions with supporters who expressed their sense of identity which forged a new sense of what the games were meant to be about.

Nonetheless, volunteering outside brought much more enjoyment. Even the athletes and supporting crews would often interact with the volunteers more. One afternoon the Scottish cycling coach had an extra bicycle with him and he allowed fellow volunteers and myself to go for a spin about the grounds during the downtime. Other occasions I found myself with other volunteers interacting with the athletes. On another afternoon a group of us had a lengthy conversation with members of the English badminton team. The most memorable experience was the group photograph taken on the last day of badminton competition. This allowed all of the volunteers the chance to interact, run around the courts and reflect on our overall experiences. This was a significant occasion where organizers brought us all together as a united group of individuals wearing our red polo shirts and grey trousers – we were a community of Clydesiders.

Feeling out of place but at home

Geographers discuss notions of in place/out of place. Cresswell (2004, p. 102) notes that 'the "outside" plays a crucial role in the definition of the "inside"'. While I often felt out of place because people were constantly asking where I was from, I was still a part of Glasgow. Having moved there for work and volunteering at the Commonwealth Games helped disguise such out-of-place feelings, and made Glasgow feel more like home. Working and volunteering contributed to an establishment of permanence, if only referring to a new (temporary) settlement in a new place. To overcome discrepancies associating whether I was in or out of place, a new-found meaning of home was a new connection to a place. Perhaps this was because I was selected to volunteer and was given the opportunity to be a part of something that defined Glasgow in 2014. Home situates our belonging despite difference, and people generate emotional connections to their home by becoming part of a community. Being part of the imagined community of 2014 Clydesiders brought together my academic and social interests. Getting involved therefore reinforced my presence and ability to connect with people when I passed other people wearing the same red polo, a Glasgow 2014 jacket or carrying the branded bag.

To put these reflections into perspective, even when I felt out of place at times, I still wanted to position myself and feel connected (or in place) by making myself feel like I did belong in Glasgow. In this case it was finding that relative cultural practice, and to me it was becoming a Commonwealth Games volunteer. I had previously volunteered in other places, but this experience took on a different meaning. Foremost, in Glasgow I was no longer a student, which I had been for ten years prior to moving to the United Kingdom. Because employment leads to some semblance of permanence, we need to connect with our new places of residence through activities that make us feel like we belong. My profession has taken me to different places and will continue to take me to places that I am not familiar with. In a fluid globalized world professionals move to places that they may know little about, and I found volunteering gave me the opportunity to get to know Glasgow, and the people from the city, Scotland and across the United Kingdom better. A symbolic event for Scotland was important for Glasgow and contributed to collective identity formation linking people and place. Such expressions are secured and transmitted through involvement and the opportunity to be a part of a spectacle in an international sports volunteering context.

Concluding remarks and future directions

This chapter outlined some conceptual points and operations based on my experiences as a volunteer at the 2014 Commonwealth Games in Glasgow. The study represented an opportunity to reflect on observations, interactions and try and get a sense of how to critically reflect on ourselves and our role as an international when volunteering at a major sporting event. Conceptual links that I incorporated focus on place, community and belonging in an attempt to position feelings and reactions. As Harris (2006) mentioned, there is a need for more work that positions the role of the individual in sport ethnography, and this is achieved through self-reflexive autoethnographies. This chapter sought to reflect on being an international migrant to a new city and how the opportunity to volunteer helped to create a sense of belonging in a new place. More self-reflective studies are needed to promote narratives that position the researcher in different social and cultural settings when volunteering. Ethnographic and autoethnographic approaches require much more development in the area of international sport and event volunteering – and it is important to place the researcher at the centre of the volunteering process. Disciplinary and conceptual perspectives add more scope to the study. My background and personal interests fall in the area of human (social) geography, so reflections noted relate to conceptual understanding of place, in place/out of place and sense of bellowing by on how I critically examined my role, my experiences and my surroundings as an international volunteer at a sporting event.

Notes

1 Clydesider is the name given to volunteers at the Commonwealth Games, similar in nature to the term 'Games Maker' used for volunteers at the 2012 London Games. In this chapter, Clydesider and volunteer will be used interchangeably.
2 A Glaswegian is a resident of Glasgow, Scotland, UK.
3 The Commonwealth Games are also referred to as the *Friendly Games*.

References

Allen, J.B. and Bartle, M. (2014). Sport event volunteers' engagement: Management matters. *Managing Leisure* 19(1): 36–50.
Anderson, B. (1991). *Imagined communities*. London: Verso.
Bale, J. and Maguire, J. (eds) (1994). *The global sports arena: Athletic talent migration in an interdependent world*. London: Frank Cass.
BBC. (2013). Volunteers set new Commonwealth Games record. *BBC News*. www.bbc.com/news/uk-scotland-21627068.
Borer, M.I. (2006). The location of culture: The urban culturalist perspective. *City & Community* 5(2): 173–197.
Carter, T.F. (2007). Family networks, state interventions and the experience of Cuban transnational sport migration. *International Review for the Sociology of Sport* 42(4): 371–389.
Castells, M. (1997). *The power of identity*. Oxford: Blackwell.
Chang, H. (2008). *Autoethnography as method*. Walnut Creek: Left Coast Press, Inc.
Clary, E.G., Snyder, M., Ridge, R.D., Copeland, J., Stukas, A.A., Haugen, J. and Miene, P. (1998). Understanding and assessing the motivations of volunteers: A functional approach. *Journal of Personality and Social Psychology* 74: 1516–1530.
Cornelissen, S. (2010). The geopolitics of global aspiration: Sport mega-events and emerging powers. *International Journal of the History of Sport* 27(16–18): 3000–3025.
Cresswell, T. (2004). *Place: A short introduction*. Oxford: Blackwell.
Darby, P. and Solberg, E. (2010). Differing trajectories: Football development and patterns of player migration in South Africa and Ghana. *Soccer & Society* 11(1/2): 118–130.
Dashper, K., Fletcher, T. and McCullough, N. (eds) (2014). *Sports events, society and culture*. London: Routledge.
Delanty, G. (2010). *Community*. London: Routledge.
Dickson, T.J., Benson, A.M., Blackman, D.A. and Terrwiel, A.F. (2013). It's all about the Games! 2010 Vancouver Olympic and Paralympic Winter Games volunteers. *Event Management* 17(1): 77–92.

Doherty, A. (2006). Sport volunteerism: An introduction to the special issue. *Sport Management Review* 9: 105–109.

Elliott, R. and Harris, J. (eds) (2014). *Football and migration: Perspectives, places and players*. London: Routledge.

Farrell, J.M., Johnston, M.E. and Twynam, G.D. (1998). Volunteer motivation, satisfaction, and management at an elite sporting competition. *Journal of Sport Management* 12(4): 288–300.

García, I., Guiliani, F. and Wiesenfeld, E. (1999). Community and sense of community: The case of an urban barrio in Caracas. *Journal of Community Psychology* 27(6): 727–740.

Grainger, A. (2006). From immigrant to overstayer: Samoan identity, rugby, and cultural politics of race and nation in Aotearoa/New Zealand. *Journal of Sport & Social Issues* 30(1): 45–61.

Hall, C.M. and Page, S. (2012). Geography and the study of events. In S. Page and J. Connell (eds) *The Routledge handbook of events*. London: Routledge (pp. 148–164).

Harris, J. (2006). The science of research in sport and tourism: Some reflections upon the promise of the sociological imagination. *Journal of Sport & Tourism* 11(2): 153–171.

Holt, N.L. (2003). Representation, legitimation, and autoethnography: An authethnographic writing story. *International Journal of Qualitative Methods* 2(1): article 2.

Jenkins, R. (2008). *Social identity*. London: Routledge.

Larsen, S. and Johnson, J.T. (2012). Toward an open sense of place: Phenomenology, affinity, and the question of being. *Annals of the Association of American Geographers* 102(3): 623–646.

McMillan, D. and Chavis, D. (1986). Sense of community: A definition and theory. *Journal of Community Psychology* 14: 9–14.

Mangan, J.A. (ed.) (1996). *Tribal identities: Nationalism, Europe, sport*. London: Frank Cass.

Manzo, L.C. and Devine-Wright, P. (eds) (2014). *Place attachment: Advances in theory, methods and applications*. London: Routledge.

Østerlund, K. (2013). Managing voluntary sport organizations to facilitate volunteer recruitment. *European Sport Management Quarterly* 13(2): 143–165.

Poplin, D. (1979). *Communities: A survey of theories and methods of research*. New York: Macmillan.

Ralston, R., Downward, P. and Lumsdown, L. (2004). The expectation of volunteers prior to the XVII Commonwealth Games 2002: A qualitative study. *Event Management* 9(1–2): 13–26.

Raymond, B.M. and Hall, C.M. (2008). The development of cross-cultural (mis) understanding through volunteer tourism. *Journal of Sustainable Tourism* 16(5): 530–543.

Ringuet-Riot, C., Cuskelly, G., Auld, C. and Zakus, D.H. (2013). Volunteer roles, involvement and commitment in voluntary sport organizations: evidence of core and peripheral volunteers. *Sport in Society* 17(1): 116–133.

Rose, G. (1995). Place and identity: A sense of place. In D. Massey and P. Jess (eds) *A place in the world*. Oxford: Oxford University Press (pp. 87–132).

Sands, R.R. (2002). *Sport ethnography*. Champaign: Human Kinetics.

Smith, A. (2012). *Events and urban regeneration: The strategic use of events to revitalise cities*. London: Routledge.

Smith, B. and Weed, M. (2007). The potential of narrative research in sports tourism. *Journal of Sport & Tourism* 12(3/4): 249–269.

Smith, K.A., Wolf, N. and Lockstone-Binney, L. (2014). Volunteer experiences in the build-up to the Rugby World Cup 2011. In K. Smith, L. Lockstone-Binney, K. Holmes and T. Baum (eds) *Event volunteering: International perspectives on the volunteering experience at events*. London: Routledge (pp. 111–125).

Sparkes, A. (2000). Autoethnographies and narratives of self: Reflections on critical in action. *Sociology of Sport Journal* 17(1): 21–43.

Sparkes, A. (2002). *Telling tales in sport and physical activity: A qualitative journey*. Champaign: Human Kinetics.

Sugden, J. (2007). Running Havana: Observations on the political economy of sport tourism in Cuba. *Leisure Studies* 26(2): 235–251.

Taylor, P.D., Panagouleas, T. and Nichols, G. (2012). Determinants of sports volunteering and sports volunteer time in England. *International Journal of Sport Policy and Politics* 4(2): 201–220.

Watson, A. and Till, K. (2010). Ethnography and participant observation. In D. DeLyser, S. Herbert, S. Aitken, M. Crang and L. McDowell (eds) *The SAGE handbook of qualitative geography*. London: Sage (pp. 121–137).

Weed, M. (2006). The story of ethnography: The experience of watching the 2002 World Cup in the pub. *Soccer & Society* 7(1): 76–95.

Wilson, J. (2000). Volunteering. *Annual Review of Sociology* 26: 215–240.

Wise, N. (2011). Transcending imaginations through football participation and narratives of the *other*: Haitian national identity in the Dominican Republic. *Journal of Sport & Tourism* 16(3): 259–275.

Wise, N. (2015). Placing sense of community. *Journal of Community Psychology* 43(7): 920–929.

Wise, N. and Harris. J. (2016). Community, identity and contested notions of place: A study of Haitian recreational soccer players in the Dominican Republic. *Soccer & Society* 17(4): 610–627.

Wong, L.L. and Trumper, R. (2002). Global celebrity athletes and nationalism: Fútbol, hockey, and representation of nation. *Journal of Sport & Social Issues* 26(2): 168–194.

Yeoman, I. (2008). *Tomorrow's tourist*. London: Routledge.

Chapter 4

The transgressive potential of international volunteering

Issues and legacies at the 2014 Cleveland/Akron Gay Games

Nigel Jarvis

Introduction

LGBTQ[1] sport events, such as the Gay Games, potentially represent a significant transgressive and alternative space in the world of sport. They can provide the opportunity for a range of complex and interconnected issues and legacies to emerge. Since the outset of the gay liberation movement in the early 1970s, organized sport events have become an integral part of developing lesbian and gay communities. There is little doubt that the considerable growth of gay sporting cultures and events over the past few decades signifies steady progress for sexual minorities in the arena of physical activity. However, there has been a scarcity of research on the full range of legacies that these types of alternative medium-sized events can have, including volunteering and more specifically related to international aspects of the phenomenon. Previous volunteer studies have tended to focus on larger mega-sport events such as the Olympics. These larger Games can often attract more international volunteers, compared to less known sport and cultural events like the Gay Games, which may have to rely on more local unpaid helpers. Thus this chapter focuses on international and local volunteer issues at the Gay Games, which emerged as part of a wider project examining a range of legacy issues associated with the 2014 Cleveland/Akron Gay Games. For this study an international volunteer is anyone who travelled from outside of the United States to specifically offer their time to help local organizers. The proportion of local or regional versus international volunteers can help to shed some light as to whether the Gay Games could potentially achieve some of their wider goals attached to the event, which took place in a rather conservative part of the country, namely Ohio. The study also demonstrates the significance of international volunteering in relation to other socio-political, sport, tourism, arts, economic and event management legacies.

The chapter is organized as follows: after the introduction a literature review on volunteering issues and legacies of events is offered. Next is the section on methodology and methods of the study, followed by a section on the Gay Games context. The results are thematically outlined with a final discussion and conclusion section.

Volunteering issues and legacies of events

There is considerable academic and applied event/destination management interest in critically investigating the legacies of events, especially sport related, due not only to their prominence within the global arena, but their associated investment costs. In times of austerity, the considerable outlay in staging a major event, makes organizers, especially cities, focus on a bid if there is significant promise of a lasting legacy. The focus of much legacy research has been on larger-scale events such as FIFA World Cups and Olympic Games (Leopkey and Parent, 2012, 2015; Roche, 2003), with a skew towards the economic issues on the host region, although there is much scepticism towards those (Cornelissen *et al.*, 2011). However, smaller and medium-sized events, or those less known that do not generate a huge amount of media interest, can potentially have significant benefit for a destination (Shipway and Kirkup, 2012).

It is thus important to investigate the broader impacts and legacies of these types of events, beyond the economic and infrastructural elements (Ohmann *et al.*, 2006). Social aspects, which would include volunteering, political and environmental legacies, are sometimes ignored and encompass a diverse range of both negative and positive aspects, felt by a number of stakeholders, such as local residents and businesses, cultural organizations, government and civic leaders, and sport groups. Any thorough assessment of an event needs to integrate and consider the full range and extent of any type of legacy (Li and McCabe, 2013). This chapter examines the dimensions of potential (international) volunteer issues and legacies associated with a medium-sized alternative sport event, namely the 2014 Gay Games, hosted by Cleveland/Akron. It investigates whether the types of volunteer legacies are similar to those associated with the better documented sport mega-events. The study is also useful for those interested in competing discourses between professional and commercialized sport events and alternative transgressive grassroots formats aimed at inclusivity and challenging heteronormative values.

Legacy is a much-used term among scholars as well as in the rhetoric promoted by destination organizations and managers, event bidders, community groups, government officials and politicians. However, the topic has only emerged since the 1980s as an area of academic interest. Since then there have been numerous studies focusing on event legacies, not only related to sport (see Benson *et al.*, 2014; Cornelissen *et al.*, 2011; Dickson *et al.*, 2011; MacAloon, 2008; Matheson, 2010; Preuss, 2007; Reis *et al.*, 2014; Ritchie, 2000; Sant *et al.*, 2013; Thomson *et al.*, 2013) but other sectors like world expositions and tourism (Foley *et al.*, 2014; Li and

McCabe, 2013; Stevenson, 2011). Mair and Whitford (2013) conclude legacy is one of the increasingly central themes explored by academics in the event field. Many conceptual papers exist on categorizing, measuring or theorizing legacies; however, a literature review reveals more empirical studies are needed on simply identifying event stakeholder and other's views on what they may actually be.

Numerous definitions of the term exist and it remains an ill-defined topic. Legacies may be identified as part of the initial bidding process but this can occur four of five years away from the actual event, so it is difficult to define and identify the full range of legacies that may develop over time. Legacy has been conceptualized as all planned and unplanned, hard and soft, positive and negative, tangible and intangible impacts and/or structures created for, and by, an event, which remain longer than the event itself, irrespective of time and production and space (Gratton and Preuss, 2008; Li and McCabe, 2013; Sant et al., 2013). Thus events can be profound history marking institutions and catalysts, with a complex set of potential legacies. Indeed, while mega-events are relatively short-lived entities they possess long-lived pre- and post-social dimensions (Roche, 2003). However, it can be difficult to attribute if future developments occur because of an event that was held five or ten years earlier. Still, it is important to collect initial impressions of legacies because they lay the groundwork for which they can be measured against in the future.

For this chapter tangibility is used to help categorize those that were identified. Tangible legacies created by sport events, such as the much contested economic spend by visitors, athletes and related officials (Li et al., 2011; Matheson, 2002), infrastructure development, and an increase in sport participation rates (Reis et al., 2014) tend to be easier to identify and quantify. These types of legacies can also relate to the number of volunteers taking part and how this may affect future intentions to continue (see Aisbett et al., 2015; Doherty, 2009), although there appears to be less research that focuses on international aspects of volunteering (Jarvis and Blank, 2011; Lockstone-Binney et al., 2010), a void that this book intends to fill. Harder to measure intangible legacies could include increasing volunteer motivations (Dickson et al., 2011; Ritchie, 2000), how volunteering may strengthen the social fabric of society (Doherty, 2009) and develop friendships and interaction between volunteers (Brennan, 2005), as well as inspirational effects, re-visit intentions and change in destination image (Li and McCabe, 2013; Preuss, 2007), networking, sense of community pride, prestige and well-being (Fredline et al., 2003; Preuss, 2007; Shipway and Kirkup, 2012), skill development (Minnaert, 2012), and generating interest to stage future events in the host city (Gursoy and Kendall, 2006). This chapter investigates both tangible and less tangible volunteer legacies.

Drawing upon the work of Giddens (1990), events can be theorized as a mechanism to celebrate a collective consciousness to overcome negative feelings and affirm resident identities. They are seen to help enact social agency, although much of the past research on events and their potentially socially progressive agendas tend to downplay their negative or contradictory features, especially with respect to aspects of injustice, inequality, social polarization and domination (Gruneau and Horne, 2016). On the other hand, Debord (1983) critiques them, arguing the associated spectacle masks ongoing issues for the socio-economically disadvantaged. This points to the fact that the legacy rhetoric often used may be difficult to achieve or is less predictable. Regardless, festivals aimed at minorities or marginalized people are important symbolic occurrences for those taking part. For example, the role gay pride parades play in contested processes of social change surrounding sexual minorities is well documented (see Kates and Belk, 2001; Markwell and Waitt, 2009), and they generally produce a range of positive legacies, including bringing volunteers together from both the straight and gay communities, outweighing negative ones that may also emerge. Gay related events, through playful and transgressive acts, help to question and challenge dominant heteronormative ideologies (Hetherington, 1997; Lee *et al.*, 2014; Waitt, 2003). They generally help facilitate the development of complex interconnections between all types of people that help characterize society in the host destination. They may change people's attitudes towards LGBTQI persons, although they may further embed stereotypes. Therefore, it is worthwhile to explore how a gay sport festival may help reconfigure opinions of sexuality through the social connections, such as volunteering, made to bring the event together.

While Pride may be the typical cultural event associated with the LGBTQI community, less is known about other types of occasions geared towards them. Compared to Pride, extraordinary one-off cases like the Gay Games for host cities occur outside of other types of annual events, and thus rarely experienced more than once in a lifetime for local stakeholders of any particular destination.

Finally, Preuss (2007) acknowledges the contentious role of benchmarking in the measurement of legacies, that is based on past experience from previous events; however, there are no published data on volunteering legacies created by earlier Gay Games, or whether how many people travel to volunteer at various events. While there are connections to past and future Gay Games as a movement, the legacies and impacts created for a particular host is specific and unique and is worthy of much scrutiny. Different events create distinct legacies even within the same city. The next section outlines the methodology and methods used for this study.

Methodology and methods

A qualitative approach was used to investigate the case study. A total of 29 local stakeholders were formally interviewed in August 2014, representing a diverse number of organizations and sectors centred around LGBT groups and other community institutions, civic leaders, the arts, gay sport leagues, tourism, philanthropic/funding bodies and the business community. In addition, conversations with 48 local residents, such as taxi and bus drivers, police officers, shop assistants, customers and employees in bars and restaurants, and people in the street when the opportunity arose, were used to complement the stakeholder data. Included in this were two Games volunteers specifically approached, although many of the stakeholders were also volunteers in more strategic roles.

Events are often criticized because they may be promoted and dominated by politicians, the media or (white) middle-class consumers (see Gruneau, 2002; Preuss, 2007). The interviews and conversations were hence conducted to strategically account for a broad and dynamic variety of communities and perspectives in the area, such as African-American, Hispanic and Caucasian, with a range of political, social, legal and economic interests and sensitivities. Most interview partners discussed their sexual identity through the natural course of the conversations, so the voices of both straight and LGBTQI citizens are reflected. By no means is this a fully representative sample of all stakeholders.

Once granted ethical approval from my university, a qualitative investigation was undertaken to address the empirical gap, examining key legacy research themes and questions identified in the literature (Fontana and Frey, 2000). Themes emerged from the interview prompts that were common to all participants, such as how they defined a legacy, before identifying particular legacies the Games may have on the area, and potential barriers to them coming to fruition. It is from here volunteering legacies emerged. These were used in part to assess the transgressive capacity of the event and its volunteers to contribute to a legacy of changing people's societal attitudes towards the LGBTQI community specifically and sexuality more generally. All formal interview participants consented their names could be used in the published paper, and all but one agreed that the conversations were recorded to allow a full and accurate transcript. Conservation quotes were written on note pads discreetly later with no names gathered, although characteristics such as job, gender and approximate age were added. The data were analysed using thematic coding, wherein interviewee responses to the researcher's questions were interrogated to identify any commonalities and differences (Silverman, 2011) about the potential (volunteering) legacies of the Gay Games for Cleveland/Akron.

The most prominent legacies to emerge were socio-political orientated, those often considered as less tangible. This was followed by a number of other legacies, in descending order, on sport, volunteering, tourism, the arts, the economy, and future events capacity. However while this chapter primarily focuses on both local and international aspects to volunteering there is some overlap with socio-political and tourism aspects that emerged and is thus difficult to separate. The next section illuminates the Gay Games as an event and discusses the social significance of it as a sporting festival.

The Gay Games context

The context of the Gay Games is introduced to those readers who may not be familiar with the growth of this significant hallmark sport tourism event, which also provides the opportunity to volunteer for both local citizens and from those further afield. Messner (1992) noted since the outset of the gay liberation movement in the early 1970s, organized sport has become an integral part of developing lesbian and gay communities. As lesbians and gay men emerged from underground bars and other covert sites in western industrialized nations, sport became a new place where they could be more visible and socialize. The contestation and clash around space and meaning, and the aspiration and desire to acquire or provide space for new types and different forms of cultural expression, such as gay sporting events like the Gay Games, is a theme that has only emerged in the sociological and cultural analysis of modern sport over the past 15 years (Symons, 2010; Waitt, 2003).

The Gay Games, founded by Dr Tom Waddell, a former American Olympic decathlete, began in 1982 and are held every four years like the Olympics. They are arguably the most popular and globally recognized sport event for the LGBTQI community. The mission of the Federation of Gay Games (FGG) (2014a), the body that oversees the movement, is 'to promote equality through the organization of the premiere international LGBT and gay-friendly sports and cultural event known as the Gay Games. They are built upon the principles of participation, inclusion and personal best'. Unlike the Olympics, the Gay Games, much like any gay sport tournament, have gone out of their way to stress inclusiveness, regardless of skill, age, gender, disability, race, class, HIV status, geographic origin and sexual orientation. Less known is that straight athletes and allies can also participate (and volunteer) in the event, a phenomenon known as 'inverse integration' (Elling et al., 2003).

Table 4.1 demonstrates the Games have now taken place in three different continents and experienced considerable growth in terms of the number of athletes competing, and countries and types of sports represented. The Games traditionally last a full week with an official opening and closing ceremony and six days of athletic competition. The Games are a privately organized event that relies on individual registrations to finance and stage each quadrennial gathering. Participant fees partially help offset the large operational costs to stage the Games, as organizers also seek sponsorship to further subsidize budgets. Much like any sport tourism event, volunteers also are important to the Gay Games; however scant volunteer data are available from previous competitions.

Table 4.1 The growth of the Gay Games

Year	Host city	Athletes	Countries	Number of sports
1982	San Francisco	1,300	12	11
1986	San Francisco	3,500	17	17
1990	Vancouver	7,300	39	27
1994	New York	12,500	40	31
1998	Amsterdam	13,000	68	30
2002	Sydney	11,000	80	31
2006	Chicago	11,500	70	34
2010	Cologne	10,000	70+	35
2014	Cleveland	8,000	50+	30
2018	Paris	15,000 est.		

Source: FGG 2014b.

The Games were co-held in the north-eastern Ohio cities of Akron and Cleveland between 9 and 16 August. For some the 2014 Games were awarded surprisingly to Cleveland/Akron in 2009, stereotypically seen as blue-collar cities in industrial decline, although Cleveland appears to be going through a strong period of urban regeneration. They beat Washington, DC and Boston, two larger conurbations traditionally seen as more gay-friendly, in addition to being more well known as international tourist destinations. Events have the potential to show off a marginal city on a global scale (Horne and Manzenreiter, 2006). Noteworthy, Cleveland hosted the 2013 National Senior Games, attracting nearly 11,000 athletes and was awarded the 2016 Republican Party Convention. As Gilbert (2014) notes these were three key developments as the area is not known as a destination for major events. Stevenson et al. (2005) state hosting the Games tends to consolidate or articulate with an already existing aspect of a city's identity, rather than forging one anew. Awarding the Games to the Cleveland area seems a brave choice because it is located in the heartland of mid-west America, perceived as a more conservative part of the nation. Ohio is consistently seen as one of the worst states for gay rights (Guardian, 2012). At the time of the Games, the state of Ohio banned same-sex marriage and did not protect individuals from discrimination based on sexual orientation or gender identity.

Stevenson et al. (2005, p. 453) further state that:

> the coupling of the politics of sexuality and civic identity/economy is crucial because it is the promised economic benefits of the Gay Games (in terms of visitor numbers including attracting national and international volunteers) that makes it attractive to cities that otherwise would almost certainly take little interest in a fringe and sometimes controversial event.

Indeed, reading the bid document, Cleveland/Akron Games organizers' main aim for the Games was to help promote LGBT issues in the region, but also to create some visitor spending. Cleveland and its organizers originally hoped the Games would inject over $60 million into the local economy (Maag, 2009); however, this was downgraded to about $40 million (Armon, 2014; Gilbert, 2014).

In the run up to the event, the cover story of *Cleveland Magazine*'s 2014 August issue, headlined as 'How Gay Are We?', focused on the inclusivity of the city in terms of living. It concluded Cleveland has a way to go with LGBT issues, although compared to some other cities in Ohio it is seen as more progressive. *The Plain Dealer*, Cleveland's main newspaper with the largest circulation in the state, daily devoted prominent news coverage of the Games for the entire week of the event. Both publications hoped the Games would have some long-lasting legacies on the area, especially on the political, legal and social fronts. However, what is lacking is further critical scholarly investigation focusing on the symbolic and transgressive potential nature of the event. A key legacy theme to explore is how the Gay Games contribute to reconfiguring attitudes about sexuality as part of wider socio-political agendas in Cleveland/Akron, in the state of Ohio, and beyond. Finally, it is imperative to explore what factors may inhibit any legacies from meeting their potential.

Past scholarly research on the Gay Games and/or LGBTQI sport and events have focused on how they are seen as part of a general celebration and display of gay culture with a marked focus on making conspicuous lifestyle statements (Hargreaves, 2000). They also constitute a powerful and public reaction to homophobic discrimination and oppression in sport, and provide a safe space for participants, friends and volunteers. On this level, then, participating and volunteering in gay sport can be seen as having emancipatory power. This is especially true for those athletes and volunteers who come from countries that discriminate against or persecute LGBT people. The global growth and development of gay sports networks and events, like the Gay Games, have transformed the way gay athletes experience and understand sport (Pronger, 2000; Symons, 2010; Waitt, 2003), although there are some critics (Davidson, 2006, 2014; Pronger, 2000; Sykes, 2006) of the role of these events in that they mirror conservative sporting institutions and do not challenge the prevalent heteronormativity of sport. Less is known about others taking part in these types of events, such as non-athletes like volunteers.

Symons' (2010) historiography of the Gay Games is useful for those wishing to develop a more comprehensive understanding of issues surrounding sport, gender, sexuality, queer and feminist studies. Her work is also relevant to those interested in exploring the development of mega-sporting events and the competing discourses between commercialization and professional sport and grassroots sports models directed towards 'sport for all' and inclusivity. However, her book fails to acknowledge the multiple legacies the events created. There is only one mention of legacy in the entire book, where the 2002 Sydney Games 'had the potential to earn a huge economic impact and a legacy about community development' (p. 179). Thus, there has been a lack of published research on the volunteering legacy of gay sport events like the Games.

The next section presents the results of the volunteer legacies that emerged, and demonstrates how they are interconnected to some wider socio-political and tourism issues. Both local and international aspects of volunteering are explored and discussed.

Results: the local and international volunteer legacies of the 2014 Cleveland/Akron Gay Games

The size and nature of volunteering and links to tourism

A total of 15 of the 29 stakeholders specifically mentioned volunteering issues and legacies as part of their interviews. Much like previous Gay Games, and other major sport events, organizers advertised the need for volunteers well before the Games. Mary (Director of Development, Gay Games) said the Games recruited over 3,000 volunteers. She did identify that the vast majority of them ('about 98 per cent') came from the immediate Cleveland/Akron and north-east Ohio region. Thus, a very small percentage of them came from other parts of the United States or internationally. There is no evidence as to whether this is higher or lower compared to previous Games. Mary said two volunteers travelled from Sierra Leone because 'one wanted to meet other volunteer workers to share ideas and learn more about LGBT people around the world ... the other wanted to come because they are an activist helping young people back in their country'.

Some stakeholders mentioned that it was hard to attract volunteers from outside Ohio and internationally because Cleveland/Akron is not a well-known destination, even within the United States. This appears to be a great challenge to attract international volunteers. Olympic and mega-sport host cities and regions are often well-established tourist destinations prior to a bid (Sant et al., 2013), and this is true for all previous Gay Games host cities (San Francisco, Vancouver, New York, Amsterdam, Sydney, Chicago and Cologne, with Paris in 2018). Cleveland/Akron is not considered a major tourist destination domestically and especially for international visitors where it is not among the top 20 cities visited (U.S. Department of Commerce National Travel and Tourism Office, 2014). Cleveland is also not known particularly as a gay destination, as it is not listed on *The Advocate*'s (Breen, 2014) annual ranking of the 25 'gayest' cities in the United States. This likely affected athlete registration numbers as well as volunteering numbers, which ultimately resulted in the down-grading of the economic impacts forecasted. Literature suggests (see Jarvis and Blank, 2011) that high tourism amenity cities may have an easier time attracting international volunteers who also may be tourists at the same time.

David (Positively Cleveland/Convention and Visitors Bureau) said Cleveland has a tourism destination image problem, which may affect either athletes or volunteers to come to take part. One respondent alluded to the fact that 'it does not hold a positive perception on a national level – we are the mistake by the lake, the burning river'. Changing this negative destination image of Cleveland was commonly referred to. Another commented that 'we cannot even get people to come to Cleveland from Los Angeles ... how are we going to attract international participants or volunteers'. Tracey (AIDS Task Force) said:

> The Games will help tourism as it breaks down people's barriers because I think when you start to talk about cities like Cleveland people think 'they are very poor and they don't have anything why would I go to Cleveland?' ... I have heard that more times than I care to count.

Michelle (Plexus/FIT) said volunteers were learning about their own city and helping to communicate this to domestic and international tourists. Wally (Consolidated Solutions) believed the Games had already changed the stereotypical view, 'just by watching the social media and seeing people from all over the world, they are having positive experiences'. While the interviews showed people were optimistic about a positive change, Li and McCabe (2013) discuss the potential of events to further embed undesirable aspects. Kristi (Cleveland Foundation) believed tourism is an important legacy; however, she felt this was lessened to an extent because registration numbers were smaller than anticipated, and that volunteers were mainly local. Still, some believed participants and the few volunteers from outside Ohio would re-visit the cities in the future.

David, and his organization (Positively Cleveland), focused on the obvious increase in immediate visitor numbers and spend as a result of the Games, referred to as a tangible legacy (Li et al., 2011; Matheson, 2002), but also the difficulty of trying to track the long-term tourism legacy. This makes it a contested issue within the literature. Part of this relates to challenging methodological and ethical issues related to researching LGBTQI people. His team had developed a LGBT tourism strategy as a result and hoped to attract specifically gay sport fans and LGBT tourists in the future. Some of those could be the few volunteers who travelled to Cleveland/Akron, although this aspect would be expected to be minimal. Destination image change and re-visit intentions are both considered as intangible legacies (Li and McCabe, 2013; Preuss, 2007). Weed (2008) identified the development of strategic sport/tourism policies and plans as another tangible legacy. This demonstrates the Games have been a catalyst for tourism planning and how tourism aspects can be interconnected to international volunteering, although minimal for Cleveland/Akron in terms of the latter. However, for future Games such as Paris 2018 it would be expected that this high tourist amenity city would attract more international volunteers.

Attracting straight volunteers

The Games attracted a range of volunteers, many of whom were straight allies. Mary (Director of Development, Gay Games) estimated just over half of volunteers were straight, which may surprise some people. She also suggested locals made up more of the straight volunteers while those coming from further afield were more likely to be gay. Respondents talked about how volunteers came from all walks of life, the young and old, and the corporate community including KeyBank and Ernst & Young. Stakeholders felt the volunteer support demonstrated that 'Clevelanders are wonderful people'. Joe (Councillor) was enthusiastic about a volunteer legacy, especially among the straight community:

> I saw, in the Games festival village, residents of mine who have maybe been in Cleveland for two or three years, who were ... this is for them. This is their introduction to volunteering in Cleveland. We had Mayor Baker who coined a phrase called 'Civitism' that we must all be ... activists for the civic good ... I saw one and said 'What are you doing?' And she said 'I really wanted to volunteer, you know we have lived in Tremont for two years and I thought this was a great chance to meet people' ... and the cool thing was that so many people who were older were volunteering. And I am going to say this, and maybe this is me revealing my own prejudices: people that I didn't think would be 'out' allies. You know we have a lot of allies – the question is are they out? GG9 has outed a lot of allies. And when you look at the generational situation I think that has been the case, and especially for a lot of our volunteers.

Two of the 46 conversations held with residents mentioned volunteering, not including the other two people who were specifically spoken to because they were helping out. A hostess in a restaurant, originally from Paraguay but who has lived in Cleveland for ten years, said 'Yeah it is great the Games are here. Some of my friends are volunteering and because of that I know lots about them. It is hard to be gay in Paraguay but not here'. A young female shop assistant, upon seeing my Games participation badge, said 'Oh I forgot to wear my badge in support ... lots of my crowd are talking about the Games ... they don't care about sexuality ... my friends all know about the Games and some are volunteering'.

Jason (Softball) was impressed by the number of volunteers and 'was curious to know how the organizers recruited them. I had 12 helping out with softball ... I talked to one kid who was doing it because of a school project'. Mary felt the wider straight community was more excited to offer their time than gay people. Luz (Women's Happy Hour) was aware that an even mix of gay and straight people were volunteering. She added, 'once the word gets out for these events and causes, people come out and help'. Michelle referred to the volunteers as a tangible legacy, although the literature points to inspiring people to volunteer as intangible.

Christen (Diversity Center) undertook sensitivity training with corporations that encouraged employees to volunteer, so that they knew how to engage with participant athletes who came from more than 50 countries and use appropriate language. Whilst registering for the event at the Cleveland Convention Center, I talked to two young women from the local area whom said their companies gave them time off from work so they could volunteer. They both identified as straight, with one stating 'my company has an active volunteer programme and I just thought this was the perfect event to be part of ... it is just so exciting!' Scott (Team Cleveland/Softball/Bowling) said he went to university campuses to try to recruit volunteers to help organize sport events. He said he did not care whether they were gay or straight, just that 'it was important to get young people in the community involved'. Mary (Director of Development, Gay Games) felt a lasting legacy in terms of volunteers was the gay community did not rely only on help from within, that we do not 'ghettoize', as the Games helped foster volunteer relations across a range of people and communities.

The Gay Games as a volunteer catalyst

The role of the Gay Games as a catalyst for increasing volunteerism appears to be under some dispute. Nelson (St. Lukes) questioned the volunteering, believing that the majority of the volunteers were already civically engaged and being drawn from the same sample that already takes part. Some interviewed referred to Gay Games volunteers as to ones that had previously done so for the Senior Games. Indeed, Valarie (Cleveland City Chief of Government & International Affairs) identified that the city possesses a volunteer data base of 5,000 from the Senior Games. This may help to explain the numbers of straight persons being part of the Gay Games. But Valarie added that the Gay Games helped increase the LGBT proportion within the city's volunteer pool. Phyllis (LGBT Center) thought many Games volunteers would also step forward for the Republican National Convention in 2016. Gursoy and Kendall (2006) identify that a less tangible legacy is to inspire additional support to stage future events in the host destination. Nelson (St. Lukes) thinks Cleveland now has the physical and volunteering infrastructure to pull off future events.

As Mike (Billiards) noted, 'many people at my work are volunteering ... they will volunteer for anything but it is great for them to see the gay community and what it is really all about'. While it appears that some new volunteers were attracted because of the Gay Games, what remains is the problem of how to accurately measure the volunteer motivation and inspiration, and what types of people took part. It appears that some new people did volunteer, likely those from corporations who allowed employees to take part in this form of civic engagement. For Minnaert (2012), questions remain whether marginalized groups gain access to skill development through volunteering. Those interviewed were unsure if people from minority backgrounds volunteered in significant numbers.

Volunteering and connections to socio-political legacies

This section discusses some of the personal legacies that were identified by stakeholders and residents, which are connected to wider socio-political aspects as well as volunteering specifically as the two cannot be separated. While the Games had a personal aspect related to starting conversations, they also allowed wider discussions and connections to be made with a diverse range of people and organizations. Valarie (Cleveland City Chief of Government & International Affairs) mentioned that the 'friendships created by those volunteers organizing the Games' are key, referred to by Foley et al. (2014) as a less considered legacy. Alana (Equality Ohio) felt the foremost legacy was 'the strengthened volunteering organizational capacity across the board, a distancing from individuals being in charge to organizations ... part of organizational unity'.

Phyllis (LGBT Center) said 'we need to tap in to the Games volunteers and capture that'. She also felt the connections and partnerships made with the volunteers in the planning of the event have helped to increase awareness of the LGBTQI community and the challenges and issues they face. Others mentioned 'coalitions' developed through volunteering. However this appears to be coalitions based in the local area, and not building that many connections to a wider network of volunteers on an international scale. The optimism was not a universal feeling. Kristi (Cleveland Foundation) did sense some 'apathy and lukewarm responses among people in the community' about the Games in terms of helping out and volunteering. Mary (Director of Development, Gay Games) even sensed some straight people were more excited to volunteer for the Games compared to gay persons.

Preuss (2007) talks of legacies in terms of what would have happened if the event had not taken place. Were the Games the catalyst for increased acceptance and integration of the gay community? Most agreed that they were; however, many felt it was hard to measure. Christen (Diversity Center) mentioned it would be worthwhile to follow up the stories of those who volunteered to hear their experiences and to see if they helped to enact social change. A few felt societal and cultural changes towards LGBTQI people were happening already, but most thought the Games had accelerated the process, especially through the wide range of volunteers who came together from different communities. Wally said 'I defy anybody to say that would have happened without the Games'. Certainly the Games are hoped to act as a catalyst to bring about wider socio-political and legal change for politicians and other key leaders.

Barriers to volunteering legacies

A concern from many stakeholders was related to loss of 'momentum' or 'political will' once the Games were over. Some key volunteer organizers had been helping for a number of years and mentioned they needed a 'well-earned vacation'. Most were optimistic the legacies created by those volunteering and organizing the event will happen but some were cautious as key individuals may resign or give up volunteering due to 'burn out'. Colleen (Neighborhood Progress) thought it was a huge concern that things would slow down and 'we lose the champions', but stressed the need to continue the dialogue between various communities in the area, and to fight for (LGBTQI) social inequalities being erased.

Alana (Equality Ohio) and Thomas (Executive Director Gay Games) both were concerned the event may not inspire new talents to emerge within the community to carry on the voluntary work. Indeed, Minnaert (2012) talks about the intangible skill development that can be developed among volunteers, as these skills can be lost if they drop out and cannot pass on their knowledge to younger generations. Mary (Director of Development, Gay Games) was somewhat disappointed the event did not attract more volunteers from outside of Ohio:

> It was great they [two volunteers] came from Sierra Leone but it would have been nicer to see others coming from a range of other countries ... where it is harder to be gay ... but it can be expensive to come to the US to take part.

Thus the cost to travel to these types of international events is expensive, not only for volunteers, but for athletes and friends. Some felt the majority of the local volunteers were mainly coming from the white middle-class community, with less from those sometimes seen as more marginalized such as African-Americans. It is noteworthy to mention that the two international volunteers who came from Sierra Leone were hoping to learn how to help marginalized LGBT people in their own country. Kristi (Cleveland

Foundation) extended the point about talent being a type of resource lacking, as well as funding and people's volunteering time and interest.

Discussion and conclusions about the transgressive potential of the Gay Games volunteer legacies

The preceding results section has identified a range of both local and international volunteer legacies and attempted to categorize their tangible nature, and briefly showed what may limit them in the future. The empirical data identify the interconnections created and the complex dimensions (Leopkey and Parent, 2012) associated with potential legacies of a less-known alternative event like the Gay Games. More specifically, it showed the relation of volunteering to both tourism and socio-political legacies.

Studies suggest smaller or medium-sized events can often have a greater benefit for a host compared to those related to mega-sport events. This appears to be the case in Cleveland/Akron. This research provides a thorough assessment of a range of possible aspects beyond the traditional focus on economic or infrastructural legacies created by larger sport events. While a vast range of socio-political, sport, volunteering, tourism, arts, economic and event management legacies were created on a macro-level, it is important to remember how the Games may also leave a personal legacy on each stakeholder. Most of the stakeholders were also volunteers themselves, leaving a potential mark on their own individual capital, developing their own skills and creating networks and friendships at the local level but at times more nationally and internationally. Knowledge about the 2014 event is to be passed on to the organizers and volunteers of the 2018 Paris Games.

Overall, the wider legacies skewed very positively, although some challenging barriers exist that may inhibit them from reaching their full potential. While a vast range of positive legacies were identified, one must remember the 29 stakeholders interviewed may have a vested interest in promoting them at the cost of others. Further, as pointed out by Gruneau (2002) and Preuss (2007), concerns about hosting an event are often marginalized or downplayed for the greater good. This project gives equal voice to all types of negative and positive aspects, exposing community anxieties and tensions, providing a balanced and revealing assessment, which Li and McCabe (2013) state is crucial for event legacy research.

Specifically in terms of volunteering the legacies from the Gay Games were largely seen as positive as well. Legacies here could be seen as both tangible and intangible. Despite some dispute about whether the same volunteers were being used for a number of events, the greater benefit appeared to be the increased awareness of LGBTQI issues in the local area. This would hope to further accelerate societal acceptance of gay people and their associated socio-political, legal and day-to-day issues they face among the wider population, especially since the majority of volunteers were straight. Tangible legacies were created simply by the number of volunteers taking part, and their associated economic spend. The spend was lessened because the event happened in a low tourist amenity destination (Cleveland/Akron), thus resulting in fewer international or even national volunteers travelling to take part. Other mega-sport events like the Olympics likely attract more international volunteers, although there appears to be scant studies providing evidence of this. Less tangible aspects emerged from motivating volunteers to possibly help out at future events, skill development, and creating friendships with other volunteers both locally, nationally and internationally. Further, volunteering helped to instil community pride as they showed off Akron/Cleveland to national and international athletes and tourists.

Preuss (2007) also refers importantly to what would have happened if the event had not taken place. Some thoughts are thus raised as to the Gay Games being a catalyst for legacies to emerge and the transformations taking place in the Cleveland/Akron community. Regardless of the event, wider societal attitudes towards sexual minorities are clearly moving in a positive direction in most developed nations. Certainly the vast majority of those interviewed believed the Games accelerated the process of change related to the wider key socio-political legacies associated with increasing awareness of the LGBTQI community, providing leverage for related legal battles in Ohio, and creating connections and alliances between gay and straight people and institutions, significantly through the volunteering networks. This was enhanced by the local nature of the volunteering base as opposed to those who travelled internationally. While this points to a largely positive position, some clear challenges remain. These include considerable barriers such as a loss of volunteer momentum once the Games finished, or people becoming comfortable with the work being completed and going back to their 'silos'.

A key challenge in the study of legacies is measurement (Egelstaff, 2014; Li and McCabe, 2013) and at what point does one gauge them because they have considerable pre- and post-social dimensions (Roche, 2003). This has significance for Cleveland and Akron. As Valarie (Cleveland City Chief of Government & International Affairs) says, 'the simple fact that the Games were in Cleveland is a legacy. We hosted the Games ... but I'd like to attend a Gay Games in 20 years now and hear people still talking about Cleveland'. However, she and many others thought the biggest takeaway is intangible, something that is hard to measure and cannot necessarily be seen. Legacies can be unpredictable. Either way, many felt this event was a profound history marking occurrence and was helping to 'rebuild our city'.

The Gay Games clearly has potential for much symbolic significance, especially through the volunteer networks that helped create and organize them. But do they have the transgressive ability to overcome negative feelings about the LGBTQI community from the outside or even within it? As Giddens (1990) stated, events such as the Gay Games have the power to affirm local resident identities. Debord (1983) is much more critical, suggesting event spectacles conceal enduring issues affecting socioeconomically marginalized people. Did the Games challenge wider existing dominant heteronormative values? The answer appears to be a qualified yes – the Gay Games can be seen as a disruptive and playful platform to challenge and question dominant heteronormative ideologies (Hetherington, 1997; Lee et al., 2014; Waitt, 2003), change attitudes towards LGBTQI people, and raise awareness about wider legal battles. Perhaps these are the most important legacies, rooted in socio-cultural and political discourses, and not just on the more traditional economic indicators. New narratives have been created in Cleveland/Akron around configurations of sexuality.

The Games helped changed societal attitudes towards LGBTQI people in the local area by bringing together volunteers from both the straight and gay communities, forming new networks and strengthening links in the host destination. Because local volunteers, who made up the vast majority of the helpers, were also from the straight community, as opposed to the international volunteers who were more likely to be gay, it is thought that this helped to change attitudes even more. Thus the lack of internationalization of the volunteer base likely aided in socio-political goals being met more quickly. This was especially important in Ohio, considered one of the least LGBT-friendly places to live and work in the United States. Further, local volunteers from a range of sectors interacted with domestic and international gay athletes who came to compete in a variety of sport events, helping to breakdown stereotypes and fostering a sense of pride in Cleveland/Akron.

The Games can contribute to tackling some immediate issues but many more remain that need to be addressed. Through the interviews with many stakeholders work still needs to be done changing attitudes and meeting the needs of those marginalized within the LGBTQI community, namely youth, seniors, trans, the homeless, those from ethnic minorities, and to some extent women and even bisexuals. Many commented that the volunteering and organizational base came from a white middle-class community, dominated by men. The voices heard in this study clearly do not want the Gay Games to be seen as the endpoint, that everything is fine, when many concerns persist. As Alana (Equality Ohio) reminded us, 'we need to have a healthy balance, we need to take the excitement that we have now and channel it into work that still needs to be done'.

Preuss (2007) talks about the importance of momentum created by an event and its volunteers, often built on emotion. The literature, grounded mainly in mega-sports, says events give politicians and other stakeholders, such as voluntary organizations, a vision. Citizens become emotionally involved. The private and corporate sectors are inspired by welcoming an extraordinary and widely-known event. While this may be true for something like the Olympics, is it the same for the Gay Games in Cleveland/ Akron? Again, the answer is a qualified yes, as concerns about a loss of momentum is a challenge that may prevent the full leverage potential of initially identified (volunteer) legacies being realized. Various funds and resources have been donated and awarded in Akron/Cleveland so future legacy work continues, although little appeared to be directly related to volunteering. Thus a fragmented approach seems to have developed and what is needed may require some type of legacy committee, although what form that takes and resource funding aspects would need to be determined. At the time of this writing no legacy committee had been established. A key focus of a committee would be to help develop the momentum of the volunteer base, whether for other gay events or more mainstream ones.

Finally, more longitudinal work is clearly needed. This study has provided insights into initial impressions of potential (international) volunteer and other legacies associated with the Cleveland/Akron Gay Games. This lays the groundwork against which they can be monitored and measured in the near future, whether two or five years or even longer. Thus it is suggested that stakeholders are interviewed again so that they can reflect and self-assess the volunteering legacies they initially identified. Interviews can further explore the continued transgressive power of the Games in challenging wider societal attitudes. One stakeholder suggested it would be important to hear the stories of those who volunteered and how they enacted change in the future, whether they were local or those who travelled from other nations. This could be especially true for those few international volunteers who came from countries with less tolerant attitudes towards LGBTQI people.

Note

1 This chapter interchangeably uses terms, from the widest ranging inclusive 'LGBTQI' (lesbian, gay, bisexual, trans, questioning and intersex) to the shorter LGBT, which was used by many of those interviewed. The word 'gay' is also used, which should be considered to represent the wider LGBTQI community depending on the context. For example, some sport clubs/leagues simply use the term gay to promote to the wider community. LGBTQI is used to represent a range of inclusive identities beyond just gay and lesbian.

References

Aisbett, L., Randle, E. and Kappelides, P. (2015). Future volunteer intentions at a major sport event. *Annals of Leisure Research* 18(4): 491–509.

Armon, R. (2014). Gay Games to boost regional economy. *Akron Beacon Journal*, 8 August.

Benson, A.M., Dickson, T.J., Terwei, F.A. and Blackman, D.A. (2014). Training of Vancouver 2010 volunteers: A legacy opportunity? *Contemporary Social Science* 9(2): 210–226.

Breen, M. (2014). 2014 gayest cities in America. www.advocate.com/travel/2014/01/06/2014s-gayest-cities-america?page=0%2C3.

Brennan, M.A. (2005). Volunteerism and community development: A comparison of factors shaping volunteer behaviour in Irish and American communities. *Journal of Volunteer Administration* 23(2): 20–27.

Cornelissen, S., Bob, U. and Swart, K. (2011). Towards redefining the concept of legacy in relation to sport mega-events: insights from the 2010 FIFA World Cup. *Development Southern Africa* 28(3): 307–318.

Davidson, J. (2006). The necessity of queer shame for gay pride: The Gay Games and cultural events. In J. Caudwell (ed.) *Sport, sexualities and queer/theory.* London: Routledge (pp. 90–105).

Davidson, J. (2014). Racism against the abnormal? The twentieth century Gay Games, biopower and the emergence of homonational sport. *Leisure Studies* 33(4): 357–378.

Debord, G. (1983). *Society of the spectacle.* London: Rebel Press.

Dickson, T.J., Benson, A.M. and Blackman, D.A. (2011). Developing a framework for evaluating Olympic and Paralympic legacies. *Journal of Sport & Tourism* 16(4): 285–302.

Doherty, A. (2009). The volunteer legacy of a major sport event. *Journal of Policy Research in Tourism, Leisure and Events* 1(3): 185–207.

Egelstaff, S. (2014). Glasgow celebrates: The 20th Commonwealth Games and their legacy. *International Centre for Sport Security Journal* 2(3): 96–101.

Elling A., Knoppers, A. and de Knop, P. (2003). Gay/lesbian sport clubs and events: Places of homo-social bonding and cultural resistance? *International Review for the Sociology of Sport* 38: 441–456.

FGG (2014a). *Mission, vision and values.* www.gaygames.net/index.php?id=56.

FGG (2014b). *History of the FGG and the Gay Games.* www.gaygames.net/index.php?id=28.

Foley, C., Edwards, D. and Schlenker, K. (2014). Business events and friendship: Leveraging the sociable legacies. *Event Management* 18: 53–64.

Fontana, A. and Frey, J.H. (2000). The interview: From structured questions to negotiated text. In N.K. Denzin and Y.S. Lincoln (eds) *Handbook of qualitative research.* Thousand Oaks: Sage (pp. 645–672).

Fredline, L., Jago, L. and Deery, M. (2003). The development of a generic scale to measure the social impacts of events. *Event Management* 8(1): 23–37.

Giddens, A. (1990). *The consequences of modernity.* Cambridge: Polity.

Gilbert, D. (2014). Interview with David Gilbert, President and CEO of Positively Cleveland (Cleveland Convention and Visitor Bureau), 14 August.

Gratton, C. and Preuss, H. (2008). Maximising Olympic impacts by building up legacies. *The International Journal of the History of Sport* 25: 1922–1938.

Gruneau, R. (2002). Foreword. In M. Lowes (ed.) *Indy dreams and urban nightmares.* Toronto: Toronto University Press (pp. ix–xii).

Gruneau, R. and Horne, J. (eds) (2016). *Mega-events and globalization: Capital and spectacle in a changing world order.* Abingdon: Routledge.

Guardian. (2012). Gay rights in the US, state by state. www.theguardian.com/world/interactive/2012/may/08/gay-rights-united-states.

Gursoy, D. and Kendall, K. (2006). Hosting mega-events modelling locals' support. *Annals of Tourism Research* 33(3): 603–623.

Hargreaves, J.A. (2000). *Heroines of sport: The politics of difference and identity.* London: Routledge.

Hetherington, K. (1997). *The badlands of modernity: Heterotopia and social ordering.* London: Routledge.

Horne, J. and Manzenreiter, W. (2006). An introduction to the sociology of sports mega-events. *The Sociological Review* 54: 1–24.

Jarvis, N. and Blank, C. (2011). The importance of tourism motivations among sport event volunteers at the 2007 World Artistic Gymnastics Championships, Stuttgart, Germany. *Journal of Sport & Tourism* 16(2): 129–147.

Kates, S.M. and Belk, R.W. (2001). The meanings of lesbian and gay pride day. *Journal of Contemporary Ethnography* 30(4): 392–429.

Lee, S., Kim, S. and Love, A. (2014). Coverage of the Gay Games from 1980–2012 in U.S. newspapers: An analysis of newspaper article framing. *Journal of Sport Management* 28(2): 176–188.

Leopkey, B. and Parent, M.M. (2012). Olympic Games legacy: From general benefits to sustainable long-term legacy. *International Journal of the History of Sport* 29(6): 924–943.

Leopkey, B. and Parent, M.M. (2015). Stakeholder perspectives regarding the governance of legacy at the Olympic Games. *Annals of Leisure Research* 18(4): 528–548.

Li, S. and McCabe, S. (2013). Measuring the socio-economic legacies of mega-events: Concepts, propositions and indicators. *International Journal of Tourism Research* 15: 388–402.

Li, S.N., Blake, A. and Cooper, C. (2011). Modelling the economic impact of international tourism on the Chinese economy: A CGE analysis of the Beijing 2008 Olympics. *Tourism Economics* 17(2): 279–303.

Lockstone-Binney, L., Holmes, K., Smith, K.M. and Baum, T.G. (2010). Volunteers and volunteering in leisure: Social science perspectives. *Leisure Studies* 29(4): 435–455.

Maag, C. (2009). Forget Chicago: Cleveland gets the Gay Games. *Time Inc.* www.time.com/time/nation/article/0,8599,1927211,00.html.

MacAloon, J.J. (2008). 'Legacy' as managerial/magical discourse in contemporary Olympic affairs. *The International Journal of the History of Sport* 25: 2020–2071.

Mair, J. and Whitford, M. (2013). An exploration of events research: event topics, themes and emerging trends. *International Journal of Event and Festival Management* 4(1): 6–30.

Markwell, K. and Waitt, G. (2009). Festivals, space and sexuality: Gay Pride in Australia. *Tourism Geographies* 11(2): 143–168.

Matheson, C. (2002). Upon further review: An examination of sporting event economic impact studies. *The Sport Journal* 5(1): 1–4.

Matheson, C. (2010). Legacy planning, regeneration and events: The Glasgow 2014 Commonwealth Games. *Local Economy* 25(1): 10–23.

Messner, M. (1992). *Power at play: Sports and the problem of masculinity.* Boston: Beacon Press.

Minnaert, L. (2012). An Olympic legacy for all? The non-infrastructural outcomes of the Olympic Games for socially excluded groups. *Tourism Management* 33(2): 361–370.

Ohmann, S., Jones, I. and Wilkes, K. (2006). The perceived social impacts of the 2006 World Cup on Munich residents. *Journal of Sport & Tourism* 11(2): 129–152.

Preuss, H. (2007). The conceptualisation and measurement of mega sport legacies. *Journal of Sport & Tourism* 12(3/4): 207–228.

Pronger, B. (2000). Homosexuality and sport: Who's winning? In J. McKay, M. Messner and D. Sabo (eds) *Masculinities, gender relations, and sport*. London: Sage (pp. 222–244).

Reis, A.C., Rodrigues de Sousa-Mast, F. and Gurgel, L.A. (2014). Rio 2016 and the sport participation legacies. *Leisure Studies* 33(5): 437–453.

Ritchie, J.R.B. (2000). Turning 16 days into 16 years through Olympic legacies. *Event Management* 6: 155–165.

Roche, M. (2003). Mega-events, time and modernity. *Time and Society* 12(1): 99–126.

Sant, S.-L., Mason, D.S. and Hinch, T.D. (2013). Conceptualising Olympic tourism legacy: Destination marketing organisations and Vancouver 2010. *Journal of Sport & Tourism* 18(4): 287–312.

Shipway, R. and Kirkup, N. (2012). Guest editorial: The impacts of legacies of sports events. *International Journal of Event and Festival Management* 3(3): 1–5.

Silverman, D. (2011). *Qualitative research*. 3rd edition. London: SAGE.

Stevenson, N. (2011). Culture and the 2012 Games: Creating a tourism legacy. *Journal of Tourism and Cultural Change* 10(2): 137–149.

Stevenson, D., Rowe, D. and Markwell, K. (2005). Explorations in 'event ecology': The case of the International Gay Games. *Social Identities* 11(5): 447–465.

Sykes, H. (2006). Queering theories of sexuality in sport studies. In J. Caudwell (ed.) *Sport, sexualities and queer/theory*. London: Routledge (pp. 13–32).

Symons, C. (2010). *The Gay Games: A history*. London: Routledge.

Thomson, A., Schlenker, K. and Schulenkorf, N. (2013). Conceptualizing sport event legacy. *Event Management* 17: 111–122.

US Department of Commerce National Travel and Tourism Office. (2014). Overseas visitation estimates for U.S. states, cities and census regions. Washington DC: U.S. Department of Commerce.

Waitt, G. (2003). Gay Games: Performing 'community' out from the closet of the locker room. *Society and Cultural Geography* 4(2): 167–183.

Weed, M. (2008). *Olympic tourism*. Oxford: Elsevier Butterworth-Heinemann.

Chapter 5

Pull factors for Perth

Developing an International Golf Volunteer Engagement Strategy (iGoVolES)

Alfred Ogle and David Lamb

Introduction

The aim of this chapter is to examine volunteer engagement in international sports events, specifically volunteerism relating to professional golf tournaments. This chapter is based on research carried out on the volunteers of the 2014 ISPS Handa Perth International, a golf tournament co-sanctioned by the PGA Tour of Australasia and the European Tour. The factors underpinning volunteering behaviour were identified in the context of the push–pull framework (Dann, 1977) in order to assess the 'pull' influence, or attractiveness, of the tournament on international volunteer participation. This study was instigated by reports of golf volunteers, defined as 'anyone who helps others in the sport without remuneration (Other than expenses)' (golfvolunteers.org, n.d.) and travels to Professional Golf Association (PGA) tournaments around the world, including Australia (Alter, 2014; PGA, 2016).

The authors have researched volunteer motivation in Perth, which is considered 'the most remote city on earth' (Albanese, 2011) and, as repeat volunteers at the Perth International,[1] had observed anecdotally no evidence of international golf volunteers at that golf tournament. Therefore, this research seeks explanations for what appears to be a single-outbound direction of international golf volunteers. The chapter begins with development of the Golf Tournament Attendee Push–Pull Factors Model (hereafter referred to as PPFM) which underpins the Golf Volunteer Engagement Strategy (GoVolES) framework. Thereafter, an overview of professional golf is provided, followed by a discussion of its role in Western Australia's (WA) tourism. Next, the material study is explicated and its findings reported. The authors then discuss the antecedents of international golf volunteerism and posit that it itself constitutes an Event Pull Factor in its own right, thereby giving rise to the International Golf Volunteer Engagement Strategy (iGoVolES).

The push–pull framework

The push–pull framework was based on Tolman's (1937) interpretation of the sign-gestalt paradigm to distinguish between emotional and cognitions motivators, which Dann (1977) crystallized into a tourism motivation theory. In the context of golf volunteering, 'push factors' are those internal psychological motivators that induce individuals to volunteer, whereas 'pull factors' are those external motivators which compel people towards volunteering for an event, often because of the attribute(s) of the event (Grimm and Needham, 2012a). Prima facie, these disparate opposing factors, in theory, are independent of each other, with the 'push factor' typically preceding the 'pull factor' (Dann, 1981), thereby necessitating examination of the former before the latter (Dann, 1977). Therefore, in the context of golf tournaments and events, this would generally hold true because a golf enthusiast would logically have a higher propensity to partake in golfing-related activities as compared to a non-golfer.

The view that the 'pull factors of a (venue) both respond to and reinforce push factor motivation' (Dann, 1981, p. 191) also resonates with the golfing context – as golf tournaments are typically held at beautiful locales (i.e. 'pull factor'). The symbiosis between the 'push' and 'pull' factors is noted by Uysal and Jurowski (1994) in tourism, and by extension also applies to golf tourism. For purposes of this chapter, therefore, the 'push factor' is defined as a keen interest in golf as a sport and a desire to spectate and engage in golf tournament activities. This definition aligns with the findings of MacLean and Hamm (2007) that a love of the game of golf is a reason for ongoing volunteerism, albeit this had the least importance among the eight factors they identified. Bang and Chelladurai (2003) even advocated that their volunteer motivations scale for international sporting events (VMS-ISE) be extended to include the factor 'love of sport'. The modified scale was subsequently validated when further studies revealed that the 'love of sport' factor is a strong motivational factor among event volunteers (see Bang and Ross, 2009; Bang et al., 2009).

On the premise that the sequential push–pull action applies to golf volunteerism, the PPFM as depicted in Figure 5.1 is proposed. The pull factors as shown in Figure 5.1 are under three main attributes: Destination, Features, WIIFM (What's in it for me) Elements.

The primary pull factor of a golf tournament is ostensibly its field of competitors, hence one of Western Australian's strategic tourism goals to draw big name players to the World Super 6 Perth (Prestipino, 2016). Given that the calibre and celebrity of the players is a major spectator draw card (Robinson et al., 2004; Chammas, 2016), the tournament venue, or 'sportscape', is an important complementary element (Wakefield and Sloan, 1995). Lyu and Lee (2013) found that the golf event spectators are likely to pursue heterogeneous leisure benefits from their engagement

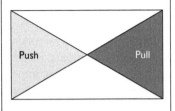

A keen interest in golf as a sport and a desire to spectate and engage in golf tournament activities including volunteering

Push

Pull

1) Location/destination (venue, accessibility, weather, safety, security, cost, ambience accommodation, hospitality)
2) Features (player calibre, brand, course layout, scenery, prestige, merchandise, golf equipment, complementary activities
3) WIIFM (What's in it for me?) elements (leisure, health, freebies, business/networking, camaraderie

Figure 5.1 Golf Tournament Attendee Push–Pull Factors Model.

with the event. Watanabe *et al.* (2013) found that spectators at Japanese professional golf tournaments were most motivated to remain at the event site by the quality of the event encompassing both the physical environment and the core products. Furthermore, Barros *et al.* (2010) found that golf tourists' length of stay is positively related to, amongst other factors, three factors that constitute elements of pull factor aspect: climate, events and hospitality.

Product innovation could be conceivably be considered as a 'pull factor', particularly when the game of golf faces threats to its popularity due to contemporary time (Vitello, 2008) and cost (*Economist*, 2015) constraints, technical difficulty (Costa, 2016), and its culture of complicated etiquette (Bense, 2016). Keipert (2016, para. 1ff.) reports that a 'Knockout Hole', a purpose-built 90-metre hole, will be part of the innovative changes afoot:

> Perth will have a golf tournament this summer but not a conventional 72-hole strokeplay event as golf's powerbrokers attempt to draw a new following via a fresh format.... The first three rounds of the tournament will resemble most others with 54 holes of strokeplay, including a 36-hole cut, before a second cut is made to the top-24 players on Saturday afternoon (with ties to be settled via a play-off). On Sunday, the remaining 24 will contest a six-hole matchplay shootout.

Moreover, Cuskelly *et al.* (2004) posit that the capability of sports events managers to identify and gauge the diversity and variability of volunteer motivation permits them to design customized strategies to sustain motivation across all the volunteers over the duration of an event. Therefore, the 'pull factors' are diverse, necessitating the need for tournament organizers and event-based sport tourism marketers to employ different techniques and approaches to increase and reinforce their customer base by providing the best pull factor fit/combination. In order to devise a holistic strategy that leverages on the optimal 'pull factor(s)', the collaboration of all stake-holders is also crucial. This is emphatically declared by the organizers of this innovative tournament (worldsuper6perth.com):

> But for the World Super 6 Perth to be a true success it needs to be embraced by Western Australia and as such a collaborative approach between the Tours, Golf WA, WA Division of the PGA, Lake Karrinyup and the entire WA golf family will be undertaken to ensure the tournament's long term success.

Implicit in the statement above is that golf volunteers, who belong to the 'golf family', should, therefore, be included in the tournament success formula. The family also extends to the community of golf enthusiasts worldwide. The recognition of the critical role that volunteers play in the success, and arguably the survival, of a tournament by all stakeholders is paramount, especially when golf represents the largest sports-related travel market[2] (Readman, 2012).

Golf Volunteer Engagement Strategy (GoVolES) framework

The Golf Volunteer Engagement Strategy (GoVolES) framework (Figure 5.2) is a strategic golf volunteer engagement framework underpinned by real-time Event Pull Factors. Represented by clockwise arrows indicating

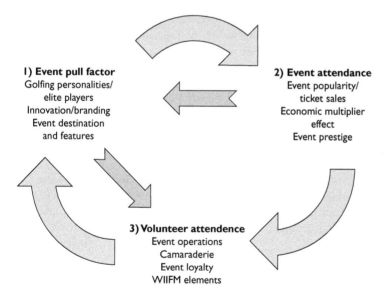

Figure 5.2 Golf Volunteer Engagement Strategy (GoVolES) framework.

the direction of influence, the premise is that the golf tournament pull factor is the primary driver of spectator attendance (this is indicated by large dark blue arrow). In turn, event attendance will attract event volunteers (this secondary driver is illustrated by a smaller lighter blue arrow). Finally, robust volunteer attendance facilitates the operationalization of the event, thereby directly enhancing the attractiveness of the event. It can, therefore, be posited that an influence cycle is formed.

The counter-clockwise arrows within the cycle represent a concurrent inverse influence dynamic: (1) Event Attendance enhances event branding, an element of Event Pull Factor; (2) Event Pull Factor attracts golf volunteer who intrinsically are 'pushed' towards the event (see Figure 5.1). Moon et al. (2011, p. 287) found that 'event quality perceptions, particularly intangible factors, positively influence the destination image' supports the counter-clockwise influence. This GoVolES is a virtuous cycle as it takes into account various environmental inputs and would apply at the tournament, city, state or national levels. GoVolES provides the basis for the development of the International Golf Volunteer Engagement Strategy (iGoVolES) which is presented at the end of the chapter.

Moital et al. (2013) propose that, in terms of spectator base, equitable management of different stakeholder expectations is imperative to ensure that local and national spectators are not displaced by the economic benefits derived from foreign and inter-state inbound spectators, which in the golfing context would be referred to as golf travellers if they engage in golfing activities in addition to attending golf tournaments (Hutchinson et al., 2009), desired by some stakeholders. This holds true in the recruitment of international volunteers: the local volunteer base must be nurtured in the first instance. Active volunteerism at the local level contributes to the camaraderie element of the WIIFM pull factor.

Volunteering at golf events

The extant literature in sports event volunteerism clearly shows the heavy reliance of such events on volunteers (Strigas and Jackson, 2003a; Zimbalist, 2010) irrespective of location as evident in the following quote:

> Volunteers are the backbone of golf tournaments worldwide – the US PGA Tour alone relies on more than 100,000 volunteers annually to run its tournaments. Though on a much smaller scale, the Aussie summer of golf also depends on a labour of love from the public.
>
> (Priest, 2015)

Given that the success of an event is based largely on the volunteers (Cuskelly et al., 2004; Getz, 2002) and their repeat volunteering behaviour (Pauline, 2011), the record high spectator attendances at PGA of America

Championships events (PGA, 2016) suggests golf volunteerism and international golf volunteerism in the United States is thriving. The apparent strength of the US PGA pull influence to spectators and golf volunteers is tantalizing, as alluded to in this quote: 'Australian golfing power-brokers are ready to lobby their American counterparts amid talk that one of the sport's four majors – the US PGA – could be played on foreign shores in the near future' (Read, 2013).

There appears to be an imbalance in golf volunteering in favour of the US PGA events despite it being the least accessible and the most costly to its volunteers. All volunteers, irrespective of the event, are typically required to commit to four full shifts approximating 16 duty hours. The PGA of America stipulates that golf volunteers must be at least of 22 years of age and purchase a mandatory volunteer uniform package (a 'custom Ralph Lauren golf shirt', vouchers for food and water from on-course concession stands, and a single discount on tournament merchandise). Volunteers receive complimentary access to the grounds throughout the seven-day PGA Championship. In contrast, the Australian PGA provide volunteers with free 'tournament branded' apparel (uniform) and merchandise, a season ticket, duty lunch and drinks, an invitation to a post-event Volunteer BBQ, and a free round of golf at the host course (PGA Australia, 2016). Whilst volunteers are required to be 18 years of age, however, younger individuals are welcomed with parent/guardian authorization.[3] Both PGAs require volunteers to commit to at least four shifts over the period of the tournament. The 2017 ISPS Handa New Zealand Open volunteer recruiters are enhancing volunteer benefits by highlighting a chance draw for a 2018 Pro-Am Tournament amateur spot, a coveted opportunity for amateurs to play a round with tour professionals. This imbalance suggest that volunteering at PGA of America events is highly attractive despite volunteers' personal expense and stringently imposed age restriction. This anomaly suggests that the PGA events perhaps have a golf volunteer pull factor that both the PGA of Australia and PGA of New Zealand do not have.

Volunteer motives

Volunteer motivation has been a dominant theme in contemporary volunteer research (Lo and Lee, 2011) encompassing mega-events (Dickson *et al.*, 2014; Duran and Hamarat, 2014) and tourism/conservation volunteering (Grimm and Needham, 2012a, 2012b). Research has also been undertaken, albeit to a lesser degree, in the areas of sports events (Lockstone-Binney *et al.*, 2014) and 'special events' (Monga, 2006). Research on volunteer motivations in the area of professional golf, however, is relatively scarce (e.g. Love *et al.*, 2011; Pauline, 2011). Strigas and Jackson (2003b) declared that the knowledge on sports volunteers' push factors was in its infancy. Their assessment still rings true a decade later despite the role of volunteers being of particular importance in professional golf event staging (Love et al., 2011). There is still a dearth of studies on golf tournaments from the spectator perspective (see Krohn and Backman, 2011; Watanabe et al., 2013) with only one specifically on professional golf spectators by Robinson et al. (2004).

Volunteers at professional golf events are typically motivated by identifiable personal rewards, but with continued engagement with successive events, motivations may change (Coyne and Coyne, 2001). This 'fluidity' (Hoye and Cuskelly, 2009, p. 174), coupled with the understanding that volunteerism can motivate individuals in various ways (Nichols and Ralston, 2012), suggests that a good understanding of those motivators and the beneficial outcomes of volunteering, such as what the individual gains from the experience, is critical (see Getz, 1991). This is clearly shown in a comparison between American and Australian volunteers in the conventions and events sectors recognized by Goldblatt and Matheson (2009), which is shown in Table 5.1. The motivators would potentially need to be accommodated if, for example, an event in Australia were to attract American volunteers.

The reasons why people make the decision to volunteer needs to be ascertained and the factors that make volunteering attractive requires identification (Costa et al., 2006). Furthermore, the inter-relationship between volunteers' motivation, experience and satisfaction, within the context of a local international event such as the Perth International, requires further research. This work is critical when one considers that this (case in point) relies on volunteer recruitment from the local community and inevitably the success of such an event depends on the participation of local volunteers (Getz, 2002). Equally, there is a diverse range of motives which determine why people decide to become volunteers and indeed there are many

Table 5.1 Australia and the United States: volunteer motivations

Australia	USA
Leisure	Recognition
Fun	Contributing to progress
Being part of a cause	New experiences
Socialization	Connections
	Futures career advancement
	Training
	Organization responds to and listen to their needs
	Various channels available for volunteer engagement including technology such as blogs and chatrooms

Source: Goldblatt and Matheson, 2009, p. 146.

different interpretations of the concept of volunteering. Cnaan *et al.* (1996) noted that most common definitions of volunteer contained four key dimensions with each dimension containing a number of variables in describing volunteers. They, however, determined that people are more inclined to associate true volunteerism with a 'pure' definition, as Jenner (1982, p. 30) describes: 'A person who, out of free will and without wages, works for a not-for-profit organization which is formally organized and has as its purpose service to someone or something other than its membership.' Lamb and Ogle (2016) confirmed observations by Cnaan *et al.* (1996) that volunteers, at least in the case a golf volunteers, did not exhibit mercenary-like intentions when engaging in volunteerism. Their findings also corroborate with the six underlying factors explaining volunteering motivation of Viking Classic PGA TOUR volunteers, namely:

1 personal enrichment;
2 altruism;
3 escapism;
4 golf interest;
5 career enhancement; and
6 prestige (Love *et al.*, 2011).

The notable difference between volunteer cohorts is the emphasis on self-benefit in the latter.

Wilson *et al.* (2005, p. 38) discovered that 'in many cases, the reasons for increases or declines in volunteering were specific to the (non-for-profit) organisation and motivated by varying degrees of altruism or self-interest'. In their research involving volunteers in a professional golf tournament, Coyne and Coyne (2001) identified that community spirit and camaraderie were key motives. Similarly, research conducted by Smith *et al.* (2003) on three sporting events based in Western Australia recognized that community related motivations were directly related to event success and to retention of volunteers. Personal experience and positive memories of an event were also significant in determining volunteer satisfaction in Coyne and Coyne's (2001) study and a number of commentators have recognized that many volunteers enjoy the 'fun' element in volunteering and see it as another form of leisure activity (Stebbins, 2009).

The international volunteer

Fairley *et al.* (2007) conducted research on the motivation of volunteers willing to travel to a location away from their place of residence at their own expense to support a sporting event in the capacity of a volunteer. The ease of international long haul travel, high discretionary income, and love for the sport has brought about 'a large number of volunteers are willing to travel, and to travel internationally, to volunteer' (Fairley *et al.*, 2007, p. 42). Bang and Ross (2009, pp. 64–65) assert that 'for popularized sporting events, people from other states or countries tend to visit the events in order to enjoy being involved', thereby possibly explaining why some volunteers are willing to travel great distances. While there has been research conducted in the area of the international sports volunteering within the mega-event (Chanavat and Ferrand, 2010; Giannoulakis *et al.*, 2007; Kim *et al.*, 2010) and golf tourism contexts (Hudson and Hudson, 2010; Kim *et al.*, 2008), there, however, is an apparent dearth of research undertaken specifically on international volunteers who have travelled from their places of residence to support a sporting event being held in a foreign locality.

Featured in a local Louisville[4] television programme, an Australian man and his wife are the epitome of the international golf volunteer, as demonstrated by the couple's volunteering behaviour:

> 'I started volunteering for the PGA in 2009 at Hazeltine. I flew over from Australia for that', said Godsell. 'We came also in 2011 and we volunteered in Atlanta'.... For Godsell, it was his passion for the sport that made him volunteer the first time, but it's the people he's met that have kept him coming back. 'I was getting to the age around about 60 and I thought, there's a few things I want to tick off in my life and if I don't start now, maybe I won't get around to it. So I thought why not go ahead and do it', said Godsell.

The impetus for Godsell was his passion for golf (push factor) but over time his motivation to continue his volunteering behaviour morphed to include the camaraderie and lifestyle factors, both identified in the Volunteer Attendance segment of the GoVolES framework.

The event and professional golf in Western Australia

Perth has had a rich history of hosting large-scale golf tournaments. The annual Western Australian Open Championship has been held at various local courses since 1921, interrupted only by the Second World War. Four Australian Open tournaments (1952, 1960, 1968, 1974) were played at the Lake Karrinyup Country Club (LKCC), and more recently the Heineken Classic hosted by the Vines Resort for 13 consecutive years beginning 1993, the Johnnie Walker Classic (2002 and 2003 at the LKCC; 2006 and 2009 at the Vines Resort), the 2007 LPGA Lexus Cup (Vines Resort) and the Perth International commencing in 2012. The Perth International was hosted at the LKCC on four occasions (2012–2014, 2016) and will be superseded by the World Super 6 Perth tournament in 2017.

Notwithstanding this heritage and having been graced by professional golf luminaries, Western Australia continues to struggle to draw the world's best golfers and golfing enthusiast despite its proximity to the burgeoning Asian golf market (Groves, 2015; 'The Future of Golf', 2014).

The Perth International was designed to be a draw card for Perth's events calendar by featuring world class golfers competing on a renowned golf course. A co-sanctioned event owned by IMG Australia and strategically linked to both the European Tour and the PGA Tour of Australasia in order to capitalize on the synergy between the two tours, the event was brought to Perth by Eventscorp (the events division of Tourism WA) to put the city back on the golfing map and encourage tourism growth and awareness of the region. The operation of the event was reliant upon a large group of 500 volunteers recruited from golf clubs in regional and metropolitan Perth and managed by Golf WA (state body for amateur golf in WA). Recruitment was via a dedicated Facebook page, 'word of mouth' (WOM) and community organizations in Perth. There appeared to be no recruitment drive for international volunteers despite the event's tourism underpinnings.

The European Tour and ISPS Handa PGA Tour of Australasia operated and sanctioned World Super 6 Perth was announced amidst much fanfare and has been heralded as a 'world-first in professional golf' (PGA Australia, 2016). Designed to 'to help lure a more attractive field' (Prestipino, 2016), an implication that can be drawn is that Perth, as a competitive golf tournament destination, had previously been deficient in attracting the biggest names in competitive golf. This 'lack of starpower depth has hurt the tournament each year' (Prestipino, 2016). Golf is strategically integral, therefore, within a larger state tourism promotion campaign led by Colin Barnett, the Premier of Western Australia and its Tourism Minister, to boost the value of tourism in WA to A$12 billion by 2020.

The research study and approach

The present study helps us understand the golf volunteer pull factors of the 2014 ISPS Handa Perth International golf tournament within the context of the GoVolES framework. By gaining a perspective of those who make the decision engage with the tournament as a golf volunteer, the range of pull factors can be determined and used to validate the proposed framework. The subsequent volunteering behaviour is pertinent given Pauline's (2011) finding that a satisfied volunteer would have a high propensity to continue volunteering for an event and that a higher frequency of volunteering at the event engenders a correspondingly high level of satisfaction.

This research is timely given the indications of declining rates of volunteering (Stott, 2014; *The Community Life Survey*, 2015; Lever, 2014;

Volunteering Australia, 2015). This ongoing study is designed to examine the relative strength of the changing forces impinging on volunteerism behaviours within the golf event milieu in Perth. An understanding of what motivates volunteers to become involved and what they gain from their experience is critical (Getz, 1991) to boost volunteerism uptake, the precipitant of international golf volunteer engagement as per the proposed iGoVolES framework later in this chapter (p. 115).

The qualitative questioning approach was underpinned by the classification model of the 'Four W's of Volunteering' (Figure 5.3), which highlights the definition, context, volunteer characteristics and motivation of volunteers (Bussell and Forbes, 2002). However, for the material study as the context was already known, the questions only pertained to the *Who*, *What* and *Why* dimensions (Table 5.2). The target respondents were volunteers who were on duty at the tournament in any capacity. The participants were recruited by the tournament volunteer co-ordinator, a volunteer himself, from his database of active volunteers via an email invitation. In that email, respondents were provided a hyperlink to the Qualtrics hosted online survey. Forty ($n = 40$) responses were received, all useable.

Results and discussion

Who

The survey respondents were predominantly male (72.5 per cent). This reflected a higher male to female volunteer ratio of male to female volunteers at the event. It might, however, simply be a reflection of a higher participation rate by men in the material survey. This finding nevertheless concurs with an apparent increasing rate of male volunteer participation over their female counterparts (Cahalane, 2014) and a general trend of

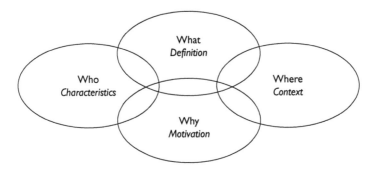

Figure 5.3 Understanding the volunteer market: the what, where, who and why of volunteering.

Source: Bussell and Forbes, 2002, p. 245.

Table 5.2 Survey questions

Who	What	Why
Age/Gender	What does the word 'volunteer' mean to you?	What are some of the benefits from volunteering for you as an individual?
Employment status	Do you recall what specifically made you first become a volunteer?	What do you think volunteers gain from their volunteering experience(s)?
Ethnicity	What environmental influence(s) might have induced your volunteering behaviour?	What were your reasons for volunteering for this event?
Place of residency	How do you think volunteers are enticed into volunteering?	What were you most looking forward to prior to the event?
Have you volunteered for this event previously?	How did you get to know about volunteering for this event in questions?	What are some of the challenges/compromises to volunteering for the recent event?
Have you volunteered for any other event of a similar nature?	How do you think your participation in the event has contributed to its success?	How can the volunteer process for this event be improved?
In what ways do you actively engage in volunteerism?	What do you think are disincentives to engaging in volunteering?	How does previous experiences (positive; negative; indifferent) influence your volunteering behaviours?

men outnumbering women in sport event volunteering (Skirstad and Hanstad, 2013). Respondent data are show in Table 5.3.

The age bracket with the most representation was the 55–64 year olds. This bracket contained the second highest proportion of female respondents (40 per cent) after the 45–54 bracket (41.7 per cent), which contained the second highest number of respondents. Whilst the largest group would appear to be primarily be made up of individuals approaching retirement (the retirement age in Australia is currently 65) and the second largest group are those in the preceding age bracket (45–54), the results would suggest that optimal time for golf volunteerism engagement is not during retirement. This despite Wilson et al. (2005, p. 38) finding that the ageing population contributed to boosting volunteer numbers in the not-for-profit sector because 'there were more retirees with time on their hands to do voluntary work'. As such, the material finding is also contrary to Won and Hwang's (2008) observation of the higher

Table 5.3 Respondent demographic data

Age bracket	Male	Female	Sub-total	Employment status	
≤18	1	1	2	Student	1
				Other	1
25–34	3	0	3	Full-time	3
35–44	7	0	7	Full-time	4
				Self-employed	2
				Other	1
45–54	7	5	12	Retired	4
				Part-time/Casual	4
				Self-employed	2
				Other	2
55–64	9	6	15	Retired	14
				Part-time/Casual	1
65–74	1	0	1	Retired	1
	28	11	40	Full-time	7
				Part-time/Casual	5
				Self-employed	4
				Student	1
				Retired	19
				Other	4

propensity for older golfers to engage in their sport compared to younger golfers as there was only one respondent who was older than 75 years of age and he appeared to be a casual golfer. The marked reduction of participation in the 75+ year age group could be attributed to the physical demands of golf volunteer work, especially given the hilly terrain of LJCC, and individuals who had 'become too old to do voluntary work' (Wilson *et al.*, 2005, p. 38).

However, when the age bracket and employment were cross tabulated, it became evident that the age bracket (45–54) constituted of four retirees, two employed on a part-time or casual basis, two under self-employment, and two others, while the pre-retirement age group (55–64) were, all bar one, already retired. The demographics of the material study, therefore, appear to concur with the literature regarding the higher propensity for retirees to engage in voluntary work in general, and golf volunteering in particular. The respondents in the 25–34 and 34–44 age brackets were mostly working full-time (70 per cent). This would suggest:

1   a strong motivation to engage in golf volunteerism despite still being in employment; and
2   a high identity salience to golfing as a sport or leisure activity.

There, however, were no female respondents in those age brackets as indicated by the literature. The underlying cause of this phenomenon should be investigated.

The findings of this study reveals flaws in the notion of a retirement age given that many respondents had already gone into retirement ahead of the prescribed age. It does indicate, however, that formal volunteering activity does increase after retirement (Zedlewski, 2007) and possibly supports the conventional wisdom held 'that most retirees want to settle in a nice retirement community, play golf, do some volunteer work, and putter [sic] around the garden' (Marston, 2010, p. 13). What, however, was revealed was that many respondents in the 55–64 age bracket (five out of nine male, five out of six female) were actively engaged in non-remunerating voluntary activities, both secular and non-secular, thereby partaking in 'productive aging' (Brown et al., 2011). While the material study did not support Goldblatt and Matheson's (2009) observation that volunteering behaviour is strong in both the young and older segments of society, the Perth event organizer should proactively engage both those segments, perhaps by heeding Sarfati's (cited in Goldblatt and Matheson, 2009, p. 145) suggestion to 'find alternative opportunities for volunteers to be engaged, other than the in-person experience'. Such a strategy could harness golf volunteers who may avoid golf volunteering due to its physical demands. As alluded to previously, the lower female participation is especially evident in the 25–34 and 35–44 age brackets. This phenomenon needs to be further investigated, particularly in comparison to participation in Ladies PGA (LPGA) events. A dominant golf volunteer gender group may not serve well as an event 'pull factor' irrespective if it is a PGA or LPGA event.

With regards to employment status, after the retirees, the second largest category of volunteers was those employed on a full-time basis. This again would seem at odds with the expectation that part-time or casual workers would have more discretionary time to dedicate to volunteerism, particularly to golf, which is highly time-consuming. Only one respondent identified himself as a student who had taken up the opportunity provided to him by his university lecturer. In terms of ethnicity, all volunteers apart from one 'Asian', a 'Mexican', an 'Italian' and an 'Australian' identified themselves as Caucasian. The data appears to echo the findings of Thoits and Hewitt (2001) that Caucasians have a higher rate of volunteering when compared to other ethnic groups. However, this participation rate is derived from a North American context, but possibly representative of a developed country, such as Australia.

All the participants involved in the study at the time the survey was conducted resided in Australia, within the geographical boundaries of Perth. This suggests that local community events are highly dependent upon the local residents as volunteers and could potentially result in 'volunteerism fatigue', because of the over-reliance for locally based events. The absence of foreign tourists represented in the sample might indicate low participation as compared to other international events such as the Abu Dhabi HSBC Golf Championships (Pinto, 2014), and the widespread volunteer tourism industry phenomenon (Holmes and Smith, 2012). With regards to lifestyle categorization, a large number of volunteers were married or partnered with children $(n = 8)$, which suggests that domestic obligations might not discourage active engagement in volunteering activities. There, however, was a preponderance of volunteers who had a spouse or partner who did not have any children or were empty nesters $(n = 24)$. Also, the assumption could be made that married people have a higher propensity to engage in volunteering when compared to unmarried/single people.

What and why

For a large majority of volunteers in this study, volunteerism was vibrant and highly relevant. Some, however, had reservations of varying degrees on the sustainability of volunteerism. 'Time' was referred to by many respondents, alluding to its significance in the context of volunteerism. For many of the volunteers involved in both events, volunteering was concerned with the giving up of their own time for the benefit of others. Typical comments included 'to volunteer is to give up your own time in order to help others who need it', 'giving your time for an event/cause you care about', and 'some one [sic] who gives of their time to help others and gets enjoyment from it'. For some, the contribution to the community was key, evidenced by the fact that many referred to volunteering as 'unpaid labour' and direct mention to the community was made in four separate instances.

The concept of volunteering still remains strong among the research participants, but for many different reasons. For the young, it seems that the key motive to volunteering is concerned with advancing their career, and for others it satisfies a need to feel worthy and acknowledged. The passion for volunteering was still evident judging by the many positive responses given concerning the meaningfulness and worth in the act of volunteering. Also, the responses indicated some linkage of volunteerism to the concept of community and for the love of the activity involved in the event, a phenomenon well documented in the literature. Experiential and personal reasons were strong, specifically with regards to enjoyment, and reference was made to the development and enhancement of a community, through the act of volunteering. To reiterate, for many their involvement was justified by the love for the primary activity (i.e. golf). Table 5.4 shows the distribution of those respondents that explicitly expressed a love for the game. This element is not only the 'push factor' in PPFM, but also the essence of Volunteer Attendance (i.e. Event Operations, Camaraderie,

Table 5.4 Respondents who love the game of golf

Age bracket	Male	Female	Sub-total
≤18	0	0	0
25–34	1	0	1
35–44	2	0	2
45–54	2	2	4
55–64	3	3	6
65–74	0	0	0
	8	5	13

Event Loyalty, and WIIFM Elements) in the GoVolES framework. This therefore has to be further investigated in order to optimise a major driver of the cycle.

The environmental influence which appeared to impart the greatest influence on the volunteering behaviour of this sample is the local golfing community. The responses suggest that the golfing community at the golf club level is highly active and effective in mobilizing volunteers for golfing events. The data suggests that the family can have a large impact on whether someone is predisposed to volunteerism. Four respondents indicated that their parents were a major influence, with many others citing friends.

In the survey volunteers were asked to reflect on their motives in volunteering. While many simply enjoyed being part of an event, a respondent, a student, sought a more prosaic outcome: gaining invaluable experience to cement and relate what he did in his studies to the reality of working in events. Personal enjoyment meant having fun and feeling happy, which resulted in a satisfying experience for many participants. They hoped their involvement in the event would stimulate community pride and wellbeing, which would make a positive contribution to the community. Also, many identified with feeling useful and others identified developing new skills and knowledge to help them in other areas of their lives.

Volunteer motives, which often determined their decision to volunteer, were focused around new friendships and the chance to meet like-minded people. Also, volunteering provided a social outlet and the opportunity to engage with other people. Some of the key benefits of involvement in an event mentioned by participants included some of the perks associated with being a volunteer such as personal contact with the golf personalities. They were able to view their heroes close up (especially those who highlighted their key motive for involvement was the love of the game) and feel part of the event, rather than merely a spectator role. They were physically involved in the event and had an identified role to play in the event, which made them feel valued and important. They took their role seriously and realized that they were integral to the success of the event and took pride in helping the event achieve a positive outcome, which resulted in feelings of self-worth, satisfaction and a sense of achievement. The findings appear to confirm that male volunteers might be more interested in instrumental reasons for volunteering, such as receiving tangible benefits and external rewards (Bang *et al.*, 2009). A key challenge to recruit volunteers for events was connected to time constraint. In addition, the bureaucracy and form-filling involved in registering to become a volunteer were frustrating for many. One respondent strongly asserted that demand-side issues pose the greatest threat to volunteerism: 'Volunteerism will die if it entails, on the part of the volunteer, a mindless morass of checklists, political correctness, safety protocols and other "arse covering" bureaucratic safeguards by those who seek the help of volunteers.' This candid view is supported by another respondent who noted that there is a level of paranoia in the community about liability borne by volunteers that needs to be redressed to mitigate apathy and passive spectatorism. Nine respondents indicated not enjoying the early start, which meant arriving at the event venue each day at 5.30 a.m. This caused problems with transport and dealing with family and other work commitments such as paid work. Even though a significant number of volunteers were retirees, they still had other regular social arrangements they had to change or rearrange which caused them problems.

Concluding remarks

The findings cannot be generalized to all event volunteers because the study was specifically on golf volunteers. The researchers did not explicitly inquire about the propensity of the respondents to engage in international golf volunteerism and, therefore, the assumption is made that there was minimal, if at all any, desire to do so. However, given that at least two respondents had travelled considerable distances from country WA to participate in the Perth International, perhaps the distance travelled should be used as a yardstick: a country WA golf volunteer could exert the same, or even more, effort to travel to Perth compared to a European golf volunteer crossing a continental border to volunteer at a golf tournament in a neighbouring EU country. The material study served to validate for the PPFM which underpinned the GoVolES framework. Apart from a family that was already in Australia on holiday that coincidentally was able to get involved with the Perth International as volunteers, there were no international golf volunteers per se over the entire duration the event was held. The authors suggest that Perth, as a golfing destination, has to strengthen its pull factors in order to create the impetus necessary to attract international golf volunteers. The international golf event stakeholders appear to have embarked on initiatives to enhance and augment Perth's Golf Event Pull Factor.

We propose the adoption of the derivative International Golf Volunteer Engagement Strategy (iGoVolES) framework (Figure 5.4) as a strategy to synthesize international volunteerism as an Event Pull Factor as evidenced by the tremendous 'pull' being exerted by the PGA of America events.

A concerted effort by the event destination informed by GoVolES to strengthen its Event Pull Factor could synthesize a new element in the form of international volunteers. An enhanced Pull Factor, on the premise that robust local volunteer representation is an antecedent of international golf volunteerism, will transform the GoVolES into the iGoVolES, whereby the mere presence of enthusiastic international volunteers morphs into an event pull factor in its own right.

The iGoVolES provides a framework to quantify the Event Pull Factor of international golf tournaments. Further investigation using both quantitative and qualitative research on the opportunity cost, personal values and HR implications vis-à-vis international volunteers on golf tournaments. With golf's reinstatement as an Olympic sport, it will have a tremendous worldwide impact particularly in countries in the developmental stages of growing the game. As part of 'the Olympic dream' (Heitner, 2015), the golf event will draw from the mature mega-event volunteerism movement. Whilst this is beneficial in accelerating the growth of the game internationally, professional golfing tournaments would naturally benefit from an influx of golf tournament attendees (refer back to Figure 5.1). Translating the 'push factor' to the iGoVolES is, however, a task for PGA

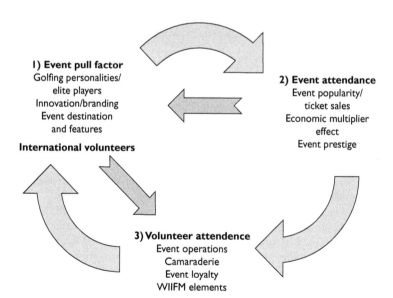

Figure 5.4 International Golf Volunteer Engagement Strategy (iGoVolES) framework.

tournament directors as, rather ironically, the summer Olympic Games presents itself now as a competitor as it vies for international golf volunteers.

Notes

1 Purportedly the 'richest prize money in Australia' in 2014 by offering an A\$1.75 million purse (Perth International, 2013; Silsbury, 2014).
2 Readman (2012, p. 166) defines golf tourism as 'travel for noncommercial reasons to participate in golf activities away from the traveler's local environment'.
3 The minimum age requirement of the European Tour is 14 years (European Tours, n.d.) and 18 years for the Asia Tour (CIMB Classic, n.d.). No volunteer age limit is mentioned on the 2017 Handa New Zealand Open website, thereby making volunteering accessible to a larger audience.
4 The Valhalla Golf Club hosted the PGA Championship in 1996, 2000 and 2014. It is one of golf's four major golf championships (the Masters played at Augusta National Golf Club, the US Open which is played at various locations in the United States, the Open Championship played at one of ten locations in the UK, and the PGA Championship which played at various locations in the United States).

References

Albanese, A. (2011). Putting world's most remote city on track for the future. www.theaustralian.com.au/business/putting-worlds-most-remote-city-on-track-for-the-future/story-e6frg8zx-1226030900688.

Alter, M. (2014). Some travel long distances to volunteer at PGA Championship. www.wlky.com/pga-championship/some-travel-long-distances-to-volunteer-at-pga-championship/27329626.

Bang, H. and Chelladurai, P. (2003). Motivation and satisfaction in volunteering for 2002 World Cup in Korea. In proceedings of the *Conference of the North American Society for Sport Management*. Ithaca, New York.

Bang, H. and Ross, S.D. (2009). Volunteer motivation and satisfaction. *Journal of Venue and Event Management* 1(1): 61–77.

Bang, H., Alexandris, K. and Ross, S.D. (2009). Validation of the revised volunteer motivation scale for international sporting events (VMS-ISE) at the Athens 2004 Olympic Games. *Event Management* 12(3–4): 119–131.

Barros, C.P., Butler, R. and Correia, A. (2010). The length of stay of golf tourism: A survival analysis. *Tourism Management* 31(1): 13–21.

Bense, K. (2016). The real reason more Americans don't get hooked on golf. www.golf.com/tour-and-news/report-more-people-are-trying-golf-its-not-sticking.

Brown, W.J., Chen, S.L., Mefford, L., Brown, A., Callen, B. and McArthur, P. (2010). Becoming an older volunteer: A grounded theory study. *Nursing Research and Practice*. DOI: 10.1155/2011/361250.

Bussell, H. and Forbes, D. (2002). Understanding the volunteer market: The what, where, who and why of volunteering. *International Journal of Nonprofit and Voluntary Sector Marketing* 7(3): 244–256.

Cahalane, C. (2014). Men overtake women as volunteer numbers return to highest in decade. *Guardian*. www.theguardian.com/voluntary-sector-network/2014/sep/05/men-overtake-women-volunteer-numbers-highest-decade.

Chammas, M. (2016). Sydney international in danger of losing its significance as crowds plummet and stars go missing. *The Sydney Morning Herald*, 12 January.

Chanavat, N. and Ferrand, A. (2010). Volunteer programme in mega sport events: The case of the Olympic Winter Games, Torino 2006. *International Journal of Sport Management and Marketing* 7(3–4): 241–266.

CIMB Classic. (n.d.). Overview. www.cimbclassic.com/Volunteers/Overview.

Cnaan, R.A., Handy, F. and Wadsworth, M. (1996). Defining who is the volunteer: Conceptual and empirical considerations. *Nonprofit and Voluntary Sector Quarterly* 25(3): 364–383.

The Community Life Survey, England 2014 to 2015. (2015). Cabinet Office. https://socialwelfare.bl.uk/subject-areas/services-activity/community-development/cabinetoffice/175974Community_Life_Survey_2014-15_Bulletin.pdf.

Costa, B. (2016). Americans want to play golf – until they try it. *The Wall Street Journal*. www.wsj.com/articles/americans-want-to-play-golfuntil-they-try-it-1457379085.

Costa, C.A., Chalip, L., Green, B.C. and Simes, C. (2006). Reconsidering the role of training in event volunteers' satisfaction. *Sport Management Review* 9(2): 165–182.

Coyne, B.S. and Coyne, E.J.S. (2001). Getting, keeping and caring for unpaid volunteers for professional golf tournament events. *Human Resource Development International* 4(2): 199–214.

Cuskelly, G., Auld, C. Harrington, M. and Coleman, D. (2004). Predicting the behavioural dependability of sport event volunteers. *Event Management* 9(1–2): 73–89.

Dann, G.M.S. (1977). Anomie, ego-enhancement and tourism. *Annals of Tourism Research* 4(4): 184–194.

Dann, G.M.S. (1981). Tourist motivation: An appraisal. *Annals of Tourism Research* 8(2): 187–219.

Dickson, T.J., Benson, A.M. and Terwiel, A. (2014). Mega-event volunteers, similar or different? Vancouver 2010 vs London 2012. *International Journal of Event and Festival Management* 5(2): 164–179.

Duran, E. and Hamarat, B. (2014). Festival attendees' motivations: The case of International Troia Festival. *International Journal of Event and Festival Management* 5(2): 146–163.

Economist. (2015). Why golf is in decline in America. April. www.economist.com/blogs/economist-explains/2015/04/economist-explains-1.

European Tours (n.d.). Volunteer roles. www.europeantour.com.

Fairley, S., Kellett, P. and Green, B.C. (2007). Volunteering abroad: Motives for travel to volunteer at the Athens Olympic Games. *Journal of Sport Management* 21(1): 41–57.

The future of golf: Handicapped. (2014). www.economist.com/news/christmas-specials/21636688-though-thriving-parts-asia-golf-struggling-america-and-much-europe.

Getz, D. (1991). *Festivals, special events and tourism*. New York: Van Nostrand Reinhold.

Getz, D. (2002). Why festivals fail. *Event Management* 7(4): 209–219.

Giannoulakis, C., Wang, C.H. and Gray, D. (2007). Measuring volunteer motivation in mega-sporting events. *Event Management* 11(4): 191–200.

Goldblatt, J. and Matheson, C.M. (2009). Volunteer recruitment and retention: An Australia–USA comparison. In T. Baum, M. Deery, C. Hanlon, L. Lockstone and K. Smith (eds) *People and work in events and conventions: A research perspective*. Wallingford: CABI (pp. 138–153).

Grimm, K.E. and Needham, M.D. (2012a). Internet promotional material and conservation volunteer tourist motivations: A case study of selecting organizations and projects. *Tourism Management Perspectives* 1: 17–27.

Grimm, K.E. and Needham, M.D. (2012b). Moving beyond the 'I' in motivation: Attributes and perceptions of conservation volunteer. *Tourist Journal of Travel Research* 51(4): 488–501.

Groves, R. (2015). Golf growth in China makes sense: dollars and cents. www. forbes.com/sites/rogergroves/2015/06/15/golf-growth-in-china-makes-sense-dollars-and-cents/#66ca6cb5328f.

Heitner, D. (2015). Golf's global impact: Teeing up the Solheim Cup and Presidents Cup. www.forbes.com/sites/darrenheitner/2015/09/14/golfs-global-impact-teeing-up-the-solheim-cup-and-presidents-cup/#66ed5d7f1b7b.

Holmes, K. and Smith, K. (2012). *Managing volunteers in tourism*. Oxford: Butterworth-Heinemann.

Hoye, R. and Cuskelly, G. (2009). Psychology of sports event volunteerism. In T. Baum, M. Deery, C. Hanlon, L. Lockstone and K. Smith (eds) *People and work in events and conventions: A research perspective*. Wallingford: CABI (pp. 171–180).

Hudson, S. and Hudson, L. (2010). *Golf tourism*. Oxford: Goodfellow Publishing.

Hutchinson, J., Lai, F. and Wang, Y. (2009). Understanding the relationship of quality, value, equity, satisfaction, and behavioral intentions among golf travellers. *Tourism Management* 30(2): 298–308.

Jenner, J.R. (1982). Participation, leadership, and the role of volunteerism among selected women volunteers. *Journal of Voluntary Action Research* 11(4): 27–38.

Keipert, S. (2016). World Super 6 golf heading to Perth. www.golfaustralia.com.au/news-world-super-6-golf-heading-to-perth-437264.

Kim, M., Kim, M.K. and Odio, M.A. (2010). Are you proud? The influence of sport and community identity and job satisfaction on pride of mega-event volunteers. *Event Management* 14(2): 127–136.

Kim, S.S., Kim, J.H. and Ritchie, B.W. (2008). Segmenting overseas golf tourists by the concept of specialization. *Journal of Travel & Tourism Marketing* 25(2): 199–217.

Krohn, B.D. and Backman, S.J. (2011). Event attributes and the structure of satisfaction: A case study of golf spectators. *Event Management* 15(3): 267–277.

Lamb, D. and Ogle, A. (2016). Motivation and engagement in local community events. In A. Jepson and A. Clarke (eds) *Managing and developing community festivals and events*. London: Palgrave Macmillan (pp. 50–68).

Lever, J. (2014), Survey: Americans' interest in volunteering and charity is precipitously declining. *Forbes* (online), 21 September. www.forbes.com/sites/realspin/2014/09/21/survey-americans-interest-in-volunteering-and-charity-is-precipitously-declining/#19aef77f4f88.

Lo, S.A. and Lee, C.Y.S. (2011). Motivations and perceived value of volunteer tourists in Hong Kong. *Tourism Management* 32(2): 326–334.

Lockstone-Binney, L., Holmes, K., Baum, T. and Smith, K.A. (2014). Event Volunteering Evaluation (EVE) project. In K.A. Smith, L. Lockstone-Binney, K. Holmes and T. Baum (eds) *Event volunteering: International perspectives on the event volunteering experience*. New York: Routledge (pp. 167–180).

Love, A., Hardin, R., Koo, W. and Morse, A.L. (2011), Effects of motives on satisfaction and behavioral intentions of volunteers at a PGA tour event. *International Journal of Sport Management* 12(1): 86–101.

Lyu, S.O. and Lee, H. (2013). Market segmentation of golf event spectators using leisure benefits. *Journal of Travel & Tourism Marketing* 30(3): 186–200.

MacLean, J. and Hamm, S. (2007). Motivation, commitment, and intentions of volunteers at a large Canadian sporting event. *Leisure/Loisir: Journal of the Canadian Association for Leisure Studies* 31(2): 523–556.

Marston, C. (2010). *Motivating the 'what's in it for me' workforce: Manage across the generational divide and increase profits*. Hoboken: John Wiley & Sons.

Moital, I., Jackson, C. and Le Couillard, J. (2013). Using scenarios to investigate stakeholders' views on the future of a sporting event. *Event Management* 17(4): 439–452.

Monga, M. (2006). Measuring motivation to volunteer for special events. *Event Management* 10(1): 47–61.

Moon, K.S., Kim, M., Ko, Y.J., Connaughton, D.P. and Lee, J.H. (2011). The influence of consumer's event quality perception on destination image. *Managing Service Quality: An International Journal* 21(3): 287–303.

Nichols, G. and Ralston, R. (2012). The rewards of individual engagement in volunteering: A missing dimension of the Big Society. *Environment and Planning-Part A* 44(12): 2974–2987.

Pauline, G. (2011). Volunteer satisfaction and intent to remain: An analysis of contributing factors among professional golf event volunteers. *International Journal of Event Management Research* 16(1): 10–32.

Perth International (2013). ISPS HANDA Perth International 2013. http://perth international.com/Portals/21/ISPA%20HANDA%20Perth%20International%20 Facts%20and%20figures.pdf.

PGA (2016). Limited volunteer opportunities remain for 2016 PGA Championship. www.pga.com/pgachampionship/news/limited-volunteer-opportunities-remain-2016-pga-championship.

PGA Australia. (2016). Volunteer. http://championship.pga.org.au/tournament/ info/volunteer.

Pinto, D. (2014). Abu Dhabi HSC Golf Championship starts off with golf's elites. *Sport 360°*, 20 December. http://sport360.com.

Prestipino, D. (2016). Revolutionary new golf event headed west to replace Perth International. www.smh.com.au/sport/golf/revolutionary-new-golf-event-headed-west-to-replace-perth-international-20160914-grg22m.html.

Priest, E. (2015). Golf digest: Volunteers are the real heroes of golf tournaments. www.news.com.au/sport/golf-digest-volunteers-are-the-real-heroes-of-golf-tournaments/news-story/8957d4e3eae9315164dafdbf390316d3.

Read, B. (2013). Australian golf to campaign for the US PGA to be played here. www.theaustralian.com.au/sport/golf/australian-golf-to-campaign-for-the-us-pga-to-be-played-here/news-story/fa4c0809e05078de11e7ed1e7d1ba2fc.

Readman, M. (2012). Golf tourism. In S. Hudson (ed.) *Sport and adventure tourism*. Binghamton: The Haworth Hospitality Press (pp. 165–201).

Robinson, M.J., Trail, G.T. and Kwon, H. (2004). Motives and points of attachment of professional golf spectators. *Sport Management Review* 7(2): 167–192.

Silsbury, K. (2014). 2014 Perth International to welcome defending champion Jin Jeong back to course. www.abc.net.au/news/2014-10-20/jin-aims-to-claim-back-to-back-perth-invitational-victories/5828434.

Skirstad, B. and Hanstad, D.V. (2013). Gender matters in sport event volunteering. Managing Leisure 18(4): 316–330.

Smith, K., Holmes, K., Store, C., Lockstone-Binney, L. and Baum, T.C. (2003). Models of sport event management and volunteer motivation. Tourism and global change: On the edge of something big. CAUTHE 2003 conference proceedings.

Stebbins, R.A. (2009). Would you volunteer? *Society* 46(2): 155–159.

Stott, R. (2014). Survey: Volunteering numbers are on the decline. *Associations Now*. http://associationsnow.com/2014/03/survey-volunteering-numbers-decline.

Strigas, A.D. and Jackson, E.N. (2003a). Motivating volunteers to serve and succeed: Design and results of a pilot study that explores demographics and motivational factors in sports volunteerism. *International Sports Journal* 7(1): 111–123.

Strigas, A.D. and Jackson, E.N. (2003b). The importance of motivational factors and demographic attitudes at the design, marketing, and implementation of successful volunteer recruitment programs: What sport and recreational professionals should investigate first. *Research Quarterly for Exercise and Sport* 74(1): A-24.

Thoits, P.A. and Hewitt, L.N. (2001). Volunteer work and well-being. *Journal of Health and Social Behavior* 42(2): 115–131.

Tolman, E.C. (1937). The acquisition of string-pulling by rats: Conditioned response or sign-gestalt? *Psychological Review* 44(3): 195–211.

Uysal, M. and Jurowski, C. (1994). Testing the push and pull factors. *Annals of Tourism Research* 21(4): 844–846.

Vitello, P. (2008). More Americans are giving up golf. *New York Times*.

Volunteering Australia. (2015). Are time poor Australians abandoning volunteering? www.volunteeringaustralia.org/2015/07/are-time-poor-australians-abandoning-volunteering/.

Wakefield, K.L. and Sloan, H.J. (1995). The effects of team loyalty and selected stadium factors on spectator attendance. *Journal of Sport Management* 9(2): 153–172.

Watanabe, Y., Matsumoto, K. and Nogawa, H. (2013). Variables influencing spectators' desire to stay at a professional golf tournament in Japan. *Contemporary Management Research* 9(3): 283–298.

Won, D. and Hwang, S. (2008). The course to tee off: Golfers' participation constraints, age, income, and leisure identity salience. *The ICHPER-SD Journal of Research* 3(2): 55–61.

Wilson, L., Spoehr, J. and McLean, R. (2005). Volunteering in not-for-profit organisations and the accumulation of social capital in South Australia. *Australian Journal on Volunteering* 1(10): 32–41.

Zedlewski, S.R. (2007). Will retiring Boomers form a new army of volunteers? *Perspectives on Productive Aging* 7. Washington, DC: Urban Institute.

Zimbalist, A. (2010). Is it worth it? Hosting the Olympic Games and other mega sporting events is an honor many countries aspire to – but why? *Finance & Development*, March: 8–11.

Chapter 6

Indirect volunteers and application of the volunteer cube

A framework for international sport volunteering?

Berit Skirstad and Elsa Kristiansen

Introduction

This chapter is not about international sport volunteers, per se, but there are a number of aspects linked to points and data from this chapter that will be useful in future international sport volunteering research using the conceptual framework outlined along with the volunteer cube framework. While defining volunteering, at one level appears to be easy, it is relatively complex to embrace all the different 'types' or segments of volunteers that exist and their lack of definition. Volunteers have generally been treated as a homogeneous group by researchers even if they are not. Further, volunteer traditions is also coloured by the context in which it occurs. Arguably, this work with local volunteers offers a new dynamic for conducting research in comparative international sporting events.

In Norway voluntary work, called *dugnad*, has a long tradition at the grassroot level (Lorentzen and Dugstad, 2011). *Dugnad* is an Old Norse word that means *help*, specifically from people working without payment (Bokmålsordboka, 2014). This tradition has existed since the twelfth century and from the sixteenth century; farmers did *dugnad* during harvest time (Lorentzen and Dugstad, 2011). Whilst it was seen as helping out a neighbour for a free meal, as industrial society emerged Norwegians started to understand *dugnad* as a collective effort for numerous causes. Voluntary work has always been embedded in social communities in Norway, and today it is seen as being one way to work together for a common goal such as raising funds for a club or hosting an event. As such, it is common for members of a sport club to raise money for their club by doing voluntary work at a sport event. This phenomenon, referred to in this chapter as *indirect volunteering*, benefits the club directly financially – and the community indirectly. Even though indirect voluntarism is vital for many sport clubs and events, indirect voluntarism has been and is still a neglected area of research. As such, we wish to fill this gap and see beyond the more investigated micro-level (the individual) by adding the meso-level (the sport club) and macro-level (the community or society).

However, for international comparative research, it is important to use the same definitions in the countries involved (Oppenheimer and Warburton, 2000 in Cuskelly *et al.*, 2006). In Norway *indirect* volunteering has been discussed for more than ten years, although it does not appear to have been picked up as a term internationally. By using the volunteer cube model by Skirstad (2012a) as the analytical framework, this chapter aims to demonstrate the role and importance of indirect volunteers by showing how indirect volunteers are valuable for sport clubs as well as sport events and the community where the event is organized. In order to do this we use the ski flying[1] 2012 World Championship and the 2013 World Cup in Vikersund, Norway as case studies.

Following the introduction, the next section outlines literature related to volunteers and volunteering and more specifically defines indirect volunteers. Next, we offer the volunteer cube as the theoretical framework for understanding volunteers and the context of the case study before outlining the data collection methods. The results are presented in accordance with the theoretical template. In the concluding section, we discuss how useful the volunteer cube is helpful for understanding all aspects of being an event volunteer and the extent to which it could be used for international sport volunteering.

The concept of volunteers and volunteering

We have several types of volunteers:

1 short- or long-term volunteers who contribute to the organization and events without receiving payment, financial or otherwise, for their services (Parent and Smith-Swan, 2013);
2 sponsor-paid volunteers or secondee: short- or long-term workforce members made available for all or part of an event but who retain their usual employment status and their employer remains responsible for their salaries, social security contributions, and insurance and for promotion (Cunningham *et al.*, 2016; Parent and Smith-Swan, 2013); and
3 indirect volunteers, these are volunteers, but the event organizer pays the sport club or other organization for the work their members do (Ferrand and Skirstad, 2015; Kristiansen *et al.*, 2014).

Many of the international volunteers at events are short-term volunteers because the event lasts only one or two days. Usually these events are organized during the weekend, so it is easier for people to be able to volunteer. It is a way of outsourcing the job on a contract with the organization, but the people who do the jobs are doing it on a voluntary basis for their organization. Consequently, this chapter will focus on indirect volunteers. This is not the only way of categorizing volunteers; Pearce (1993) introduced the term 'core' volunteer to describe the involvement and commitment levels of volunteers in non-profit organizations. Cuskelly *et al.* (2006) applied this conceptualization to sport volunteers and contended that core volunteers usually hold a formal office, often as board or committee member, are seen as leaders, and typically commit to high levels of involvement and commitment. Others again define core volunteers as 'formal' volunteers in contrast to 'informal' volunteers (Heinemann, 1999). Doherty (2009) used the distinction between 'planning' and 'on-site' volunteers at events. Ringuet-Riot *et al.* (2014) used the division between 'core' and 'peripheral' volunteers based on self-reported levels of involvement and commitment in sport organizations. Finally, Nichols (2005) wrote about very experienced volunteers who have a great deal of local knowledge, and whom he called 'stalwarts' because of their acquired experience, local knowledge and long-term commitment over decades.

In a pioneering article on volunteering, Wilson (2000, p. 233) concludes that 'one problem is that the generic term "volunteering" embraces a vast array of quite disparate activities'. Furthermore, Wilson (2000, p. 215) defines volunteering as 'any action in which time is given freely to benefit another person, group or organisation'. Later, Hustinx *et al.* (2010) identified three layers of complexity or challenges with the concept of volunteering. One of these problems was the one of definition, which we have discussed. The two other challenges were the problem of disciplinary heterogeneity or the different meanings and functions that are connected to the phenomenon and the lack of a good theory. Skirstad (2012a), building on the research by Hustinx *et al.* (2010), which gave the inspiration through their three layers of complexity for the development of the volunteer cube, is used here as a framework to better understand sport volunteering. The complexity of the concept may be due to the different motives that lead volunteers to volunteering. Recent literature (e.g. Kiviniemi *et al.*, 2002; Treuren, 2014) holds that the typical volunteer may volunteer for several reasons. Marta *et al.* (2006) found that Italian youth volunteers with multiple motivations are more likely to stay committed longer than those with only one reason for volunteering. This finding is in contrast to Kiviniemi *et al.*'s (2002) research, which found that a multiplicity of motivations gives rise to dissatisfaction and loss of commitment. One has to bear in mind that these investigations were both made on social volunteering, which may be different from event volunteering. At a sports mega-event, the main focus is to organize a successful event and to be part of it (Dickson *et al.*, 2014), and people from abroad will also want to get involved (see also Wise, Chapter 3, this volume). Treuren (2014), who looked at five different events of which two were car races, and the others not within sport, discovered that over 75 per cent of the volunteers at all these events reported at least two motivations.

In the last two decades, knowledge on volunteering has expanded, especially in the area of events, many of which would cease to exist if it were not for volunteers. Event volunteerism is a typical ad hoc form of participation, where the event is the central point. Terms like 'episodic' voluntarism, first used by MacDuff (1991), or 'revolving-door,' 'plug-in' and 'drop-by' (Dekker and Halman, 2003; Putnam, 1995), or reflexive voluntarism (Hustinx and Lammertyn, 2003) are in contrast to the traditional concept of voluntarism (a more collectivist type) and describe this activity. Event volunteers are usually involved with annual events, often over many years. A recent study on event and retention (Hyde *et al.*, 2016) categorized event volunteers according to their experience. 'Novice' included first timers, 'transition event volunteers' were persons with 2–4 years of experience and 'sustained event volunteers' had 5–6 years of consecutive experience with the event. Studies of event volunteering have been apt to focus particularly on volunteers' motivation and satisfaction (Allen and Shaw, 2009; Love *et al.*, 2011; Skille and Hanstad, 2013; Treuren, 2014; Wollebæk *et al.*, 2014), volunteer experiences (e.g. Kodama *et al.*, 2013; mega-events (e.g. Costa *et al.*, 2006; Dickson *et al.*, 2014; Tomazos and Luke, 2015), the economic value of volunteering (e.g. Davis, 2004; Solberg, 2003), the meaning of media representation (e.g. Bladen, 2010), and recruitment and retention of volunteers (e.g. Lee *et al.*, 2014; Neufeind *et al.*, 2013; Treuren, 2009, 2014). The majority of these studies have been done on a micro-level – that is at the individual level and not necessarily in an international context. The meso-level, the organizational level, for example the sport clubs, has been studied only by a few (e.g. Studer and von Schnurbein, 2013; Wicker and Hallmann, 2013) and the macro-level, the societal level with values, policies and social capital affecting volunteering, by even fewer (Kristiansen *et al.*, 2015).

The volunteer cube model as the theoretical framework

The three analytical approaches, which will be explained in detail directly below, are the basis for the volunteer cube framework (Skirstad, 2012a). As a prerequisite, the conceptual framework of volunteering (Hustinx *et al.*, 2010) is used in order to define which type of volunteering we investigate. The volunteer cube model (Figure 6.1) is used as a framework to characterize voluntarism as a phenomenon which develops over time and builds bridges for various levels of analyses. The framework includes 'a set of assumptions, concepts, values, and practices that constitutes a way of viewing reality' (American Heritage, 2011). The model is easy to remember and apply, and is useful as an organizing device in empirical research. The purpose of the model is to illustrate and explain the complexity of volunteering in sport events by using these approaches:

1   the life-cycle of the volunteers approach;
2   the individual, the organization and the society/community level approach; and
3   the volunteer stages and transitions model approach.

This gives three possible life-cycles of volunteers (antecedent, experience and consequences) multiplied with three levels of analyses (individual, organization and society) multiplied with five stages the volunteer goes through (nominee, newcomer, emotional, experienced and retiring), which then equals 45 different possibilities for a volunteer, and doubles if you consider gender.

I The 'life-cycle of volunteer's approach'

This approach includes the phases in the life course of volunteers, the stages that unfold over time, and the process of antecedents, experience and consequences (see bottom right of Figure 6.1 marked with 1). The antecedent stage regards individual, organizational and societal features that exist before a person becomes a volunteer. The experience stage looks at the contacts between the volunteer and her/his organization (i.e. satisfaction and integration with the activity and the organization) whereas the outcomes are the results of the interaction of the first two stages (i.e. the length of volunteering). According to Wilson (2012), this

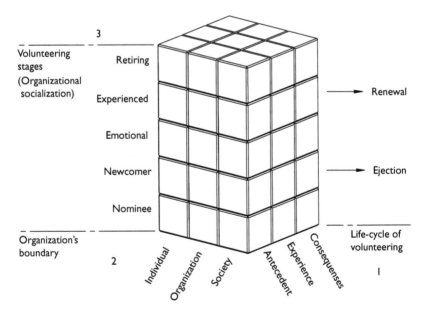

Figure 6.1 The volunteer cube.

stage is the least researched. The consequences stage focuses on change in attitudes, knowledge and behaviour among volunteers due to their volunteering.

2 The three levels of analysis (individual, organizational and community/society) approach

First, at the individual level, the approach concentrates on the individual. Second, the organizational level is included in the process model as many volunteer activities take place in co-operation with community-based organizations, Finally, at a broader community or societal level, the model considers the linkages between individuals and the social structures of their societies (see bottom left of Figure 6.1 marked with 2) (see also Omoto and Snyder, 2002).

3 The volunteer stages and transitions model (VSTM) approach

The transition model includes all stages volunteers go through in their involvement with the organization (nominee, newcomer, emotional involvement, established volunteering and retirement) and the processes from one stage to the other (Haski-Leventhal and Bargal, 2008) (see top left of Figure 6.1 marked with 3). This process model is not a theoretical model, but a logical way to order empirical data (Wilson, 2012). The VSTM model may represent a conceptual model from which the organizational socialization of other volunteers can be better understood. It binds together motivation, satisfaction, rewards and costs, which were previously studied separately. In this process, new members attain new attitudes, values, knowledge and learn certain behaviours in order to participate as organizational members. In short, organizational socialization is also the process of 'sense-making' in a new environment (Weick, 2001). Haski-Leventhal and Bargal (2008) added two more stages to their socialization so they ended up with five: the nomination phase (when one thinks about making contact with the club); the newcomer phase (when the person starts working and learning at the event); the emotional and experienced volunteer phase (from inexperienced to experienced volunteer); the established volunteer and consequences of volunteering; and lastly, the retirement phase. Volunteers should also be characterized according to the different stages they are in as a volunteer. Volunteers leave on their own account or are ejected due to three main obstacles:

1   not fitting in with the group;
2   unfavourable attitudes from their social environment; and/or
3   a lack of suitability between the individual and the organization.

Haski-Leventhal and Bargal (2008) discovered differences between new-comers, active volunteers and veteran volunteers. These transitions do not happen simply because time elapses, but there are processes that lead volunteers from one stage to another, dependent on the volunteer's experiences.

Volunteering is not a fixed concept; it changes during the period of volunteering. People may start to volunteer for certain reasons and continue for others. Some people prefer to volunteer locally at events in their community, while others look for opportunities abroad and seek international volunteering opportunities as a way of following the sport. The cost and benefits may change over time as well as volunteers' relationships with others and their perceptions and attitudes (Haski-Leventhal and Bargal, 2008). This is why volunteering should be viewed in the context of the stages volunteers are in. Volunteers usually start locally before looking for possibilities abroad. Some who are really 'bitten by the bug' continues to move around from one international mega-event to the next one, and that can be quite expensive. They have been called 'event gypsies' or 'Games gypsies'[2] by Parent and Smith-Swan (2013). 'Nomad' is another term which also refers to people move from one place to the other. Eventers or roving people could also be a collect term for this group of volunteers and employees who move around from one event to the next. Sport events are dependent on many of these experienced people who go from one international event to another and know what to do.

In order to show how the volunteer cube can be used as a framework, we will use data gathered from interviews with volunteers in Vikersund, Norway, and the analysis of local and national press coverage in the years leading up to the 2012 and 2013 ski flying events. These events are one-off events with a mix of young and old volunteers. The interviewees came from accreditation, hospitality, parking, security, distribution, medical aid, logistics, the organizing committee, volunteers' management, and food service. Before applying the model, some context about volunteering in Vikersund and the data collection is offered.

Volunteer context in the case study of Vikersund

One of the world's biggest ski flying hills is located in Norway in a small community named Vikersund with 3,000 inhabitants and situated a one-and-a-half-hour drive away from the capital Oslo. For those not so familiar with ski flying, ski flying hills are bigger than normal ski jumps. The world record set on this hill in 2015 is 254 metres. Over the years, Vikersund as a host community (where all local clubs together manage to pull it off) has organized four world championships (1977, 1990, 2000 and 2012) and nine world cup events (1980, 1983, 1986, 1995, 1998, 2007, 2009, 2011, 2013 and 2015). During major events, one-third of the inhabitants in Vikersund become volunteers (Kristiansen *et al.*, 2014). The hill is reflective of people's identity in Vikersund, and to create successful events reflects the quality of their community (Kristiansen *et al.*, 2014).

The ski jumping facility is owned by the Foundation Vikersund Jumping Centre, which again is owned by the municipality, the county and Vikersund sport club. The organization has only one full-time employed person – the event depends predominantly on volunteer labour. Where volunteering occurs is also important, as all volunteer activities are based on interpersonal relationships with other volunteers. The love for the sport is what volunteers have in common, and for specific events such as ski jumping, people will travel to international competitions. In Norway, some of the most eager members work on a weekly basis on the ski jump, regardless if they host an event that year or not. The volunteers' optimal reward is a membership in Club 246.[3] These members are genuinely interested in ski jumping, and they regularly travel to the four other venues in Europe (in Obersdorf, Germany; Kulm, Austria; Planica, Slovakia; and Harracov, Czech Republic) in order to study technical peculiarities in the different hills and gain expertise in an international setting.

Data collection in Vikersund

The methodology adopted for this chapter was qualitative and the research methods used was interviews and archival research. As such, data was collected from three different sources, two series of interviews and an archival research of newspapers, during the period January 2012 to January 2013, and covers volunteers in Vikersund at both the World Championship 2012 and the World Cup 2013. During the 2012 FIS World Championship we interviewed eight volunteers at different locations (e.g. the venue, café, restaurant), wherever was convenient for the interviewee. The same interview guide was also used when conducting 11 more interviews in 2013 (see Kristiansen *et al.*, 2014, for more information). In addition we collected interviews conducted by the local newspaper *Bygdeposten* during the 2012 FIS World Championship (a total of 24). These interviews were published daily in a section they labelled 'Voluntary Chat' (see Table 6.1), and these were used to supplement our interview data collection as the questioning by the journalist was very similar to that used with our volunteer respondents. By using the interviews from the local newspapers, we doubled the numbers of interviewees to look for stronger consistencies across the findings (Eisenhardt and Graebner, 2007). The data set was analysed using content analysis and pattern matching (cf. Miles and Huberman, 1994; Yin, 2003). The process was done manually by the research group, and key aspects were compared and contrasted using a table approach (e.g. Table 6.2; see Miles and Huberman, 1994). The emerging findings constitute our higher-order themes, that is, our results, which are presented below.

Overall, indirect voluntarism is for the volunteers one way of express-ing, celebrating and reinforcing their commitment to, and identification with, the local community. In total 48 interviews were analysed; 24 archi-val interviews and 24 face-to-face interviews (full details can be seen in Table 6.1).

Table 6.1 outlines details of interviews, which includes the indirect vol-unteers and the race director ($N=48$). In addition to newspaper interviews during the World Championship in 2012 (24 volunteers; ten women and 14 men), the authors conducted interviews with volunteers during the World Championship in 2012 (eight volunteers; five men and three women) and the World Cup 2013 (15 volunteers; 11 men and four women).

Findings: Vikersund volunteers and the volunteers cube

In this section, findings from Vikersund are presented and placed in the volunteer cube. The 48 interviews provide insights in the role and import-ance of indirect volunteers and the volunteering process. In the following, indirect volunteers (Ferrand and Skirstad, 2015) are grouped according to where they are in the volunteer process of life-cycle and the three levels of analysis (individual, organizational or community/society). The results will be displayed according to the different stages volunteers occupy in their socialization processes and the motives on the different levels, as indi-vidual, sport club and community.

The first phase of socialization process: the nomination phase

Table 6.2 highlights the motives for the *nomination phase*, which starts when the person makes the first contact with the organization, but before she or he starts volunteering. In Vikersund the persons were either motiv-ated to take part by the sport club, the schools, their parents or their friends. This phase was explained by a young man as 'I was a spectator last year, and then I decided to join the volunteers next year. I am coming from football, and I have just moved to Vikersund' (male volunteer, age 23). Another expressed that it was in an impulse – more like a sudden idea 'so I sent an email one night and 10 minutes later I had a job' (male volun-teer, age 43). Sometimes, becoming a volunteer simply means signing up at an Internet platform provided by the organizer.

At the sporting events most of the training happens on the job. Big events such as World Championships require the organizers to arrange training for the volunteers. Most participants volunteered to help their

Table 6.1 Indirect volunteer details

Year	Gender	Age	Position	Volunteer since ...
2012*	Female	17	Organize queuing	First time
2012*	Female	16	Tickets	First time
2012*	Male	15	Groomer	First time
2012*	Male	22	Parking	2011
2012*	Female	22	Guard	First time
2012*	Female	18	Kiosk	2011
2012*	Female	18	Service	2011
2012*	Female	22	Hostess	2009
2012*	Male	24	Venue service	2000
2012*	Female	22	Hostess/waiter	2010
2012*	Male	52	Icing of track	2011
2012*	Male	41	Guard	First time
2012*	Male	36	Driver	2000
2012*	Female	35	Kiosk	First time
2012*	Female	45	Secretariat	First time
2012*	Male	46	Groomer	1977
2012*	Male	48	Arena adds	1990
2012*	Male	47	Marketing	2011
2012*	Female	48	Ceremonies/pub	2005
2012*	Male	59	Guard	2007
2012*	Male	55	Security	First time
2012*	Male	62	Official	2011
2012*	Male	60	Lift	First time
2012*	Male	52	Groomer	2000
2012	Male	20	Groomer/media	2007
2012	Male	56	Guard	2009
2012	Male	46	Rigging/guard	2007
2012	Female	54	Accreditation	2011
2012	Male	43	Food service	First time
2012	Male	49	Ticketing	First time
2012	Female	35	Parking	2011
2012	Female	52	Security	Decades
2013	Male	58	Parking	1977
2013	Male	53	Parking/security	1981
2013	Male	23	Parking	First time
2013	Female	75	Food service	1979
2013	Female	55	Food service	1994
2013	Male	74	Security	1970
2013	Male	63	Security	1983
2013	Male	39	Medical aid	2007
2013	Male	17	Logistics/driver	2011
2013	Male	39	Logistics	2011
2013	Male	41	Org Committee	2011
2013	Male	29	Accreditation	2009
2013	Female	69	Accreditation	2011
2013	Female	44	Hospitality	2000
2013	Male	68	Head volunteer	1970
2013	Male		Race Director	

Notes
The interviewees marked as 2012* was interviewed by the local newspaper, one each day during the World Championship in 2012.

Table 6.2 Motives on individual, sport club and community level in the nomination phase

Individual	Sport club	Community
Access to the labour market	Spectator at an event – curious about taking part	Not so present at this stage
Get to know others	Member in a club	
Curriculum Vitae (CV)		

sport club with their expenses. Then it was close ties between formal membership and volunteering (Wollebæk *et al.*, 2014). On the question why they volunteer, this response from one of the volunteers seems quite typical: 'It's a little of everything: the biggest ski jumping hill, just in front of my living room. The sport club is the most important. But it is much intertwined' (male volunteer, age 53).

The second phase: the newcomer phase

The *newcomer* phase is the next stage, where the person is in the early stages of volunteering (see Table 6.3). This phase is characterized by learning. The interviewed volunteers all expressed that it is important to get the necessary information in order to accomplish their tasks satisfactorily. One male felt that he could have received more training as 'the first days were turbulent with a crowd and I did not handle my computer task quickly enough to avoid a crowd' (male volunteer, age 54). On the other hand, a few of the volunteers expressed that they become almost overwhelmed with new experiences, as a newcomer at the World Championship uttered: 'I think it is exiting to learn something new … and the hill is very important for us, but it is almost too much to learn as a first timer!' (male volunteer, age 23).

Table 6.3 Motives on individual, sport club and community level in the newcomer phase

Individual	Sport club	Community
Learn new skills	Money for the club	The ski jump is important
CV		
Future employment		
External factors (family, friends)		
Outfit not important		

Others had more collective reasons (Hustinx and Lammertyn, 2003) to volunteer:

> I like to work with goods, because then I can drive the four wheel thing, it is a 16 year age limit. It is fun when something happens in the community, and it is that big, we like to have it well done.
>
> (Male volunteer, age 17 year)

For him being a volunteer meant having an opportunity to drive! However, he further revealed a traditional approach (Hustinx and Lammertyn, 2004) to voluntarism, whereas both influences from family and the identity with the local community were used when he explained to us why he volunteered:

> My stepfather is my boss here. It is good environment. There are many young people who are groomers, they are alpine skiers and also some who sell goods in the kiosks. We use to be together when we are off duty as well, and then we are in the facility. When I was young I used to come with the school. This creates identity feeling.
>
> (Male volunteer, age 17)

He continued: 'Last year when I was ploughing snow, I met someone who I have worked for afterwards. I have met lots of useful contacts in the network, all from the community'. 'This is much better than being at school. The teachers think it is good that we take part. Some classes go here and have a picnic.'

The third phase: emotional or experienced volunteer

Table 6.4 focuses on the third phase of the volunteer process, which concerns the experiences of the volunteers that either make them volunteer in the future or not. The model distinguishes between two different types of turnover: early ejection because of unsuitable volunteers or at the end of the event. At this stage you find the *emotional volunteer*, and the most

Table 6.4 Motives on individual, sport club and community level in the experienced phase

Individual	Sport club	Community
Relationship with other volunteers	Accomplishment Stalwarts Loyalty, solidarity	Part of the community detached Ensure the success of the event Pride
Retention or not	Over- or under-burdened	
High commitment	Recognize volunteers	

prominent change in this period is the volunteer's relationship with other volunteers. At this stage they are highly committed. This is the time for bonding and creating social capital (Putnam, 1995).

> This is social. All my friends do it. All the friends I have now are connected to the hill in one way or other. When we do voluntary work we are all the same, if you in your civil life are policeman, priest, or manager. We support our community in this way, but that I do not think so much about it. I have been the leader of the handball group, and we have earned some money [for the sport club].
>
> (Female volunteer, age 55)

Another volunteer respondent chose to use a quote by the Nobel peace prize winner Albert Schweitzer in order to illustrate the joy felt during volunteering: 'Imagine if every person had a bit of volunteer work in their lives, we would change the world' (male volunteer, age 56). One of the volunteers standing at the parking area added 'I had never seen a ski jump [much laughter]. When the world record was set, I saw the jump on TV when I came home. We do it for the social environment; we have the same sick humour' (male volunteer, age 53).

Compared to many volunteers at other events (Skirstad, 2012b; Skirstad and Hanstad, 2013) these volunteers do not receive too many extrinsic rewards. 'We have to pay 500 NOK for the jackets, but we received the hats, buffs, and a backpack' explained a volunteer (female volunteer, age 69). Another volunteer added 'the jackets with the advertisement we have bought ourselves, which is hard for others [in society] to understand. They do not understand the concept of *dugnad*' (female volunteer, age 44). One woman working in the accreditation said 'the first year I bought a fleece sweater and we got a college sweater'.

The fourth phase: established volunteer and consequences of voluntarism

At the fourth *stage*, you find the *established volunteer* when the affiliation transition happens as the volunteers enters the senior ranks (see Table 6.5). In this phase, volunteers can experience burnout or they may question the volunteering. Fortunately, the volunteers in 2013 benefited from a new cafeteria where they could eat and warm up during the competition. Earlier they lacked that facility. One of the established volunteers said with a laugh 'Every year we say we will never do [12-hour shifts] again, and there we go again' (female volunteer, age 55). To have somewhere to warm up in between their shifts was appreciated. 'This has started to be a life-style' added a female volunteer (age 75).

Table 6.5 Motives on individual, sport club and community level in the established phase

Individual	Sport club	Community
	Bonding with other volunteers	Life-style Bridging
Social capital	Knowledge resource	Rural and non-commodity mentality or two worlds colliding, the business and the rural
Burn out? Intention to leave		Obligation to the community
'We can do it' 'Don't pick on us'		Attachment to the event

During the World Championship in ski flying, a special event organizer, Sponsor Link, was hired to take care of the most important guests and visitors. Usually Sponsor Link works as a travel agency and brings Norwegians to major sport events abroad (World Cup, World Championships), and their international VIP-treatment provoked the locals and it caused conflicts as mentioned in the interview:

> They have not understood the Vikersund mentality, the rural and non-commodity mentality. They came from Oslo and treated the people from Vikersund as farmers, and they corrected them all the time. The table cloth and the napkins should be like so and so.... Then the VIPs up there were drunk so they did not mind anyway.
>
> (Male volunteer, age 39)

This description reveals a collision between the business world and the volunteers. The next year the volunteers refused to do volunteer work for Sponsor Link, and that was a clear message to the organizer – it is important to have stable contexts to retain as many volunteers as possible. They also need to feel that they are in charge and able to find meaning in the work. For organizers to listen to their volunteers leads to a retention rate of approximately 90 per cent (Kristiansen et al., 2014). To enable volunteers to change tasks or move up in their volunteer careers can help as well. Another possibility in order to keep people motivated is to take some time off and return to volunteer later in life.

The retiring volunteer (the fifth phase) is not observed in this case study since only volunteers who were actively involved were interviewed. No retirees were approached or tracked down.

Discussion and conclusion

In order to understand volunteering in Norway, you need to appreciate the concept of 'indirect volunteering' at events. This is because indirect volunteering constitutes much of the volunteering undertaken in Norway, particularly at sport events. The motives for the different levels have been shown in Tables 6.2, 6.3, 6.4 and 6.5. In the beginning the important motive of the volunteers are to get money for their sport club, but other motives became more important the longer the volunteer had been involved in the event. Volunteers taking part in several events get to know each other well and create a good network of friends and they call on each other for help at other events when necessary. Some of these networks do internationally develop into 'event gypsies' (Parent and Smith-Swan, 2013), where the employees and volunteers go from one international mega-event to another. We hope to substitute the name for this group with event nomads. There are two types of these nomads, one who posits special knowledge and become regular workforce in the organizing committees, and then it is the volunteers who do it for the joy and the experience.

While indirect volunteering is considered volunteer activity in Norway, others tend to react to our use of volunteers in this connection. For example FIS Race Director for ski jumping remarked in 2013:

> then it is not volunteer work anymore. As I say, volunteer's work for free, that is the definition.... But with major events, like here in Norway, we don't have any problem with volunteers, it is a huge pressure from over the world to come and volunteer. There is also another problem, if you don't have a major event every year, it is very hard to keep the staff, alive, and then every second or third year you will have to start from scratch.... It might be, you have to stay together when you are such a small community, with little potential sources for volunteers, then you stay together.

The response of the FIS race director is ambiguous. Indirect volunteering needs to be counted as a voluntary activity since the persons who do the jobs are not paid, but their organization is contracted to have the work done. It is also interesting that he emphasizes how to retain indirect volunteers, and the advantage of Norway. The idea about raising this question was to find out how this is categorized internationally.

An important aspect of the volunteer cube is that each volunteer can find his or her mini cube inside the volunteer cube. As such the volunteer cube model may present a framework for understanding volunteers, the changing nature of involvement through the different phases of organizational socialization, and the life-cycles of the work of a volunteer. By using the cube, one can track volunteers in their volunteer development. You can, for example, be an old person starting to volunteer late in life, and will accordingly have different motives than a young volunteer. Furthermore, children are recruited very early in Vikersund as the schools bring them to the venue. The common effort of the community – and all involved stakeholders (school, entrepreneurs, local companies, the organizing committee, and so forth) – makes these events a success. Young children may be introduced to volunteer work by their parents. Children start with easy volunteer tasks, and then follow their interests to have different tasks or eventually enough experience to have leadership positions. They are raised in an indirect volunteering culture. Voluntary spirit flourishes in Vikersund and this World Cup in ski flying shows that claims that community spirit is disappearing are terribly wrong.

The usefulness of considering volunteers' different phases of involvement when reviewing the motives for volunteer work was confirmed – a person's volunteering behaviour, motives and activities are not constant. Individuals adapt their volunteering behaviours to fit their life situation and motivations and commitments to volunteer (see Tables 6.2, 6.3, 6.4 and 6.5). We consider community both as context and process, as Omoto and Snyder (2002) did. They looked at community as 'a psychological entity or conceptualization that we [they] believe is likely to have significant consequences for understanding voluntary efforts and broader civic participation' (Omoto and Snyder, 2002, p. 848). There seems to be interplay between the community context and the activities of the event volunteers.

If you do not specify, for example, which sport or club shall get the money you have worked for, the money is distributed to the organizing committee. About half of the volunteers are indirect volunteers according to the daily director of the event. Indirect volunteering was meaningful to the volunteer – even cleaning the toilets was seen as important and explained to us with pride. Moving away from the community was not seen as a reason to stop volunteering – some who study abroad come back to volunteer for ski flying events. Volunteers are motivated by what Treuren (2014) calls associative-supportive motivation and labelled enthusiastic volunteers for whom it is important that the event will be a success. Some of these very motivated people go abroad to other similar events to gain further experience and ideas of improving the event.

What is pertinent here is that the old core group of volunteers was extended by many young volunteers because of the 2012 World Championship (see Table 6.1). Both new and old volunteers worked long hours in order for the event to be successful. These findings are supported by Schlesinger et al. (2013), who investigated volunteer commitment specifically to a community sport club. They found that one's attachment and obligation to the group is likely to override both working conditions and late hours. None of these factors prevented them from volunteering the next time Vikersund hosted a major competition. What flourished in Vikersund is what we will call traditional or collective volunteering (Hustinx and Lammertyn, 2003). The volunteers might start out with individualistic motives (such as to gain access to the labour market), but gradually become motivated due to pride in the community.

This chapter has defined voluntarism and examined the indirect volunteering in Norwegian sport events in order to reveal important aspects of volunteerism at sport events. By using the voluntary cube template in presenting our findings, we could differentiate motives between various volunteers in their life-cycle, and the stages and processes the various volunteers go through in their socialization to the event and the linkage to the sport club and community. Interest for the sport club appears to be connected to the community at the macro level. From the onset we questioned if volunteers who work for the benefit of their sport club consider themselves 'real' volunteers. Our interviewees confirmed that they do – as long as they do the work for free and the clubs are paid, they are still volunteers.

Future research should clarify if indirect volunteers are used internationally. Do other countries except Norway and Sweden (see Kristiansen *et al.*, 2014) use volunteers in order to provide money for their sport club, and do they name them volunteers? By defining volunteers more specific international research can help in mapping the phenomena. Furthermore, there is a need to find out newcomers' experience of events versus those of experienced volunteers. In order to learn how volunteers' motives changes during their life-time, it would be relevant to undertake longitudinal and interdisciplinary research on volunteers in events so that the reflections and insights are broadened and challenges can be explored from different aspects and across disciplines.

Notes

1 The discipline of sky flying is an offshoot of ski jumping.
2 Gypsy is a derogatory word, so we are eager to use another concept.
3 The club was founded ahead of the World Cup Races in 1993 (Finsrud, 2011). The upper limit of members is 246, like the hill record at that time. Only a quarter of the members in Club 246 are from Vikersund. World record holders or international medallists may also become members.

References

Allen, J.B. and Shaw, S. (2009). 'Everyone rolls up their sleeves and mucks in': Exploring volunteers' motivation and experiences of the motivational climate of a sporting event. *Sport Management Review* 12: 79–90.
American Heritage. (2011). *Dictionary of the English language*, fifth edition. Boston: Houghton Mifflin Harcourt. www.ahdictionary.com/.

Bladen, C.R. (2010). Media representation of volunteers at the Beijing Olympic Games. *Sport in Society* 13(5): 784–796.

Bokmålsordboka (2014). Universitetet i Bergen i samarbeid med Språkrådet. www. nob-ordbok.uio.no/perl/ordbok.cgi?OPP=+dugnad&begge=+&ordbok=begge.

Costa, C.A., Chalip, L., Green, C. and Simens, C. (2006). Reconsidering the role of training in event volunteers' satisfaction. *Sport Management Review* 9: 165–182.

Cunningham, I., Dawes, G. and Bennet, B. (2016). *The handbook of work based learning*. London: Routledge.

Cuskelly, G., Hoye, R. and Auld, C. (2006). *Working with volunteers in sport: Theory and practice*. London: Routledge.

Davis, L. (2004). Valuing the voluntary sector in sport: Rethinking economic analysis. *Leisure Studies* 23(4): 347–364.

Dekker, P. and Halman, L. (2003). *The values of volunteering: Cross-cultural perspectives*. Norwell: Kluwer Academic/Plenum Publishers.

Dickson, T.J., Benson, A.M. and Terwiel, F.A. (2014). Mega-event volunteers, similar or different? Vancouver 2010 vs. London 2012. *International Journal of Event and Festival Management* 5: 164–179.

Doherty, A. (2009). The volunteer legacy of a major sport event. *Journal of Policy Research in Tourism, Leisure and Events* 1(3): 185–207.

Eisenhardt, K. and Graebner, M.E. (2007). Theory building from cases: Opportunities and challenges. *Academy of Management Journal* 50: 25–32.

Ferrand, A. and Skirstad, B. (2015). The volunteers' perspective. In M.M. Parent and J.-L. Chappelet (eds) *Routledge handbook of sports event management*. London: Routledge (pp. 65–88).

Finsrud, G. (2011). *Club 246. Vikersund 2013*. 6 September. www.vikersund.no/om-vikersund/organisasjonskomite/club-246/.

Haski-Leventhal, D. and Bargal, D. (2008). The volunteer stages and transitions model: Organizational socialization of volunteers. *Human Relations* 61(1): 67–102.

Heinemann, K. (ed.) (1999). *Sport clubs in various European countries*. Stuttgart: Hofmann Verlag.

Hustinx, L. and Lammertyn, F. (2003). Collective and reflexive styles of volunteering: A sociological modernization perspective. *Voluntas* 14(2): 167–187.

Hustinx, L. and Lammertyn, F. (2004). The cultural bases of volunteering: Understanding and predicting attitudinal differences between Flemish Red Cross volunteers. *Nonprofit and Voluntary Sector Quarterly* 33(4): 548–584.

Hustinx, L., Cnaan, R.A. and Handy, F. (2010). Navigating theories of volunteering: A hybrid map for a complex phenomenon. *Journal for the Theory of Social Behaviour* 40(4): 410–434.

Hyde, M.K., Dunn, J., Bax, C. and Chambers, S.K. (2016). Episodic volunteering and retention: An integrated theoretical approach. *Nonprofit and Voluntary Sector Quarterly* 45(1): 45–63.

Kiviniemi, M.T., Snyder, M. and Omoto, A.M. (2002). Too many of a good thing? The effects of multiple motivations on stress, cost, fulfilment, and satisfaction. *Personality and Social Psychology Bulletin* 28(6): 732–743.

Kristiansen, E., Skille, E.A. and Hanstad, D.V. (2014). From community based identities to individual benefits for volunteers: Comparison of three sporting events. *Scandinavian Sport Studies Forum* 5: 47–68.

Kristiansen, E., Skirstad, B., Parent, M. M. and Waddington, I. (2015). 'We can do it': Community, resistance, social solidarity, and long-term volunteering at a sport event. *Sport Management Review* 18(2): 256–267.

Lee, Y.J., Won, D. and Bang, H. (2014). Why do event volunteers return? Theory of planned behavior. *International Review on Public and Nonprofit Marketing* 11: 229–241.

Lorentzen, H. and Dugstad, L. (2011). *Den norske dugnaden: historie, kultur og fellesskap*. Kristiansand: Høyskoleforlaget.

Love, A., Hardin, R.L. and Koo, G.-Y. (2011). Effects of motives on satisfaction and behavioral intentions of volunteers at a PGA tour event. *International Journal of Sport Management* 12(1): 86–101.

MacDuff, N. (1991). *Episodic volunteering: Building the short-term volunteer program*. Walla Wall: Washington, MBA Publishing.

Marta, E., Guglielmetti, C. and Pozzi, M. (2006). Volunteerism during young adulthood: An Italian investigation into motivational patterns. *Voluntas: International Journal of Voluntary and Nonprofit Organizations* 17(3): 221–232.

Miles, M.B. and Huberman, M. (1994). *Qualitative data analysis: An expanded sourcebook*. Thousand Oaks: Sage.

Neufeind, M., Güntert, S.T. and Wehner, T. (2013). The impact of job design on event volunteers' future engagement: insights from the European Football Championship 2008. *European Sport Management Quarterly* 13(5): 537–556.

Nichols, G. (2005). Stalwarts in sport. *World Leisure Journal* 47(2): 31–37.

Omoto, A.M. and Snyder, M. (2002). Considerations of community: The context and process of volunteerism. *American Behavioral Scientist* 45: 846–867.

Parent, M.M. and Smith-Swan, S. (2013). *Managing major sports events: Theory and practice*. London: Routledge.

Putnam, R.D. (1995). Bowling alone: American's declining social capital. *Journal of Democracy* 6(1): 65–78.

Ringuet-Riot, C., Cuskelly, G., Auld, C. and Zakus, D.H. (2014). Volunteer roles, involvement and commitment in voluntary sport organizations: Evidence of core and peripheral volunteers. *Sport in Society* 17(1): 116–133.

Schlesinger, T., Egli, B. and Nagel, S. (2013). 'Continue or terminate?' Determinants of long-term volunteering in sports clubs. *European Sport Management Quarterly* 13(1): 32–53.

Skille, E.A. and Hanstad, D.V. (2013). Who are they and why do they do it? The habitus of sport event volunteers in Norway: Volunteers at the European handball championship for women 2010. *Sport in Society* 16(9): 1135–1148.

Skirstad, B. (2012a). Challenges for theories of volunteering in sport. Paper presented at EASM Conference, Aalborg, Denmark.

Skirstad, B. (2012b). Kjønn utgjør en forskjell. [Gender makes a difference]. In D.V. Hanstad (ed.) *Ski-VM 2011. Planlegging og gjennomføring [The Ski World Championship 2011: Planning and implementation]*. Oslo: Achilles (pp. 181–204).

Skirstad, B. and Hanstad, D.V. (2013). Gender matters in sport event volunteering. *Managing Leisure* 18(4): 316–330.

Solberg, H.A. (2003). Major sporting events: assessing the value of volunteers' work. *Managing Leisure* 8(1): 17–27.

Studer, S. and von Schnurbein, G. (2013). Organizational factors affecting volunteers: A literature review on volunteer coordination. *VOLUNTAS: International Journal of Voluntary and Nonprofit Organizations* 24(2): 403–440.

Tomazos, K. and Luke, S. (2015). Mega-sports events volunteering: Journeys with a past, a present and a future. *VOLUNTAS: International Journal of Voluntary and Nonprofit Organizations* 26(4): 1337–1359.

Treuren, G. (2009). The associative-supportive motivation as a factor in the decision to event volunteer. *Leisure/Loisir* 33(2): 687–711.

Treuren, G.J. (2014). Enthusiasts, conscripts or instrumentalists? The motivational profiles of event volunteers. *Managing Leisure* 19(1): 51–70.

Weick, K.E. (2001). *Making sense of the organization.* Oxford: Blackwell.

Wicker, P. and Hallmann, K. (2013). A multi-level framework for investigating the engagement of sport volunteers. *European Sport Management Quarterly* 13(1): 110–139.

Wilson, J. (2000). Volunteering. *Annual Review of Sociology* 26: 215–240.

Wilson, J. (2012). Volunteerism research: A review essay. *Nonprofit and Voluntary Sector Quarterly* 41(2): 176–212.

Wollebæk, D., Skirstad, B. and Hanstad, D.V. (2014). Between two volunteer cultures: Social composition and motivation among volunteers at the 2010 test event for the FIS Nordic World Ski Championships. *International Review for the Sociology of Sport* 49(1): 22–41.

Yin, R.K. (2003). *Case study research: Design and methods.* Thousand Oaks: Sage.

Part II

International sport volunteering and sport and development

Chapter 7

International Development through Excellence and Leadership in Sport (IDEALS)

The Namibia and Liverpool John Moores University programme

Tom Fletcher and Danny Cullinane

Introduction

International Development through Excellence and Leadership in Sport (IDEALS) is a UK Sport programme designed to establish a high quality, progressive and co-ordinated sports leadership development exchange programme between UK universities and their international partner institutions. Since its inception in 2006, the IDEALS programme has grown year on year. The aim of the programme is to inspire the next generation of globally aware leaders through sport. Furthermore, the programme offers higher education students the opportunity to add value to their degree programme, enhance global awareness and develop leadership skills (UK Sport, 2016a).

The IDEALS initiative is linked to ten universities and a number of sport National Governing Bodies (NGBs) across the UK. The programme is currently operational in Zambia, Namibia and Tanzania, involving local organizations, universities and Sport-for-Development (SFD) projects overseas. Since 2006, more than 350 British students, 60 university staff members and 30 young professionals (those working in the sporting environment) have participated in the programme. The programme is directly supported by the participating organizations and International Inspiration (IN). This is an international development charity, which was born from the London 2012 Olympic and Paralympic Games, with the aim of inspiring and transforming the lives of young people around the world through the power of sport (UK Sport, 2016a).

Liverpool John Moores University (LJMU) has been involved with the IDEALS programme since 2007. UK Sport agreed to start a programme in Namibia with BA (Hons) Sport Development and BA (Hons) Sport Coaching students undertaking volunteer placements with various sport-related Non-Governmental Organizations (NGOs) at the end of their second year. The Sport Development degree programme develops students' knowledge and skills to help them understand and influence sport and sport development in public, private and voluntary sectors. The Sport Coaching programme develops student's specific professional and technical skills to enhance coaching performance in sport and physical activity. These students also develop an emerging expertise in leadership.

The success and sustainability of the IDEALS Namibia programme depends upon the availability of a pool of LJMU students (judged based on their capability of benefiting from participation in this type of learning experience). Namely, that they are able to enhance their employability skills through learning from, and contributing to, the development of others. Recruitment for the IDEALS Namibia programme has only been open to the Sport Development and Sport Coaching second-year students, due to the context of the placements and alignment with the students' previous learning experiences. Initial information is provided by staff and IDEALS alumni who give presentations to students at the beginning of the academic year in September. The selection process is via an initial application form, followed by interviews in October which use motivation, competence and scenario-based questions (i.e. Why do you want to go? What skills and experiences will you bring? What do you want to take away? If you were asked to act in this particular way, what would you do?). The interview panel is chaired by the co-ordinating university staff member, with the alumni students from the previous year making up the panel. Decisions also take into account team dynamics, the likely contribution of the group, the potential personal development as well as existing skill sets. Whilst gender equality is desirable, the selection process has resulted in years where there have been 5:1 ratios in favour of both female and male students. More typically though there is an equal gender split.

What this programme does is deliver on the employability agenda as employers expect graduates to have developed their skills prior to employment (Done and Mulvey, 2013), and many employers still express dissatisfaction with the generic employability skills of graduates (AGR, 2011). This emphasizes work experience as being imperative in order to be 'employable'. Recent research discovered that work experience was looked upon highly by employers and is considered to be as important as degree qualifications when it came to choosing between job applicants (*Independent*, 2015). Such overseas experience, notably of different cultural contexts, is increasingly used as differentiating factor in graduate recruitment and selection (Plum, 2008).

Consequently, this chapter provides an examination of the IDEALS programme in Namibia. From the perspective of the international student volunteer, the chapter will explore how the initiative has impacted on the individual's personal and professional development. Furthermore, it will examine the role the local placements play in the community and the challenges they face in providing services in a wider SFD context and consider the development of the IDEALS programme over the past ten years and the extent to which it has achieved its aims and objectives.

The chapter is organized in the following way. The next section offers a brief contextual exploration of concepts relevant to IDEALS Namibia. These, alongside outlines of the country and host placements, provide a sense of the scope of the programme. Two key concepts involved in the IDEALS Namibia programme are examined further: leadership and cultural awareness. Findings from an analysis of student volunteer participants' weekly reports are then assessed to reveal some chronological patterns of engagement. An examination of how the programme has developed further opportunities for the student volunteers over its life cycle follows, leading on to some concluding points on the nature of such programmes and considerations for any similar activities.

Volunteering and Sport for Development

Volunteering is a choice people make and is a donation of their own time (Holmes and Smith, 2009). Motivations to volunteer are complex, and relate to a range of conceptual factors underpinning drivers to volunteer, such as for solidary, purposive or material reasons. Solidary reasons are related to social interactions; purposive incentives include the desire to do something beneficial for society or an organization; and material reasons are the tangible rewards or special privileges that volunteers may receive as a result of their work (Caldwell and Andereck, 1994). Whilst initial reasons for volunteering may differ widely, sport volunteering not only benefits the individuals immediately involved, but can also have a wider impact on the community, and provide attractive potential for social gain (European Commission, 2007). This social development derives from participatory mutually beneficial interactions between individuals and groups, thus highlighting the importance of sport programmes and initiatives (Schulenkorf, 2013).

International volunteering opportunities for young people have increased greatly over recent years, but as Jones (2011) has indicated, there needs to be a more nuanced view of the diversity of experiences available and the potential benefits and disadvantages that can accrue. McGloin and Georgeou (2016) usefully distinguish between different types of approaches, and the key differentials that distinguish each model. Using such an approach, the IDEALS Namibia programme can perhaps be seen as being under the banner of 'Short-term International Volunteering' (Lough, 2008).

Many individuals will commence volunteer work as a means to gain experience and to enhance their curriculum vitae. Furthermore Handy *et al.* (2010) identified that students use volunteering as a means of signalling desirable work qualities to a potential employer, therefore having competitive advantage over other job applicants. It is also widely acknowledged that sport participation has been linked to increased self-esteem, leadership skills, empowerment, and personal and professional development (Kidd and Donnelly, 2007; Levermore, 2008).

Whilst sport development is still a contested term, Houlihan (2010) usefully conceptualizes it into three main areas of activity: improving the quality of and access to sport; talent identification and development; and using sport as a means to tackle social issues. The latter includes activities frequently identified as being SFD. Kidd (2008) recognizes the overlap of activities between the terms but distinguishes Sport Development as often being run by sports organizations and targeting people who want to be involved in sport, whilst SFD is often (but not always) led by non-sporting organizations with less concern for people becoming active sports players. Globally, government agencies and NGOs are increasingly acknowledging the role of sport and physical activity in addressing social issues and promoting social cohesion (Schulenkorf, 2013), and so SFD is increasingly appearing as a vehicle for social change (Jarvie, 2011). In the IDEALS Namibia programme, whilst the majority of the activities would be labelled as Sport for Development, there are also some core activities which would be recognised as more traditional mass participation sport development, and a small part as the early stages of elite sport development.

IDEALS Namibia

Namibia, LJMU's partner in the IDEALS programme, is a large and sparsely populated country, home to 2.4 million people. It is a geographically, ethnically and linguistically diverse society, and enjoys a high degree of political, economic and social stability. For the IDEALS Namibia programme the country's geography and its historical legacy has some important, if hidden, impacts that perhaps makes the country an easier place for volunteers from the UK to feel comfortable. In addition to English being the official language, vehicles drive on the left as they do in the UK. For much of the year Namibia is in the same time zone as the UK. Whilst the placements take place during the Namibian winter, the weather is in fact often better and far more predictable than a British summer, with very limited rainfall and daytime temperatures of around 23°C. The IDEALS activities take place in a township of the capital city, Windhoek. In the city there are many 'familiar' sights to western eyes at the shopping malls, cinemas, private gyms and fast food outlets. However, whilst this gives a sense of ease, the existing socio-economic and cultural differences within the country and with the UK are perhaps magnified by comparison. These include the more restricted access to the education system; the lack of a structured Physical Education in the curriculum, due to limited opportunities for structured physical activity by many of the population; the digital divide in technology; and the more obvious physical juxtaposition of rich and poor communities.

Institutional stakeholders in IDEALS Namibia

The hosts' role in managing placements is multi-faceted, including: the provision of practical sports development experience to students from LJMU; increasing the capacity of partner NGOs to deliver their programme of activities; and support for development of HIV/AIDS curriculum resources (a critical public health issue in Namibia). It is recognized that the use of sport as a tool to engage children in health education programmes can improve the likelihood of information retention, empowerment and attitude change (Levermore, 2008; Laureus, 2010). Each host placement has unique situational contexts to address but this also offers an array of opportunities that can enable students to both learn new skills and develop those they already have.

Over the past nine years, students from LJMU have been hosted by five local sport and community organizations. All of these have vibrant activities in the main township of Katutura, immediately adjacent to the northern districts of Windhoek. Of these five, three also run nationwide programmes (SCORE, Special Olympics Namibia and the Namibian Football Association's 'Galz and Goals' programme), and whilst the other two organizations (Physically Active Youth [PAY] and Frank Fredericks Foundation) primarily deliver activities in Katutura and Windhoek, they are also involved in other programmes that reach across the country. All believe in the benefits of sport for wider social gains, and were therefore selected as LJMU partners because of the excellent quality of work they already provide. A notable shared element of the placements is that they shape the local programme of activities. This is important as it allows each placement to focus on ensuring they get the maximum value of the student volunteer's input. Whilst a dialogue is encouraged between the students and the placement as the programme develops each year, it is the placement that determines what is done and when.

NFA 'Galz and Goals'

Launched in 2009, the NFA 'Galz and Goals' project is a partnership between the Namibia Football Association and Unicef. It aims to empower girls aged 10–15 to make healthy choices in life through participation in football leagues and festivals that integrates life skills, HIV/AIDS education and healthy living. The programme is uniquely aimed at the girls of Namibia, who are generally lacking in opportunities to participate in organized sports, and particularly seeks to use football as a tool to promote individual health and foster social change (Unicef, 2012). Furthermore, the programme has developed a curriculum for use by teachers, coaches and parents, to help communicate and teach the benefits of healthy lifestyles. As Namibian women and young girls are disproportionally affected by the HIV epidemic, the curriculum includes information on HIV/AIDS, drug and alcohol abuse and gender discrimination (Unicef, 2012).

Frank Fredericks Foundation

The Frank Fredericks Foundation is a non-profit organization dedicated to the development of Namibia's young talented athletes. It was set up by Frank Fredericks (who was a world champion in athletics in the immediate years after the country gained independence and became a sporting icon), who has continued to play a major role in sporting administration internationally. One part of the Foundation helps provide opportunities for young athletes to further their education by creating scholarships. It also educates participants in the areas of management, finance, marketing and investment opportunities, which can then further support and develop their sporting careers. Another part helps develop and support volunteers to increase the level of access to sports (such as athletics and volleyball) young people have in and beyond schools.

Physically Active Youth

Physically Active Youth (PAY) is a community-based after-school project that focuses on the development of young people in Katutura. The programme incorporates a holistic approach to child development by combining academic work (tutoring) with physical activity and sport, life skills, gender and HIV/AIDS education. The programme operates in a friendly environment, where help and support is always on offer for any issues the children have relating to their personal development. This programme is particularly important given the present situation regarding youth access to higher education.

In order for Namibian high school students to access higher education, they must pass two mandatory exams, one in Grade 10 and a second in Grade 12. Students who fail the exams are barred from post-secondary studies. Approximately half of all Namibians who sit the Grade 10 exam, and around 40 per cent of those who reach Grade 12, fail the exams. This creates a large population of unemployed, unskilled youth who are consequently at increased risk of lapsing into reckless behaviour such as substance abuse, criminal activity and/or unsafe sexual conduct. Traditionally, non-white schools continue to lack resources, teachers and facilities to prepare students for these exams. Students in the PAY programme receive two hours of academic tutoring followed by an hour-long sport and physical activity session, Mondays through Thursdays. Fridays are reserved 'open days' with a different theme (e.g. life skills, gender, environment) each week.

Special Olympics Namibia

Special Olympics Namibia (SON) is part of a global organization catering for intellectually disabled athletes, from the age of eight. SON represents and supports the intellectually disabled athletes of Namibia. The mission of SON is to provide year-round sports training and athletic competition in a variety of Olympic-type sports, for children and adults with intellectual disabilities. It aims to provide these groups with continuing opportunities to develop physical fitness, demonstrate courage, experience joy and participate in the sharing of gifts, skills and friendship with their families, other SON athletes and the community. SON also works closely with volunteers and local schools, both mainstream and those catering for disabled pupils, in an effort to break down negative stereotyping and promote unified sports participation.

SON is also affiliated with the Fédération Internationale de Football Association (FIFA) through the Football for Hope Project, which was piloted in 2006 in Namibia, Tanzania and Botswana. Since the 2010 FIFA Football World Cup in South Africa, SON has also been responsible for the running a 'Football for Hope' legacy centre, consisting of an all-weather artificial floodlit surface, changing rooms and community buildings, as well as a site office.

SCORE

SCORE is a non-profit NGO from southern Africa which has as its objective the development of communities and empowerment of individuals through sport and recreation. Its mission is to use sport to provide children and youth with valuable skills and opportunities, to help them both succeed in life and contribute to their communities (SCORE, 2016). Whilst it runs a national programme, in Windhoek SCORE is based primarily within the low-income areas of Katutura, and works in both local schools and throughout the community.

Central to SCORE's intervention methodology is the utilization of local sports leaders who implement activities, and drive the sport and development process in their own communities. By providing access to new sports opportunities and increasing participation, SCORE builds stronger and healthier communities by promoting equality, friendship, partnerships, exchanges and fair play. SCORE's core programmes and key projects are largely funded by donor organizations and government departments.

Nonetheless, the organization faces an ongoing challenge to sustain and grow funding, in order to increase its capacity to implement existing projects.

The development of student participants in IDEALS Namibia

Induction for selected students (and participating staff) takes place over two days, at a host UK university involved in the IDEALS programme. The purpose of the induction is to impart information about UK Sport, the projects and the host country, and to help students settle into their projects and host country quickly. It also allows students and project staff to meet, interact and exchange information and experiences. An important element of the pre-departure induction is the opportunity to address concerns and to highlight both similarities and differences in cultural context. All UK participants are asked to sign a code of conduct (which is circulated at the induction course) requesting students to adhere to a minimum standard of behaviour to ensure the professionalism of the programme.

The IDEALS Namibia programme has sought to facilitate student development in several strands, through: sports and coaching leadership, practical skills development and cultural awareness (UK Sport, 2016b). In this section, a brief exploration of some activities pertinent to leadership and cultural awareness will follow, including the process of reflection that underpins student development.

Leadership

Leadership in IDEALS is not just seen as being an innate characteristic of an individual, but a construct of social factors, processes and settings (Vella *et al.*, 2010). The IDEALS Namibia programme gives students opportunities to access the consideration, practice and development of leadership in different ways. The most common of these are through direct participatory action, exposure to different leadership styles, and by engaging in discussion and debate with host nation peers.

The most obvious leadership activity is by students directly taking on the role of a leader within one of the placement's programmes. As such, students are often responsible for programme delivery and development and have to come up with the best ways to reach particular priorities set by the placement. This has included talent identification programmes for children with disabilities, sport specific coaching schemes and often activities tied into wider programme aims such as exploring gender equality roles or healthy living. The students are also expected to be able to take charge in delivering quality sessions themselves and facilitating the delivery of such by others. Students gain immediate feedback and advice from placement hosts and partners on their performance, and use this to build on their capabilities. As students have already undertaken modules in sports delivery, this is often the simplest area for them to register development.

A key feature of the IDEALS Namibia programme is through observing leadership styles displayed by the placement hosts. Contact with experienced practitioners has frequently been commented on by students as a major area of learning and inspiration. In these cases, the students as international sport volunteers initially shadow then assist in the delivery of sessions led by experienced local coaches and development workers, in parallel with running their own session during the first few weeks. Students are encouraged to reflect on these experiences and to question their own assumptions and principles on which they make judgements. In some instances, this has led on to further informal mentoring of students by hosts, and to continuing friendships beyond the lifetime of the student's direct engagement in the programme.

Students are also encouraged to co-lead activities with local peers, such as heading up 'Youth Leads' programmes in local secondary schools. They are enabled to subsequently share their experiences with peer leaders from the host country, and by discussing issues and ideas with them, the students are able to explore what is understood by leadership in different cultures. From this, new constructions of what a leader can be are built around a shared generational understanding. The power of conversation as a means of engaging and developing such identities has been an important strength of the programme, building on local experiences of community development. An additional benefit of this approach has been to develop the capacity of the host placement to increase sustainability in their own programmes, as the peer leaders gain access to skills and knowledge that they might otherwise find difficult to locate. However, this is not an automatic benefit, and there has to be a conscious and continual reflection of whether these benefits are actually real, or indeed appropriate (Spaaij et al., 2016).

Cultural awareness

Kay and Bradbury (2009) have shown that a structured volunteering programme in the UK may have the capacity to foster what they have termed 'social connectedness'. This is viewed as an ability for volunteers to engage with others and have an increased awareness of other's needs in their own community. The IDEALS Namibia programme seeks to take this type of approach into a global scenario. However, the achievement of such outcomes, as indicated by Lough (2011), requires the right conditions for this to happen.

The aforementioned UK induction programme plays an important role in this. Before students travel to their partner country at the end of May, they attend the induction weekend in late February. At this event, students are exposed to overseas views of how British culture appears, and how their own actions may be interpreted. UK Sport invites practitioners from the host countries to visit and lead discussions about their country, so that the students can find out more and ask questions. The induction schedule also utilizes experts from international development organizations who share their experiences and highlight the opportunities and pitfalls they have faced. This includes issues of language, behaviour and dress-codes. This is followed by an in-country induction in the first days of the pro-gramme, which reinforces and extends these issues. Students are provided with a geographical and historical tour of the townships where they will be working, giving them the chance to go on guided visits of the National Museum of Namibia to learn more about the nation's history and culture (as presented locally rather than from a UK perspective), and engage with local speakers about everyday life in Namibia. These have covered a range of perspectives, including presentations from senior government officials, young people living with HIV and Namibian sports internationals. Stu-dents are also encouraged to participate in local cultural activities whilst they are in country, including events such as festivals for the International Day of the African Child, and attending international football matches and music concerts.

A final thread in this strand is for students to organize an event using sport that brings together young people from different communities in Katu-tura and Windhoek. The students are responsible for working with all the host placements to deliver a day-long festival that reinforces the partnerships forged by IDEALS, between the hosts and the UK stakeholders. These are often held in celebration of a major international event such as the Olym-pics, Paralympics or Commonwealth Games, but uses local as well as global games and activities to construct the day's programme of events.

Several reports have identified that this aspect has been a successful part of the IDEALS programme. A survey in 2010 of IDEALS participants across all the programmes showed that 86.2 per cent of participants reported that their placement had contributed to increased skills in inter-cultural communication. A report commissioned by UK Sport from Powell (2011) evaluated two of the IDEALS objectives, cultural awareness and raising students' skills through international awareness. Powell (2011, p. 10) concluded that 'participation ... develops a range of sought after employability skills in the form of communication, team working, innova-tion and creativity and problem-solving'. It has also been evident that the lengthy placement has allowed greater awareness to be developed. The first year of the programme lasted for six weeks, and the unanimous feedback from placements, staff and students was that this was not long enough to permit a deeper understanding of the work and the culture. Consequently, in all subsequent years the programme has lasted eight weeks.

Research methods

When the students are in Namibia, the programme requires participating students to record and submit a weekly individual reflective report on their activities. The cohort also prepares a group report outlining their perceived shared highlights of the week. This reporting process was instigated to serve a number of purposes, building on the accessing of volunteer diaries that has proven illuminating in earlier SFD programmes (Sugden, 2006). First, it provides a formal means for students to record and communicate what has been happening, and so begin to consider and understand the requisite professional skills that are likely to be encountered in their career. Second, the reports form a record of events that, with editing, can be shared with other stakeholders to inform them of the students' progress. In turn, the stakeholders have been able to react to these reflections and tailor future activities at placements to account for specific issues that have emerged, beginning a potential for co-creation of meaningful experience (Nicholls *et al.*, 2010). Monitoring of the reports has also facilitated iden-tification of ongoing tensions within student groups, or emerging dif-ficulties for the students that they have not been able to openly articulate. Finally, the reports have allowed analysis of the student experience in their own words, revealing patterns and dynamics of individual development.

There has been no set format for the structure of the reports, encourag-ing the students to express themselves individually. Whilst the students have been familiar with reflective models, such as Gibbs (1998), Johns (2000) and Kolb (1984), the students have often developed their own indi-vidual approaches to structuring their reflections. These have included the use of photos as a starting point for reflection, the adoption of slogans as media-style 'headlines', a binary approach of good and bad, and identifica-tion of the 'emotions of the day' to bring an internalized focus on what is seen as most relevant. The weekly reports would normally be in the range of about 1,500 words to 3,000 words, but for some students they did extend to over 5,000 words per week, providing a depth of insight into what mattered to each student. For some, recording in detail a key event was most important, while for others logging of the daily routine and how the placement fitted into their whole day was their focus.

As the IDEALS programme matured, the second author began to inves-tigate these reports to identify student earning, patterns of activity, areas of concern, and to inform future practice The reports were collated and uploaded into QSR NVivo (2.0.161) to facilitate the handling and analysis of the data. The final data set consisted of 319 weekly reports that were submitted by students (n = 47: 29 female, 18 male; age range from 19 to 26 years old) participating in the programme from 2008 to 2015. The reports were read and re-read prior to coding using an inductive thematic analysis and six-stage process outlined by Braun and Clarke (2006).

Findings

Five themes emerged from the analysis, involving a noticeable temporal progression that outlined a likely trajectory students followed in their volunteering experience. These are, in turn: novelty; practical delivery and logistics; concern for participants and feedback; extending impact; and finally, reflection and departures. Most students have covered these points in their reports, although not all at the same speed, in the exact same sequence or with the same intensity or depth of experience.

The first theme captures the personal novelty of the student's situation and primarily occurs in the first week's reports. Immediate and obvious differences between the UK and Namibia are often to the fore, and variances between students' expectations and the reality of their actual experiences are also commented upon. These include everything from the first sighting of baboons on the side of road from the airport, to socio-cultural aspects such as quickly getting used to welcomes through the mastering of complex handshakes. It projects the excitement and adventure. Students are often passive but excited recipients of the experiences at this stage:

> Something that I have noticed during my first week here is the attitude that Namibians have, in particular those living within Katutura township. They are always so polite and friendly, greeting you whenever they see you and asking how you are.
>
> (Bobby, Week 1, 2008)

The second theme sees the focus quickly shift onto more practical activities. This is frequently recording the elements of delivery and session planning, and on the mechanics of what is to be done: scheduling, organizing and co-ordinating efforts. The students are seen as becoming more active agents of their own experiences. However they will be often be applying their ideas from a model that is built on their own cultural experiences and modus operandi in the UK. Fears of not being at the right standard are often implied:

> One of the most interesting and testing sessions for me was a volleyball session we had to take, where we had been given no equipment and the school had none either. I was leading the session as volleyball is my stronger area of expertise. It was very challenging as there is only so much volleyball you can do with no balls.... This was very challenging for both of us but I think we managed to pull it off and keep the children engaged.
>
> (Tina, Week 2, 2010)

The third theme focuses on the participants, and the immediate response to feedback after holding successful sessions. Attachments to individuals begin to become clear as friendships are made. Daily patterns are mentioned less. Students start to show signs of adaptation in their approaches to practical delivery. This is evidenced in an easing of the rigours of a formalized structuring of sessions, a relaxation of preoccupation with what were initially seen as barriers and obstacles (such as a lack of equipment or limited dedicated facilities), and the taking on board of ideas from the placement hosts and peer leaders. An acceptance of other ways of achieving goals is explored, and a sense of creativity blossoms as students begin to find other ways of getting things done:

> Again the children really seemed to enjoy the session and asked if they could take part in more rugby in the next lesson! ... From what we have seen of Kiki as a coach and as 'head' of the NAM-VIP's he is a real inspiration and brilliant at what he does.
>
> (Eric, Week 4, 2011)

The fourth theme of extending impact emerges further into the volunteering programme, as the more adept students begin to show a sense of exploring the challenges that exist, and considering ways in which they can make a specific difference. They will explore ideas of innovation and sustainability, questioning how things are done with an aim of finding solutions. They will also have developed a high level of trust with their peer leaders, and will refer to exchanging ideas and responsibilities. Weaker students at this stage more often make continuing reference to the routine, identifying specific standout events rather than underlying issues:

> Before the session I noticed one of the children was in a wheelchair. I was slightly frustrated and annoyed that the teacher straight away put the brakes on his wheelchair and told him that he would just have to watch. When I told the teacher that he would be able to partake in the session too she looked very shocked and surprised.... This is a subject that I feel very strongly about as I feel no child should ever be excluded from participating in sport because of their disability. I made sure that I changed or adapted all elements of my session so he could partake and used him as one of the demonstrators for several of the skills.
>
> (Whitney, Week 6, 2013)

The final theme of reflection and departure contains a broader sense of reflection on the whole period. This is embedded in the realization of the finality of leaving and the inevitable separation from those that they have worked with. A sense of attachment and responsibility for the participants and placements is often expressed through concerns for what will be continued to be provided, coupled with a desire to maintain contacts, to return, and the desire to have a legacy in place. There is also often a sense of confusion and frustration that emerges. Students recognize that they have had access to higher levels of influence in their placements than they may have previously had encountered in the UK, within which they have probably been effective. But in considering their return, they identify that these opportunities to hold similar positions may be more difficult to obtain. A sense of the limits is placed on the limited time available:

> Last day of placement (sad times)!!!!!!! The morning started with our IDEALS debriefs, and to be honest it was good which shocked me. I personally found it interesting to see how like-minded we were as a team. I just hope that the things discussed today could be put in place or at least worked towards to make a better experience for the future students, but more so the organisations.
>
> (Tom, Week 8, 2014)

It is worth recording that the increasing availability, reliability and capacity of the Internet in Namibia over the lifespan of the programme has radically altered certain aspects of the experience, especially in communication. It is now far easier for students to maintain contact with friends and family at home: the sense of distance, delay and the time spent apart is consequently much reduced, and the immediacy of relating stories has increased. This has meant that whilst there is greater sharing there is perhaps less selectivity in picking out what are the key incidents.

As a positive, it has also meant that communications with the placements can begin before the students leave the UK, and be more easily maintained on their return (see Lough et al., 2014), primarily through social media. These virtual contacts have increased greatly in the decade since the IDEALS programme begun, and it has gone beyond the first simple sharing of experiences through photos and personal updates to include for example detailed and complex preparation resources for sport sessions and educational programmes.

The development of the IDEALS Namibia programme

The IDEALS Namibia programme has undergone many developments as it has evolved, in response to changing conditions on the ground as well as ongoing learning from the students' experiences as international sport volunteers. This section examines the dynamics concerning:

1   students' return to university education;
2   the emerging Team Leader role; and
3   employment opportunities.

Students' return to university education

In the first two years of IDEALS Namibia, students were able to formally reflect upon their overseas experience as part of an optional module that examined personal and professional development. This was taken up by all the IDEALS participants, which suggested that the experience had been of personal value. In later iterations of the degree this option module was not available, and so to give greater relevance to the student's experiences, other ways of embedding IDEALS into the programme have been sought. Some students have been able to extend their experiences into the curriculum in their final year. The most common method has been through an individually negotiated project, in which students identify and manage year-long projects and then reflect on the outputs and outcomes. For IDEALS alumni who have taken this possibility, examples have included translating their delivery experiences into local schools' physical education, using the lessons from cross-curricular delivery in Namibia to apply in the UK. Another student has set up a virtual resource bank of school lesson plans and other resources to share with leaders in both Namibia and the UK. Students have also undertaken dissertation projects exploring similarities and differences between sport and education delivery, perceptions of physical activity, and even critiquing the value of sport in a society where certain basic provisions are not universally available.

On a wider basis, at the start of the each academic year, the returning cohort have led practical sessions for new first-year students, exposing them to different activities, acting as role models for what progress students can make through engaging in such opportunities, and discussing about their experiences and personal development.

Emerging Team Leader role

A key development within the IDEALS Namibia programme has been that of the Team Leader role. It was already known from the first two years of delivery that the first weeks in country had to be supported well. Whilst the local induction plays a considerable part in helping the transition to a new country, for the first two years, a member of university staff accompanied the students in the early weeks to support the settling in process, and ensure that the logistics were all in place. In discussions between the stakeholders, it became apparent that this facilitating role might be better implemented using someone whom the students could associate with more closely. By having access to someone who themselves had gone through a similar adjustment process, and had more closely related characteristics regarding age and educational experiences, it was hoped that students would be able to be more open and share their concerns. It would also provide an opportunity for the person in that role to take on greater responsibility in leadership, one of the key aims of the IDEALS programme.

The first iterations of the role used master's level students who had previously been part of the IDEALS Namibia programme. In later years, students who had been involved the previous year were considered the way forward. This was popular amongst IDEALS alumni, and on average 50 per cent of the returning students would express an interest and apply to be selected for this role. Selection for this role was by application, and then interview by university staff members. Further training has been provided by UK Sport alongside other participants in similar roles on the other IDEALS programmes. Team Leaders will now spend three weeks accompanying the student group: the first week is spent supporting familiarization, the second in ensuring that activity patterns are in place and being met, and the third in consolidating standards and helping the students to set their own expectations in conjunction with the placements.

Employment opportunities

IDEALS has been a powerful tool to develop student's skills for the workplace. A UK Sport survey in 2012, covering the full range of IDEALS programmes (including Ghana, Namibia, Tanzania and Zambia), showed that students from these programmes have had enhanced employment opportunities. A total of 82 per cent of the alumni contacted in 2012 stated that IDEALS had helped them gain their first or current post, and 100 per cent of the alumni were either employed or in postgraduate education.

For the IDEALS Namibia alumni, there are a range of job roles that they have gone into. Some are more in alignment with the traditional exit routes of the degrees, such as teachers (of secondary level Physical Education and primary education) or as local council and national governing body sport development officers. Others have deployed their skills into other community-based jobs such as firefighters. Furthermore, some students have been employed to run SFD programmes overseas. This has resulted in a few now living abroad to work in development programmes, with one even changing nationality.

Discussion and conclusion

As indicated above, the IDEALS Namibia programme would be recognized as delivering activities within the field of SFD. This is not an unproblematic area (Darnell, 2007), as issues of conflict, power and dependability, and neo-colonialism have all been identified (Hartmann and Kwauk, 2011; Lindsey and Banda, 2011; Giulianotti, 2011). We do not go into these more thoroughly here but, at the very least, a sensitivity to the impact of these should be in place in any considerations. To enable year-on-year delivery, the IDEALS programme has taken a pragmatic approach in which these issues are recognized and in discussion with the host placements, the limitations that they impose are worked within.

For many of the IDEALS Namibia partners, the primary concerns have simply been issues of financial and organizational existence and stability. Several local organizations have survived extreme financial challenges since 2007, and understandably have had to prioritize their actions and support to these issues. Therefore, any international volunteering programme has to recognize the burden that a partnership may create as well as the benefits it may bring. This requires balancing a degree of expertise in sustainability and diligence against a pragmatic realism of potential longer-term benefits. Consequently, having the right co-ordinating organization (in this case, UK Sport) is vital to facilitate in-country organizational capacity on a year-by-year basis.

Indeed, there are many overseas organizations that facilitate their own volunteer programmes, and there appears little local co-ordination or control of them. In the timespan of IDEALS Namibia, UK students have had regular contact with both organized and independent volunteers from other countries (such as Canada, Norway, the United States, Germany and the Netherlands). The standards of co-operation, objectives and ownership of these programmes vary greatly, and this places a large strain on placement hosts. This emerges from handling the different expectations and demands of overseas organizations for which they have little spare capacity to deal with, through to the direct undermining of work already undertaken through overseas agencies setting up their own high-profile but often temporary interventions.

Whilst a volunteer programme brings a short-term addition to resources in terms of workload capacity and potentially expertise, translating that into longer-term benefits can be difficult for local partners. Often peer leaders who gain skills and knowledge become more employable, and if successful in gaining employment they usually cannot then volunteer. This has translated into a high turnover of paid and unpaid local staff, and thus a reduction in the transfer of expertise and the exchange of knowledge to what could have been expected. Indeed, only two paid staff who were in Namibian host organizations in 2007 are still working with the IDEALS partners (one of these individuals has changed organizations). For the UK volunteers, this can lead to a sense of frustration when they realize that creating something sustainable is reliant on a very fragile structure. As referred to elsewhere, and indicated in this case study, sport volunteer programmes can play a significant role in developing social capital. Morgan (2013) identifies that engagement needs to be longer term to accumulate social capital and even where an individual inherits a relatively high level of social capital this needs to be reinvested, exchanged and developed to maintain.

The involvement of international volunteers can allow local placements to use this as a lever to show that what they do is of recognizable good quality and has an impact. It can be a form of individual and organizational empowerment through the exchange of ideas. Volunteer students therefore need to understand the wider impact that their conduct and input may have for an organization, long beyond the duration of their visit. However, it can also lead to suspicions from other local bodies that the placements have access to many other resources such as finances and so conversely make it more difficult for them to access funds.

The evaluations of the IDEALS Namibia programmes that have been undertaken have all been about the UK student experience and development. Whilst there is scope for exploring the impact this programme may have had on host placements, the resources to do so have been limited. Taking on board Coalter's (2010) message, the benefits of the IDEALS experience also reinforce the importance of considering from the outset how to monitor and measure impact and expected outcomes. Once a programme has started, it becomes very hard to disentangle established ways of working. Although Sabatier (1988) recommends that any policy-type intervention requires at least ten years for its impact to be seen, over such a long time frame, the environment within which the programme works has significantly changed. Local variations and changes in financial stability, key personnel and the introduction of new higher-specification facilities have all had an unknown level of impact on IDEALS Namibia.

In essence, it is already known that successful volunteer programmes require a huge amount of investment and work over an extended period (Smith et al., 2014). The IDEALS Namibia experience would confirm that. Whilst it could therefore be suggested that any new volunteer programmes of this type should identify a long-term commitment before starting so that the resourcing can be secured, the sheer difficulty for local placements just to continue to be in existence and serve their core function has to be recognized as a limiting factor. However, there are tangible benefits for all partners. Students who have the right combination of motivation, learning, skill set and support are able to take longer-term benefits from such experiences – and through exchange placements are able to extract valuable short-term capacity and longer-term peer-learning.

References

Association of Graduate Recruiters (AGR). (2011). Graduate recruitment survey 2011.

Braun, V. and Clarke, V. (2006). Using thematic analysis in psychology. *Qualitative Research in Psychology* 3(2): 77–101.

Caldwell, L.L. and Andereck, K.L. (1994). Motives for initiating and continuing membership in a recreation-related voluntary association. *Leisure Sciences* 16: 33–44.

Coalter, F. (2010). The politics of sport-for-development: Limited focus programmes and broad gauge problems? *International Review for the Sociology of Sport* 45(3): 295–314.

Darnell, S.C. (2007). Playing with race: *Right to Play* and the production of whiteness in 'Development through Sport'. *Sport in Society* 10(4): 560–579.

Done, J. and Mulvey, M.R. (2013). *Brilliant graduate career handbook*, 2nd edition. Harlow: Pearson Education.

European Commission. (2007). *White paper on sport*. Brussels: European Commission.

Gibbs, G. (1988). *Learning by doing: A guide to teaching and learning methods*. London: FEU.

Giulianotti, R. (2011). The sport, development and peace sector: A model of four social policy domains. *Journal of Social Policy* 40(4): 757–776.

Handy, F., Cnaan, R.A. Hustinx, L., Kang, C., Brudney, J.L., Haski-Leventhal, D., Holmes, K., Meijs, L.C.P.M., Pessi, A.B., Ranade, B., Yamauchi, N. and Zrinscak, S. (2010). A cross-cultural examination of student volunteering: Is it all about résumé building? *Nonprofit and Voluntary Sector Quarterly* 39(3): 498–523.

Hartmann, D. and Kwauk, C. (2011). Sport and development: An overview, critique, and reconstruction. *Journal of Sport & Social Issues* 35(3): 284–305.

Holmes, K. and Smith, K. (2009). *Managing volunteers in tourism: Destinations, attractions and events*. Wallingford: Elsevier Butterworth-Heinemann.

Houlihan, B. (2010). Introduction. In B. Houlihan and M. Green (eds) *Routledge handbook of sports development*. Abingdon: Routledge (pp. 5–8).

Independent. (2015). Leading employers prefer work experience over grades says new research. www.independent.co.uk/news/education/education-news/leading-employers-prefer-work-experience-over-grades-says-new-research-10286829.html.

Jarvie, G. (2011). Sport, development and aid: Can sport make a difference? *Sport in Society* 14(2): 241–252.

Johns, C. (2000). *Becoming a reflective practitioner: A reflective and holistic approach to clinical nursing, practice development and clinical supervision*. Oxford: Blackwell Science.

Jones, A. (2011). Theorising international youth volunteering: Training for global (corporate) work? *Transactions of the Institute of British Geographers* 36(4): 530–544.

Kay, T. and Bradbury, S. (2009). Youth sport volunteering: Developing social capital? *Sport, Education and Society* 14(1): 121–140.

Kidd, B. (2008). A new social movement: Sport for development and peace. *Sport in Society* 11(4): 370–380.

Kidd, B. and Donnelly, P. (2007). *Literature reviews on sport for development and peace, sport for development and peace*. www.righttoplay.com/moreinfo/aboutus/Documents/Literature%20Reviews%20SDP.pdf.

Kolb, D. (1984). *Experiential learning: Experience as the source of learning and development*. Englewood Cliffs: Prentice Hall.

Laureus. (2010). *What sport can do for Africa & what Africa can do for sport*. London: Laureus Sport for Good Foundation.

Levermore, R. (2008). Sport in international development: Time to treat it seriously? *Brown Journal of World Affairs* 14(2): 55–66.

Lindsey, I. and Banda, D. (2011). Sport and the fight against HIV/AIDS in Zambia: A 'partnership approach'? *International Review for the Sociology of Sport* 46(1): 90–107.

Lough, B. (2008). International voluntary service. In T. Mizrahi and L. Davis (eds) *Encyclopedia of social work*, 20th edition. Oxford: Oxford University Press and National Association of Social Workers.

Lough, B. (2011). International volunteers' perceptions of intercultural competence. *International Journal of Intercultural Relations* 35(4): 452–464.

Lough, B.J., Sherraden, M.S. and McBride, A.M. (2014). Developing and utilising social capital through international volunteer service. *Voluntary Sector Review* 5(3): 331–344.

McGloin, C. and Georgeou, N. (2016). 'Looks good on your CV': The sociology of voluntourism recruitment in higher education. *Journal of Sociology* 52(2): 403–417.

Morgan, H. (2013). Sport volunteering, active citizenship and social capital enhancement: What role in the 'Big Society'? *International Journal of Sport Policy and Politics* 5(3): 381–395.

Nicholls, S., Giles, A.R. and Sethna, C. (2010). Perpetuating the 'lack of evidence' discourse in sport for development: Privileged voices, unheard stories and subjugated knowledge. *International Review for the Sociology of Sport* 46(3): 249–264.

Plum, E. (2008). *Cultural intelligence: The art of leading cultural complexity*. Cambridge: Middlesex University Press.

Powell, L. (2011). IDEALS evaluation 2011: A report to UK Sport on short-term overseas projects and cultural intelligence: Developing graduates for the 21st century.

Sabatier, P.A. (1988). An advocacy coalition framework of policy change and the role of policy-oriented learning therein. *Policy Sciences* 21(2–3): 129–168.

Schulenkorf, N. (2013). Sport-for-Development events and social capital building: A critical analysis of experiences from Sri Lanka. *Journal of Sport for Development* 1(1): 25–36.

SCORE. (2016). About. www.score.org.za/about/.

Smith, K.A., Baum, T., Holmes, K. and Lockstone-Binney, L. (eds). (2014). *Event volunteering: International perspectives on the event volunteering experience*. London: Routledge.

Spaaij, R., Oxford, S. and Jeanes, R. (2016). Transforming communities through sport? Critical pedagogy and sport for development. *Sport, Education and Society* 21(4): 570–587.

Sugden, J. (2006). Teaching and playing sport for conflict resolution and co-existence in Israel. *International Review for the Sociology of Sport* 41(2): 221–240.

UK Sport. (2016a). People development. www.uksport.gov.uk/our-work/international-relations/people-development.

UK Sport. (2016b). IDEALS Namibia 2016: Programme handbook. Unpublished.

Unicef. (2012). www.unicef.org/infobycountry/namibia_51687.html.

Vella, S.A., Oades, L.G. and Crowe, T.P. (2010). The application of coach leadership models to coaching practice: Current state and future directions. *International Journal of Sports Science & Coaching* 5(3): 425–434.

Chapter 8

International sport volunteering and social legacy

Impact, development and health improvement in Lusaka, Zambia

Fiona Reid and Jennifer Tattersall

Introduction

This chapter will outline initial findings from research undertaken with Zambian non-governmental organizations (NGOs), volunteer peer leaders and other participants in an international sport volunteer social regeneration project. While some of the benefits for UK sport volunteers in similar programmes have been previously documented, less is known about the benefits for the hosts (Ingram, 2011). Therefore, this chapter focuses on the impact of the International Development through Excellence and Leadership in Sport (IDEALS) Advanced project on the destination communities in Lusaka, Zambia. The IDEALS Advanced Project is a volunteer-placement sports-based leadership development exchange programme for young people between the UK and UK Sport's International Development partner countries (see also Fletcher and Cullinane, Chapter 7, this collection). UK student volunteers are paired with communities in Lusaka where Zambian peer leaders (ZPLs) from Sport in Action (SIA) and EduSport have been delivering sport and health education programmes in conjunction with their visiting counterparts since 2006 (Reid and Tattersall, 2013). Findings are critically evaluated to establish the extent to which social impacts have been achieved and which groups and individuals have been most affected by the project. Further, the social legacy of IDEALS is examined and the authors question whether the international sport volunteering project reflects the values of those controlling and sponsoring the project rather than the perspective of the host community (Levermore and Beacom, 2012). Finally, the chapter closes with suggestions for future research into international volunteering in sport for development settings.

Research framework

In 2005, London was awarded the 2012 Olympic Games and part of the bid included a commitment to create an Olympic legacy throughout the world, not just in the UK (Jenkins and France, 2014). Significantly increased funding was therefore channelled into sport for development projects in a number of countries and UK Sport devised the IDEALS programme to further enhance their work (UK Sport, 2009b). This programme had two strands, IDEALS Professional for developing sport professionals in the UK and Africa and IDEALS Advanced for students in higher education in UK universities to undertake volunteer placements in African countries to develop their leadership skills and enhance their global awareness before beginning their professional careers in sport (UK Sport, 2009b). This chapter will focus on the case study of the IDEALS Advanced programme looking at the impact of international volunteering in Lusaka, Zambia.

There are three key characteristics of volunteering: that it should be done willingly, that it should not be done primarily for financial reward (although there may be some recompense) and that it should be for the common good (wider than for one's family or close friends) (Hockenos, 2011). A particular volunteer would be somewhere on a spectrum on each of the characteristics. A sport volunteer carries out the volunteering outlined above in the context of sport. An all-encompassing definition of sport and physical activity applies to the use of the term sport in this chapter. Sport includes 'all forms of physical activity that contribute to physical fitness, mental well-being and social interaction. These include play; recreation; organized, casual or competitive sport; and indigenous sports or games' (United Nations, 2003, p. 2).

The concept of legacy has been widely used in relation to sport and sport events in recent years. Preuss et al. (2007, p. 86) define legacy as 'all planned and unplanned positive and negative, intangible and tangible structures created by and for a sport event that remains for a longer time than the event itself'. Legacy has been defined in relation to sport events, but it can also apply to a sport development programme. In relation to the international legacy of London 2012, a programme of activities over a number of years (similar to leveraging) was designed to leave a lasting legacy (Jenkins and France, 2014). This idea of sustained impacts deriving from a sport intervention gives the main difference between short-term outcomes and a true legacy which would be over a longer time frame (Taks, 2013). A social legacy could consist of the intangible components (see Preuss et al., 2007) but can also include themes of power relations, urban regeneration, socialization and human capital when examining the impacts on communities (Taks, 2013). In terms of sustainability, the triple bottom line approach differentiates between the social, economic and environmental components of legacy (Elkington, 1994).

Legacy is not an uncontested term and it can be difficult to identify and assess. One particular issue is that different stakeholders are affected differently by exactly the same aspects of an event or programme. Exactly the same intervention can produce both positive and negative impacts for different people – or even for the same person at different times (Preuss, 2015). Sometimes this has been described as a double-edged sword (Fredline *et al.*, 2003). Social legacy is rarely planned for and even more rarely is it assessed and monitored effectively (Foley *et al.*, 2012). In the UK, there is no consensus on key social outcome measures resulting from culture and sport interventions. Recently suggested are employment and economic productivity, civic participation, improved health, reduced crime, increased social capital and improved education outcomes (Taylor *et al.*, 2015; Fujiwara *et al.*, 2014). Globally, Taks (2013, p. 125) listed the social impacts of such events as changes being made to: collective and individual value systems; behaviour patterns; community structures; and lifestyle and quality of life.

Sport for development projects suffer from a lack of understanding of social impacts (Kay, 2009). UK Sport (2009c) indicated that the evaluation of its International Sport Development Programmes would be based on measures of:

- efficiency (e.g. cost per activity, cost per participant, ratio of staff to participant);
- effectiveness (outputs and outcomes – e.g. impact of participation on individuals in areas of physical health, life/leadership skills, AIDS awareness and behaviour, improved self-esteem/confidence);
- strategic outcomes (e.g. broader impact of programmes on community, improved perception on quality of life, improved attitude towards another culture).

They recommended using the manual for the monitoring and evaluation of sport for development projects written by Coalter (2006) following field-work in four sport for development programmes in less developed countries. Coalter (2006) explains that rather than achieving outcomes, development should be understood as a process and therefore, the impact of that process of development (whether through sport or by other means) could not be measured though an outcome evaluation method. He advocates process evaluation – and collaborative work where the community both structures and contributes to the tools of assessment and where the wider process of development is to be measured. This does not exactly match the UK Sport indicators above.

Sherraden *et al.* (2013) suggested regarding international student volunteering programmes, the hosts rarely had a significant voice. For example, volunteers were often selected by the university (not by the host organization) and while there was training and preparation for UK Volunteers, the same attention was not paid to host communities or receiving organizations. This lack of attention to host communities was noted across all forms of research into international tourism (Wearing and McGehee, 2013). However, perhaps it is too simple to draw a line between host communities and incoming international volunteers. In analysing a more complex interaction between hosts and visitors, Holmes *et al.* (2010) identified four factors of setting, time commitment, level of obligation, and remuneration to form a framework for evaluating the interactions between international volunteers and communities.

UK Sport International Development Programmes were evaluated in 2014 and a report highlighted several issues with the sport for development concept (Jenkins and France, 2014). They commented on the wide variety of organizations involved and their differing aims and objectives. They concluded that there is a need to develop greater theoretical understanding of the conditions, structures and processes through which sport can promote development (Lyras and Welty Peachey, 2011). The World Bank categorizes countries by their level of development on economic indicators. The countries with the highest levels of those indicators such as GDP, are termed first world or the Global North, those with the lowest levels are referred to as the less developed countries, or the Global South (Levermore and Beacom, 2009). Those countries with a low level of development are the focus of international development aid from those in the Global North. International sport for development programmes have been both praised for utilizing sport as a universal language and criticised for maintaining either old colonial power relationships or generating new power imbalances between the 'Global North' and the 'Global South' (Develtere and De Bruyn, 2009; Hartmann and Kwauk, 2011; Jarvie, 2011).

While there is a widespread belief that sport can be a useful tool in international development (United Nations Sport for Development and Peace Working Group, 2011), there is less evidence to support this. Coalter (2010, pp. 113–114), in assessing impacts of two programmes, concluded that 'there is no clear and systematic "sport-for-development effect"'. In addition, he asserted that there is also no identifiable 'sport effect' as most development programmes included other types of intervention, not purely sport. In addition, there is not a clear conceptualization of what might constitute improvement (and therefore development) within the sport for development literature (Black, 2010).

Sport development can be divided into two types according to its overarching objective. Where its main aim is to improve sport performance or participation levels, it is known as development *of* sport, and where the aim is to use sport to achieve other social, economic or political aims such as improved education or health, it is known as development *through* sport (Houlihan and White, 2002). Coalter (2009) coins the terms 'sport plus' (development of sport) and 'plus sport' (focus on social development through sport) to differentiate between the two types.

The United Nations Sport for Development and Peace International Working Group (2006) identified that sport programmes could contribute to the following aspects of sport for development:

- individual development (improves health, social skills, organisational ability);
- health promotion and disease prevention;
- promotion of gender equality;
- social integration and development of social capital;
- peace building and conflict prevention or resolution;
- post-disaster trauma relief and normalization of life;
- economic development;
- communication and social mobilization.

UNSDPWG (2011, p. 14) outlined five reasons why sport was an appropriate vehicle for achieving the Millennium Development Goals (MDGs):

- Sport has special qualities for engaging young people. Many young people want to be involved, making it a powerful tool for development.
- Sport attracts those who do not respond to other approaches.
- Sport can deliver development outcomes, either as an incentive (e.g. in some programmes children can play sport if they attend school) or through direct delivery (e.g. certain sport-based games act as HIV-AIDS educational tools).
- Sport helps establish productive relationships with adults. Young people are more willing to listen to adults when they have a close relationship with them through sport, than in formal settings where adults are more authoritarian.
- Positive experiences from sport can transfer to other contexts. Young people use the benefits they get from sport in their lives as a whole. Team sports in particular build discipline and self-control to develop personal and social skills.

One specific MDG is to combat HIV/AIDS. Mwaanga (2012, p. 181) sets out the rationales for using sport to combat HIV and AIDS in Sub-Saharan Africa: 'Sport for moral development; Sport as a positive diversion; Sport as a hook; Sport as a means to foster empowerment; Sport as a means to improve health for people living with HIV/AIDS.' Mwaanga (2012) continues to criticize the evidence base for measuring the effectiveness of sport's contribution to programmes. He explains that unequal power relations give credibility to positivist research and facts over other forms of evidence, which may exist in different stakeholders' understandings (Kay, 2009; Jeanes, 2013). He calls for a change in the way that research is carried out to recognize the different voices that should be heard with sport for development. This case study utilizes qualitative research methods to enable a clearer picture of the social legacy of an international volunteering sport-for-development intervention in the local community to be identified.

In 2016, the MDGs were replaced by 17 Sustainable Development Goals (SDGs). The United Nations Office on Sport for Development and Peace outlines how sport can contribute to achieving each of the SDGs (United Nations Office on Sport for Development and Peace, 2016). In the Declaration of the 2030 Agenda for Sustainable Development (United Nations, 2015, p. 10/35) sport is highlighted:

> Sport is also an important enabler of sustainable development. We recognize the growing contribution of sport to the realization of development and peace in its promotion of tolerance and respect and the contributions it makes to the empowerment of women and of young people, individuals and communities as well as to health, education and social inclusion objectives.

Research process and approach

In order to understand the social impacts and legacy for the communities affected by IDEALS, an interpretivist approach was used. The research was based on 'critical realism', which emphasizes the importance of each individual's perception of an independent reality (Ormston *et al.*, 2014, p. 20). The research focused on understanding the perspectives of the Zambians in the communities, and in particular the peer leaders (Kay, 2009). Practical gathering of information about the communities impacted by sport for development is extremely challenging (Jeanes and Lindsey, 2014), furthermore Kay (2012) notes that it might even be culturally impossible for researchers from a different culture.

Interviews and informal discussions were held in Lusaka. These were either digitally recorded and then transcribed, or written into detailed field notes at the time of interview. Interviews were conducted in Zambia between 2011 and 2015. In total, 37 ZPLs, 50 UK Volunteers and staff, eight Zambian NGO staff members, four teachers from the IDEALS sites, one Zambian community sport coach and one Zambian community leader were interviewed. All interviews and discussions were in English, and only the data obtained specific to social impacts and social legacy has been used in this chapter. The material was then interpreted through developing themes which were identified from the literature and also from the materials collected. There were some limitations to this research. The questions asked and the themes investigated were generated by the researchers and theories of sport development or sport for development. The ZPLs did not suggest their perspectives or questions. Those Zambians that the second author had known for the longest were possibly able to speak most freely as trust had developed between them over the years. However, by the fact that those individual peer leaders were still in that role in the project in some cases ten years after their first involvement may indicate that the author was speaking to a very particular group – those who had not moved on into different careers. There are no interviews with ZPLs who may have moved on very quickly. Confidentiality was protected and consent was obtained from those formally interviewed. Pseudonyms[1] are used throughout the chapter to protect anonymity, and in some instances staff cannot be identified by their organization. The next section of the chapter will detail the case study followed by the research findings.

The IDEALS project in Zambia

Zambia already has a large sport for development presence in both local and international agencies (see Lindsey and Banda, 2011; Lindsey and Grattan, 2012), with many of the organizations concentrating on HIV/ AIDS education and prevention (Mwaanga, 2010). This is similar to the IDEALS Advanced programme, the focus of this chapter, which offers university students the opportunity to volunteer during their summer vacation in order to add value to their degree programme, enhance their global awareness and develop their leadership skills and make a difference in the communities they visit as a reciprocal exchange of ideas and culture (UK Sport, 2009b). The additional capacity provided by the volunteers supports the local NGO's work and allows both staff and volunteers from the UK and the hosting country to undertake professional development as they work alongside each other. A group of universities in the UK have been at the core of the IDEALS project in Lusaka, Zambia and annually up to 40 students volunteer there for an 18-week period (three groups for six weeks each). The universities involved are known as the Wallace Group and are Durham, Loughborough, Bath, Northumbria, Cardiff Metropolitan, St Andrews and Stirling. Each of the universities selects a group of four or five current students, through a process of written application and oral and practical interview. They must have a strong background in sport or PE teaching and be able to work with young people and deliver quality sports sessions.

IDEALS in Zambia works alongside two NGOs – SIA and EduSport, who organize and administer activity programmes. Both have broad aims to use sport and activity to better people's quality of lives with a specific focus on HIV and life skills education. Criticisms of the concept of sport being a useful tool in this process have been focused on the low level of understanding of why the participation in sport or involvement in sport activity should lead to lower infection rates of HIV/AIDS (Long and

Sanderson, 2001). Both organizations use the peer-leader method to facilitate sport and health education. Peer-leader education in relation to HIV/AIDS has been found to be an effective way to influence the behaviour and decision-making of young people (Kay *et al.*, 2012). HIV/AIDS life skills that are developed through sport come through the process of a participant's subjective interaction with coaches, leaders, teammates, parents, friends and organizations (Banda, 2011; Mwaanga, 2010). For example, social support through mentorship programmes and youth peer support is present in all sport programmes at EduSport and SIA.

The aims of the IDEALS Advanced project, while professing to focus on partnerships and reciprocity, are clearly based on UK international development policy and the needs of UK Volunteers. The core values of IDEALS have remained 'aiming to build mutual respect and understanding between young people from the UK and Zambia'. These core values are, according to UK Sport (2006, p. 8):

- Mutuality and reciprocity – Working together with a shared responsibility (resources, skills, knowledge and experience) for the project.
- Partnership – An equitable balance between the partner organisations including shared agendas, purpose, resources and accountability.
- Sustainability – To have a long-term impact upon the communities within which it is operating and to develop sustainable networks.
- Global citizenship – Gaining an understanding of global factors and local issues which are present in all our lives, localities and communities through learning about their position and role in relation to the world in which we live.
- Diversity and equity – Ability to be included in the programme irrespective of background or resources.
- Personal development – Willingness to work in different ways and to be receptive to new ideas and demonstrate an openness to change.

Furthermore, in 2016, based on the Wallace Group (2016) report, the aims of the project were listed as:

- To provide university students the opportunity to add value to their degree programme and develop their leadership through short term volunteer placements in an overseas environment.
- To enable the Wallace Group of Universities to develop long term mutually beneficial relationships between the UK and Zambia.
- To enhance leadership and sports specific development for Zambian young people, leaders and organizations.
- To build capacity and knowledge sharing between the UK HEIs and Zambian organisations and capture good practice examples through case studies and reports.

The IDEALS project offers practical experience for UK students in delivering PE and sports coaching. It aims to develop the volunteers' leadership abilities, citizenship skills and cultural understanding and to contribute to the mentoring and training of peer leaders in Zambia. Overall, there is an ambition to make a positive impact on the lives of the children and young people in Lusaka through the sport and activity programmes. Additionally, it develops inter-university links, connects students, develops cross-cultural understanding, and has been found to increase the employability of students who have volunteered (Powell, 2011).

UK Volunteers have training over a series of events during the academic year in the UK and fundraise to support their participation in the IDEALS programme which is also partly funded by UK Sport and the universities. Once in Lusaka, the UK Volunteers join with ZPLs. ZPLs are local volunteers and based at a specific site or location – for example a school or compound. The sites are either run by SIA or EduSport and are distributed throughout Lusaka, all in very deprived communities. Table 8.1 shows the names of the sites, their nature and the NGO responsible for sport activity at that site. Throughout the year, ZPLs deliver an activity programme at their site, which involves both Zambian games and specific sports. During the 18 weeks when IDEALS is involved, pairs of UK Volunteers team up with a ZPL at a specific site/placement location. The ZPLs works alongside three different pairs of UK Volunteers as they change every six weeks. A regular highlight and key focus for UK Volunteers, ZPLs and children is the Wallace Tournament, in which placement sites compete against one another in the four sports of football, netball, volleyball and basketball.

Two team leaders (more experienced, returning UK Volunteers) spend the entire 18 weeks of the project in Lusaka and are the key support and organizing team for the UK Volunteers. They are also the point of contact between the UK Volunteers and NGO staff, as well as link between the UK Volunteers and the university staff and directors. In addition, university staff members (in paid positions) take turns to spend around three weeks at a time living with, observing and supporting UK Volunteers, or just joining in as required. Each NGO has a management and staff structure, and an office base in Lusaka. Office and management staff work alongside UK Volunteers as necessary and more closely with university staff members. Across the diverse range of staff and volunteers from both Zambia and UK, a mix of different interactions and engagements occurs throughout the annual project and to a lesser extent beyond that time.

The IDEALS project and wider sport for development in Zambia have been the subject of research and evaluation reports. For example, UK Sport commissioned annual evaluations of IDEALS (White and Goshall, 2006, 2007, 2009) and internal annual summary reports (Campbell, 2008; UK Sport, 2010, 2011, 2012b, 2013), a student employability study (Powell, 2011), and a ten-year evaluation in 2015 (Banda, 2015). These highlighted

Table 8.1 IDEALS placement sites in Lusaka from 2006 to 2016 (sites were involved at various times, for different lengths of time)

Placement site	Format	NGO responsible	Activities/aims
Munali	Cluster of approximately seven government and community schools (around Munali Secondary School)	Sport in Action	One of SIA's centres for sports excellence
Fountain of Hope	Community school and centre for street kids	Sport in Action	Sport delivered in afternoon, often with social messages
Chipata	Open community school (government school in poor and densely populated area)	Sport in Action	School sport, PE and Zambian traditional games plus disability attention
St Patrick's	Government school (all girls)	Sport in Action	PE and school sport
Mtendere	Community school	Sport in Action	School sport
Burma	Government school	Sport in Action	School sport
Chibolya	Government school	Sport in Action	School sport
Kalingalinga	One government school and two community schools	EduSport	Sports and PE sessions in schools and community sports ground
Chawama	Group of schools in district	EduSport	School sport and community sport
Bauleni	Group of schools close to pitches	EduSport	Mainly community sport – football
Chilenje	Two government schools and one community school	EduSport	Sports and PE sessions in schools and community sports ground
Ngombe	Group of schools and community sports ground	EduSport	Mainly football and netball

Sources: adapted from Banda, 2015; Reid and Tattersall, 2013; UK Sport, 2006, 2009a, 2012a, 2014, 2016.

issues, mostly from the perspectives of the UK universities or students, for example, identify that there was insufficient training about HIV/AIDS for UK Volunteers prior to arriving in Lusaka. Banda (2015) gave a more critical insight and brought up difficulties relating to mutuality, reciprocity and local decision-making that limited the impact of the project on the communities in Lusaka.

In 2015 the first Zambian National Sport Development Conference was held in order to coincide with the tenth anniversary of the IDEALS project. This Conference was supported by the Zambian Government, Ministry of Youth and Sport, Ministry of Education, Science, Vocational Training and Early Education and it was hosted at the Olympic Youth Development Centre (OYDC) in Lusaka. At the conference it was stated that over the ten years of IDEALS, approximately 150 ZPLs and community coaches received education through workshops or coaching clinics. Furthermore, it was also claimed that over 3,000 children attending the after-school sports had developed leadership skills and health and life skills through IDEALS (Zambian Government, 2015). Whilst the status of sport for development and the local NGOs had risen due to the involvement of international partners and funders such as UK Sport to enable this to take place (Banda, 2015) and the descriptive statistics are impressive (albeit a lack of clarity of evidencing the statistics) what is less clear is to what extent has the education offered been effective as there has been little attempt to assess the learning and aims/goals of IDEALS as indicated earlier in the chapter.

Social impacts through IDEALS

As would be expected the aims of the IDEALS project reflect a UK-centric view of international development and of sport development. It is also clear that much of the knowledge of the project relates to the UK Volunteers, meaning that there is limited understanding of the NGO and community perspectives. Hence the focus of this chapter is on the host communities (i.e. the people in Lusaka who experience the international volunteering). The programme is managed year-round by EduSport and SIA, however there is no clear data from either NGO on the numbers or impacts of their programmes either for the period when UK Volunteers are visiting or throughout the year. It is apparent that there are hundreds of children and young people who attend the sport programmes in the schools and communities where UK Volunteers and ZPLs are coaching sport. The numbers of children attending are very varied – even from day to day or week to week in the same place. Where the coaching takes place within a compound there can be a structured class, but suddenly 100 (or so) extra young people can appear from around the compound and join in. It is also unclear whether this is a phenomenon because of the *mzungu*[2] presence or that this is a normal occurrence.

There are three main stakeholder groups of people in Zambia who are impacted by the IDEALS project: the ZPLs, Zambian NGO (paid) staff and the children taking part in the sporting activities. This section will discuss each stakeholder in turn. ZPLs are volunteers from their community who deliver the sports and activity programmes. They are young leaders who give their time and energy to teach, coach and motivate the next generation of young people. They are in education if circumstances allow, but may also be out of education and without paid employment. Each ZPL has a slightly different story and living situation, but generally they are similar to the young people they coach and are either in school or further education or would like to be. ZPLs become part of the activity programmes through different avenues. Most have been participants in the community sports programme themselves, they have shown an interest in teaching and often been inspired by another peer leader who taught them. ZPLs are volunteers and some reasons and motivations for becoming a peer leader are reported as:

> I was inspired by my facilitator and thought of becoming one in my community.
>
> (Francis, ZPL from Kalingalinga)

> I became a peer leader because I had so much interest in sport and I really wanted to help in the development of the kids.
>
> (Peter, ZPL from Munali)

> I was always interested to assist working with and teaching young people.
>
> (Brian, ZPL from Mtendere)

For those who have been participants in the NGO programme they can ask to become a peer leader or they can be invited by an existing peer leader who identifies their potential. Some ZPLs take on the role as they have finished their education (either completed or unable to pay further) and want something to do, for example:

> Being a peer leader is something to do and I love sports.
>
> (Mary, ZPL from Munali)

> The kids see me as a role model, and the kids listen to me.
>
> (Lembe, ZPL from Kalingalinga)

> I finished school and had nothing to do ... (I have) been a peer leader for one year ... it is something to do and I love sports ... the kids respect me and see me as a role model.
>
> (Daniel, ZPL from Chilenje)

Some ZPLs hope that SIA or EduSport will support their education or that they will gain a sponsor from the IDEALS students, to enable them to continue their studies. There is clearly a dynamic between ZPLs and the UK Volunteers with some ZPLs and UK Volunteers becoming 'best of friends' during their six-week encounter and then remain in occasional contact through social media. Although the ZPLs are very different culturally, geographically, socially and educationally from the UK Volunteers, both groups speak highly of the mutual learning that takes place and impacts on each other. For example, Mark (UK volunteer) explained that 'there is no better way of learning about different perspectives'. Lembe (ZPL from Kalingalinga) spoke about the UK Volunteers and said: 'you're like a catalyst ... (we) teach each other – plant knowledge in each other's heads'. Gemma (UK Volunteer) suggested that 'good friendships based on mutual respect and understandings are the perfect base for learning to occur both ways'. Sophie (UK Volunteer) spoke highly of the Zambian children she encountered: 'The attitudes are incredible. Positivity in the face of hardship, fun, appreciative and willingness to learn are all attitudes that I hope I personally can learn from and attempt to develop into my pupils in this country.'

More subtle changes and benefits are in areas such as enhanced global awareness and cultural intelligence. ZPLs spend time with UK Volunteers and this allows dialogue and cross-cultural learning to take place. Zambians and UK Volunteers are able to describe and explain their different daily lives and for each to express their future plans and goals. They gain knowledge and become more mindful of cultural differences through their cross-cultural interactions and experiences. It is not known what the ZPLs' perception of the cultural differences implies for their future behaviour and decision-making. The interviews were not able to glean information of enough depth for that. Each year, ZPLs are offered continuous professional development workshops tutored by UK Volunteers and staff members. These are normally on a topic of particular expertise of the individual tutor from the UK, although sometimes that is mapped to a request from NGO or UK Volunteers (from a previous year) for a particular subject. An example was a goal-setting workshop for ZPLs in 2014. This was identified as a need by previous years' volunteers and staff. However, during delivery of the workshop it became clear that a Western concept of goal setting – with structured thinking and SMARTER criteria was not part of the dominant Zambian culture.

In the longer term, ZPLs may be supported by UK Volunteers on their return to the UK, by sponsoring them through further education or supporting them as they complete their higher or further education whilst maintaining a commitment to the sports delivery at their site. This investment can come from a number of external sources and last for a varying length of time. Individual 'alumni' of IDEALS support different ZPLs, either directly, or via associated charities (e.g. Umutima and Perfect Day Foundation) or formally through the NGOs. This investment in their education would allow ZPLs to complete their secondary education and/or to take on further study or practical training. This could mean completing year 12 (end of secondary school) or training to be a teacher or learning a trade. By the very nature of this type of investment in people, their ability to engage with and complete the education pathway they are put on will then determine the longer-term impact on their lives and livelihoods.

A few ZPLs have had the opportunity to visit the UK and take part in the IDEALS induction process. This is seen as a real honour and something peer leaders aspire to be asked to do. Additional benefits of being a peer leader include one or two being selected for other foreign exchange programmes. Four ZPLs are notable examples of where starting with Edu-Sport or SIA as a peer leader has allowed them to seize opportunities that have arisen and given them life experiences well beyond their home environment. Jacob (ZPL from Kalingalinga) was supported through higher education in the UK and is now working in Lusaka. Robert (ZPL from Kalingalinga) has been able to travel to the UK as an ambassador for the project and undertaken a placement in Norway. He also spent a year studying sport development and management at a university in Norway (UK Sport, 2012c). Esther, a ZPL from St Patrick's, explained that she 'finished school but (I could) not afford to study so (I) work for SIA. (I have) now worked for four or five years'. Esther wanted to work for SIA because she 'loves the children … I want to be a teacher … I hope SIA will pay for a course so I can become a teacher'. She has now progressed to be a site co-ordinator for her school/area (a paid position). Further, Esther has been to Finland to work on a specific project and to Brazil for a football project at the World Cup. One of the aims of the IDEALS project is the development of ZPLs (Wallace Group, 2016).

Some of the desired behaviour changes (desired by the UK Volunteers and the NGO staff and IDEALS Project management team) are improvements in timekeeping, coaching planning, organization and structure and the sport-specific coaching content. In particular UK Volunteers expressed frustration that valuable time appears to be wasted through cancellation of sessions, poor timetabling of classes and that ZPLs and school staff were not following the prearranged plan. This is noted repeatedly in the IDEALS Summary Reports (Campbell, 2008; UK Sport, 2010, 2011, 2012a, 2013). A cultural difference appears to exist here between Zambians and people from the UK. Instead of agreeing a time to meet, or a length of time for a lesson, in Zambian culture this is a more free-flowing concept where a meeting is at some point in the morning (or day), or a lesson can continue as long as it needs to. This conceptual difference between 'Zambian time' and 'UK time' is not fully understood by either group.

Through discussion with Robert (ZPL based in Kalingalinga) we learnt of his change in attitude to timekeeping and punctuality. There is an inherent attitude to time and punctuality in Zambia which means that being somewhere 'on time' as it is seen in the UK, is of very little consequence in a Zambian culture. Through interaction with UK Volunteers, Robert has come to see that more can be done and achieved if some level of timekeeping and routine is developed. He explained:

> If I set a time I'll be there, definitely be there and if I am late I'll call him before so he knows, before I'd say he'll wait for me, but how many times will he wait? It is wasted time.

This is a big change in the behaviour of ZPLs, which became more evident over the 18 weeks of the project, at a number of other sites (e.g. Chipata and Fountain of Hope) and in different ZPLs. Samuel, a senior NGO staff member, said 'Zambian (peer) leaders up their game, for example in terms of being punctual. Trying to align themselves to Northern ideological views about how projects go'. However, what is less clear is the extent to which this continues after the UK Volunteers have left. Year-on-year evidence suggests that the change of behaviour is not permanent for most ZPLs, as when volunteers return the following June timekeeping is not at the desired level. These behaviour changes are looked for in ZPLs as a sign of their suitability for further investment (for example, in funding for education) or in opportunities for paid work. Exceptional ZPLs such as Robert appear to retain the behaviour changes and these are the ZPLs that may be selected for further development.

The impacts on ZPLs depend on their own input and the placement site (different sites tend to have an expectation and norm as to what is expected of the ZPLs). At IDEALS sites where the ZPLs are rarely present or show little engagement there is limited impact on the ZPLs. The level of engagement depends on a number of factors such as the ZPL's character, commitment, time available, language ability and personal relationship with the UK Volunteers amongst other things. At those placement sites where UK Volunteers and ZPLs are enthusiastic, committed and open to work hard and learn from one another, then significant impacts on both are evident.

The project had personal impacts on a number of ZPLs. For instance, Levy (ZPL at Fountain of Hope) was living on the street and when he became a peer leader, this gave him the opportunity to have a home, obtain schooling and find employment. Charles (ZPL at Kalingalinga), explained that his involvement in the project gave him a form of community status, stating 'everyone knows me'. Furthermore, this was echoed by Francis (ZPL in Kalingalinga) who said 'I feel like a celebrity' in the community. Overall the ZPLs interviewed positively conveyed that the IDEALS project had a strong social impact on them due to spending time with international sport volunteers from the UK.

The programmes undertaken by the Zambian NGOs are year-round sport-for-development projects that work with schools and community groups on HIV education and sport. These programmes have a strong focus on peer leaders and use peer leaders from within communities to deliver their aims to children and young people. Overall, the NGO staff generally responded to questions or discussions with positive comments about the involvement of IDEALS but almost never give any constructive suggestions for improvements to the project. There is also little evidence of any project monitoring by the NGOs. This is despite EduSport's involvement in a detailed four-year evaluation project with Brunel University for one of its other programmes – Go Sisters (Kay *et al.*, 2012). In that, innovative methods of evaluating impacts on the peer leaders and participants were used, including ongoing training of NGO staff to conduct the evaluation and monitoring independently of the researchers.

The involvement of IDEALS and UK Sport appears to have had some impact on senior staff within the NGOs. Consequently, there is increased prestige and funding for the organizations not only from the UK but also from the Zambian Government. For example, the founder of the NGO SIA (Clement Chileshe) is now the Director of the OYDC, reflecting his status increasing over the duration of the IDEALS project. The NGO staff numbers have also increased since 2006, although IDEALS is not their only project. In the interview with Stanley, a senior NGO staff member perceived that ZPLs have been able to progress in their careers. The NGO did not have a tracking system in place, so he did not have evidence of where the ZPLs moved on to, but he felt he had seen an improvement for them on the ground. He indicated that the capacity of the organisation had grown with more participants in programmes, more ZPLs and more young ZPLs. His comments on evaluating the impact of the programmes on the ZPLs revealed the lack of focus on the details. When asked, he reflected that it was 'hard to tell the impact (IDEALS) had as you are dealing with people's lives. When we look back to 2006 and where we are today, it is just another thing completely'. He continued 'you can just see!' the differences in ZPLs over the time of their involvement.

Other NGO senior staff members explained:

> We very happy with the programme, it is very good, (we) see capacity build of the peer leaders, but would like more scholarships and sponsorship.
>
> (Fred)

> See the impact, don't need statistics, see on the participants and on the peer leaders. When they call you *mzungu* that is good but when they

call your name and invite you to their house – then you know you've had an impact ... don't doubt you are having an impact – I know you are ... keep coming, you do make a difference.

(Leo)

Some children and young people have been participants in the programme and then become young leaders, ZPLs and then site co-ordinators, progressing through a pathway. Of course this pathway is only available to a few. UK Volunteers get to know particular children who are regular attenders – particularly if they are in the sport performance orientated programmes – and speculatively, there might be a greater impact on them. A few children return year on year, but we do not know what impact the UK Volunteers have had on them. It is suggested that the presence of the UK Volunteers has the greatest impact on the ZPLs, an important effect on the NGO staff but limited impact on the children and communities. Despite the short time that each UK Volunteer is in Lusaka, there appears to be a lasting impression on both UK Volunteers and ZPLs. Levy (ZPL from Fountain of Hope) supports this by stating that 'I stay in touch with past students. They are like a family' (UK Sport, 2012d, p. 4).

The many layered and multi-faceted nature of the project allows for a broad but also sometimes a deep level of interaction and engagement between individuals and groups. Short and intense, as well as longer and more gradual relationships develop between ZPLs, UK staff and volunteers, NGO staff and other staff such as teachers in Zambia. It is these different relationships and interactions which shape the impact of this sports development project and are the key to explaining and understanding the social legacy of the sports volunteering initiative. Social legacy will be discussed next.

Social legacy

For the social impacts discussed in the section above to be considered legacy, there has to be an element of sustainability or longevity. Often the concept of legacy is used in relation to one single event. In this case study, the legacy is of a long-term programme which is a series of 18-week events that take place annually. The legacy is difficult to assess within the timescale of just ten years, as it would be better done over a number of decades. There were also unclear legacy targets set when the project began, for the research to be measured against. However, in this section, an attempt will be made to assess the extent to which any of the social impacts already identified could be considered a legacy. The legacy could comprise of both positive and negative impacts which could result from the same intervention. Since 2006 there have been improvements in general population-level health, education and infection rates of HIV/AIDS in Zambia, but it is not possible to link the contribution of one small project to these big datasets (Central Statistical Office, 2015).

The IDEALS project has brought with it a number of new facility developments, including multisport facilities at four SIA sites and new netball courts. Increasingly, past UK Volunteers have contributed to the upgrading of sporting infrastructure. In 2016, there were at least three different ongoing building projects to construct a netball court, a beach volleyball court, a kitchen and a toilet block (Warburton, 2016). The infrastructure constructed could be viewed as a longer term impact as the facilities will still be available for use in a number of years. However, Banda (2015) notes that the participation rates in sport are much higher when the UK Volunteers are involved and that the competitive structure is focused around that time. It may be that the new facilities are not needed outside the visits of the UK Volunteers. In addition, refurbishment of one of the courts built has already been required (after five years) and it is questionable whether they are sustainable in the longer term. The summary report compiled by SIA (UK Sport, 2012a) highlights the infrastructural improvements as important for performance and safe participation. There is certainly an appetite from UK Volunteers to contribute through infrastructure projects and this has been increasing over the life of IDEALS.

Another legacy for the Zambian communities involved in the IDEALS project has been attributed to paintings at the school or site facilities. Generally, the assistance of the UK Volunteers is welcomed, and walls have sometimes been painted by UK Volunteers with their names, or the project's nickname for the site (or with the name of their university on it). This is sometimes photographed by the UK Volunteers, perhaps with them and some Zambians standing in front of it – thus providing the UK Volunteers with a permanent memento of their visit. Lisa (UK Volunteer) explained: 'It looks nice to have a photo of it on your wall.' However, Lembe (ZPL from Kalingalinga) was upset by the practice 'because it's *my* community. Just because *mzungu* come and buy paint does not mean (they) can write (their) name on walls'. In an IDEALS Summary Report (UK Sport, 2011, p. 10), it is further noted that while the painted walls are 'a lovely legacy for the IDEALS groups', the communities have commented that they may be 'a little messy and sometimes not very professional'. The report went on to recommend that in the future, wall owners should be consulted about the designs and should be active participants in the painting.

Sports equipment such as footballs, basketballs, basketball hoops, netballs and volleyballs, nets/net-posts is donated or replaced annually by UK Sport and the universities. While photographs of players competing in the tournaments in university strips make for excellent publicity material, the reality is that young people cannot continue to have access to the sporting equipment if these programmes are not maintained. UK Volunteers often find that as well as the official equipment that they transport from their universities, ZPLs and children ask for clothes and other equipment. Replica football shirts and trainers are highly prized by the young Zambians. UK Volunteers may choose to return home with only the clothes they are wearing.

These gifts of equipment and clothing do not last long enough to become a legacy. But is the act of giving and receiving something that remains for longer in the psyche of the donor and recipient? For example, does the UK Volunteer remember giving and being able to help the poorer Zambians and does the young Zambian always remember the visitor from the UK who had so much more than them? Could this be a legacy of inequality? The messages sent to the local communities are of an influx of equipment and better-off UK Volunteers. One local community leader was asked what support the community would most like to have. His answer did not mention the need for footballs, nor a netball court, but instead 'garbage and drainage'. Perhaps in terms of international development, consideration of what the communities themselves most desire must be taken into account before aid money is spent on what the donor wishes to support. A change from a top-down approach where the donor offers what it thinks is best, to a bottom-up approach where the local community decides what kind of assistance is most appropriate (Banda, 2015; Black, 2010) would result in a more sustainable lasting legacy.

The greatest impact of the IDEALS project is on the ZPLs who spend the most time with UK Volunteers. In terms of the long-term legacy, it is less clear who might remain affected. However, the impact is not evenly distributed and depends on a number of factors, in particular the ZPLs and their engagement with the project. The way that behavioural changes occur could be further researched. The close working relationship between ZPLs and UK Volunteers appears to be an important factor, but the mechanisms influencing behavioural change and cross-cultural development are less clear. Education seems to be a central aim – both for the ZPLs but also as a means of creating impact. Education by its nature has a longer term impact and that could definitely constitute a legacy. The NGO staff had no evidence for believing that the ZPLs had been impacted, but they felt this had been the case.

Conclusion and recommendations

This case study has illustrated the small but significant impact that an international sport volunteering project can have on communities. Findings illustrated that investment was appreciated by the host community as it enhanced their sport participation programmes and allowed sport performance to be improved. The ZPLs were able to access education and training which otherwise would not have been available to them – giving some of them opportunities to develop their careers. The changes in their own behaviour that the ZPLs reflected upon and that were noticed by UK Volunteers could be important in allowing the sport coaching and health messages to be better conveyed, for example by more organized sessions, better content within coaching sessions and improved timekeeping. However, could all of these impacts be viewed as continuing a power imbalance between the Global North and the Global South? Is it the wish of the Zambian host communities to improve in that way or is it rather the focus of the UK agencies? In that case, the social legacy could be instead interpreted as one of aid from the UK and imposition of Western cultural norms and values on the communities.

Bearing in mind the fact that the same interventions can have both positive and negative impacts on different people, it is very hard to evaluate the social legacy of the programme. Instead we suggest that the evaluation of projects should be built in to the development of them in the first place and that those impacted (the hosts) should design the evaluation tools and determine the aims and objectives to be measured. Process evaluation could be a very valuable tool if desired by the host community. The involvement of local researchers from the community, or training of those on the programme to be evaluators, should be a priority for future research. Researchers from outside the culture may not be the best-placed people to discover impacts or interpret changes in behaviour or conduct interviews.

Notes

1 Common names from Lusaka and UK have been assigned to those interviewed – no real names are used.
2 *Mzungu* means white person.

References

Banda, D. (2011). Sport in action: Young people, sex education and HIV/Aids in Zambia. In B. Houlihan and M. Green (eds) *Handbook of sport development*. London: Routledge (pp. 323–336).
Banda, D. (2015). *Process evaluation of IDEALS Advanced programme 2015*. London: UK Sport.
Black, D. (2010). The ambiguities of development: implications for 'development through sport'. *Sport in Society* 13(1): 121–129.
Campbell, F. (2008). *IDEALS summary report 2008*. London: UK Sport.
Central Statistical Office. (2015). *Zambia – demographic and health survey 2013–14: Key findings*. Lusaka: Zambian Government.
Coalter, F. (2006). *Sport-in-development: A monitoring and evaluation manual*. London: UK Sport.
Coalter, F. (2009). Sport-in-development: Accountability or development? In R. Levermore and A. Beacom (eds) *Sport and international development*. London: Palgrave Macmillan (pp. 55–75).

Coalter, F. (2010). Sport-for-development: Going beyond the boundary? *Sport in Society* 13(9): 1374–1391.

Develtere, P. and de Bruyn, T. (2009). The emergence of the fourth pillar of development aid. *Development in Practice* 19(7): 912–922.

Elkington, J. (1994). Towards the sustainable corporation: Win–win–win business strategies for sustainable development. *California Management Review* 36(2): 90–100.

Foley, M., McGillivray, D. and McPherson, G. (2012). Policy pragmatism: Qatar and the global events circuit. *International Journal of Event and Festival Management* 3(1): 101–115.

Fredline, E., Jago, L. and Deery, M. (2003). The development of a generic scale to measure the social impacts of events. *Event Management* 8: 22–37.

Fujiwara, D., Kudrna, L. and Dolan, P. (2014). *Quantifying the social impacts of culture and sport*. London: Department for Media, Culture and Sport.

Hartmann, D. and Kwauk, C. (2011). Sport and development: An overview, critique, and reconstruction. *Journal of Sport & Social Issues* 35(3): 284–305.

Houlihan, B. and White, A. (2002). *The politics of sports development*. London: Routledge.

Hockenos, P. (ed.). (2011). *State of the world volunteerism report*. Denmark: United Nations Volunteers.

Holmes, K., Smith, K.M., Lockstone-Binney, L. and Baum, T.G. (2010). Developing the dimensions of tourism volunteering. *Leisure Sciences* 32(3): 255–268.

Ingram, J. (2011). Volunteer tourism: How do we know it is 'making a difference'? In A. Benson (ed.) *Volunteer tourism: Theory framework to practical applications*. London: Routledge (pp. 211–222).

Jarvie, G. (2011). Sport, development and aid: Can sport make a difference? *Sport in Society* 14(2): 241–252.

Jeanes, R. (2013). Educating through sport? Examining HIV/AIDS education and sport-for-development through the perspectives of Zambian young people. *Sport, Education and Society* 18(3): 388–406.

Jeanes, R. and Lindsey, I. (2014). Where's the evidence? Reflecting on monitoring and evaluation within sport-for-development. In K. Young and C. Okada (eds) *Sport, social development and peace*. Bingley: Emerald Group Publishing Limited (pp. 197–217).

Jenkins, S. and France, J. (2014). *Final evaluation of the International Inspiration programme*. UK: Ecorys.

Kay, T. (2009). Developing through sport: Evidencing sport impacts on young people. *Sport in Society* 12(9): 1177–1191.

Kay, T. (2012). Accounting for legacy: Monitoring and evaluation in sport in development relationships. *Sport in Society* 15(6): 888–904.

Kay, T., Jeanes, R. and Mansfield, L. (2012). *Evaluation of Go Sisters Zambia: Year 3 annual research report*. London: Brunel University.

Levermore, R. and Beacom, A. (2009). *Sport and international development*. London: Palgrave Macmillan.

Levermore, R. and Beacom, A. (2012). Reassessing sport-for-development: Moving beyond 'mapping the territory'. *International Journal of Sport Policy and Politics* 4(1): 125–137.

Lindsey, I. and Banda, D. (2011). Sport and the fight against HIV/AIDS in Zambia: A 'partnership approach'? *International Review for the Sociology of Sport* 46(1): 90–107.

Lindsey, I. and Grattan, A. (2012). An 'international movement'? Decentring sport-for-development within Zambian communities. *International Journal of Sport Policy and Politics* 4(1): 91–110.

Long, J. and Sanderson, I. (2001). The social benefit of sport: where's the proof? In C. Gratton and I.P. Henry (eds) *Sport in the city: The role of sport in economic and social regeneration*. London: Routledge (pp. 187–203).

Lyras, A. and Welty Peachey, J. (2011). Integrating sport-for-development theory and praxis. *Sport Management Review* 14(4): 311–326.

Mwaanga, O. (2010). Sport for addressing HIV/AIDS: Explaining our convictions. *Leisure Studies Association Newsletter* 85(March): 61–67.

Mwaanga, O. (2012). Sport for addressing HIV/AIDS: Examining rationales. In K. Gilbert and W. Bennett (eds) *Sport, peace and development*. Champaign: Common Ground (pp. 179–192).

Ormston, R., Spencer, L., Barnard, M. and Snape, D. (2014). The foundations of qualitative research. In J. Ritchie, J. Lewis, C. McNaughton Nicholls and R. Ormston (eds) *Qualitative research practice*, 2nd edition. London: Sage (pp. 1–26).

Powell, L. (2011). *Short-term overseas projects and cultural intelligence: Developing graduates for the 21st century*. London: UK Sport.

Preuss, H. (2015). A framework for identifying the legacies of a mega sport event. *Leisure Studies* 34(6): 643–664.

Preuss, H., Seguin, B. and O'Reilly, N. (2007). Profiling major sport event visitors: The 2002 Commonwealth Games. *Journal of Sport & Tourism* 12(1): 5–23.

Reid, F. and Tattersall, J. (2013). Exploring some different perspectives within a sports project in Africa. In G. Reid and J. Lee (eds) *Social justice in sport development*. Eastbourne: Leisure Studies Association (pp. 17–34).

Sherraden, M., Bopp, A. and Lough, B. (2013). Students serving abroad: A framework for enquiry. *Journal of Higher Education Outreach and Engagement* 17(2): 7–43.

Taks, M. (2013). Social sustainability of non-mega sport events in a global world. *European Journal for Sport and Society* 10(2): 121–141.

Taylor, P., Davies, L., Wells, P., Gilbertson, J. and Tayleur, W. (2015). *A review of the social impacts of culture and sport*. London: Department for Media, Culture and Sport.

UK Sport. (2006). *IDEALS advanced handbook*. London: UK Sport.

UK Sport. (2009a). *IDEALS advanced handbook*. London: UK Sport.

UK Sport. (2009b). *International sport development: IDEALS*. UK Sport. http://webarchive.nationalarchives.gov.uk/20090105001140/http://uksport.gov.uk/pages/ideals/.

UK Sport. (2009c). *International sport development: Monitoring international sport development*. http://webarchive.nationalarchives.gov.uk/20090105001140/http://uksport.gov.uk/pages/monitoring_and_evaluation/.

UK Sport. (2010). *IDEALS summary report 2010*. London: UK Sport.

UK Sport. (2011). *IDEALS summary report 2011*. London: UK Sport.

UK Sport. (2012a). *IDEALS advanced handbook*. London: UK Sport.

UK Sport. (2012b). *IDEALS summary report 2012*. London: UK Sport.

UK Sport. (2012c). *IDEALS peer leader case study 1*. London: UK Sport.

UK Sport. (2012d). *IDEALS peer leader case study 2*. London: UK Sport.

UK Sport. (2013). *IDEALS summary report 2013*. London: UK Sport.

UK Sport. (2014). *IDEALS advanced handbook*. London: UK Sport.

UK Sport. (2016). *IDEALS Zambia 2016, volunteer handbook*. London: UK Sport.

United Nations. (2003). *Report from the United Nations Inter-Agency Task Force on Sport for Development and Peace*. Geneva: United Nations.

United Nations. (2015). *Resolution 70/1 transforming our world: The 2030 agenda for sustainable development*. Geneva: United Nations.

United Nations Office on Sport for Development and Peace. (2016). *Sport and sustainable development goals*. www.un.org/sport/content/why-sport/sport-and-sustainable-development-goals.

United Nations Sport for Development and Peace International Working Group. (2006). *Sport for development and peace: From practice to policy*. Toronto: United Nations.

United Nations Sport for Development and Peace Working Group. (2011). Session II: Sport as a catalyst for achieving the MDGs – implementation perspective. *2nd International Forum for Peace and Development*. www.un.org/wcm/webdav/site/sport/shared/sport/pdfs/Reports/10-11.05.2011_UN-IOC_FORUM_Geneva_REPORT_EN.pdf.

Wallace Group. (2016). *Wallace Group Zambia: About the Wallace Group*. www.wallacegroupuniversities.com/about/4587968166.

Warburton, P. (2016). Wallace Group blog: My 2016 visit to Zambia – brief but memorable! www.wallacegroupuniversities.com/blog/4590438188/My-2016-visit-to-Zambia-%E2%80%93-brief-but-memorable/10846689.

Wearing, S. and McGehee, N.G. (2013). Volunteer tourism: A review. *Tourism Management* 38: 120–130.

White, A. and Goshall, C. (2006). IDEALS evaluation 2006, report to UK Sport. London: UK Sport.

White, A. and Goshall, C. (2007). IDEALS evaluation 2007, report to UK Sport. London: UK Sport.

White, A. and Goshall, C. (2009). IDEALS evaluation 2009, report to UK Sport. London: UK Sport.

Zambian Government. (2015). *Zambian National Sport Development Conference 2015 Programme*. Lusaka: Zambian Government.

Chapter 9

Learning about sport for development and peace through international volunteers

Mike Bartle and Peter Craig

Introduction

This chapter aims to extend an understanding of the role of international volunteers involved in sport for development and peace (SDP) programmes and activities. At one level, it is a logical extension of neo-liberalism attached to the value and legacy of sport as a tool for international development (Sugden, 2014). Assumptions about international volunteer competencies legitimize the practice of accessing globally mobile human resources as a new relational field mediated within powerful social, political and international forces as part of a deepened sense of globalization. This is evident in Olympic movement focus upon SDP, the growth of sport for peace organizations utilizing volunteers and the increased profile of volunteer motilities. Calls to engage sport volunteers in a culture of peace create new levels of privilege and expertise, however, Darnell (2011) warns of the potential threats to understanding how such engagement supports inequalities and struggles.

This chapter, therefore, seeks to understand how international sport volunteers are able to transgress national boundaries in ways which few countries are able to withstand – surreptitiously, economically and culturally. Accompanying such globalized access and egress is the proliferation of international non-governmental organizations which offer the promise of new trans-national support and identities, introducing and utilizing the potency of sport to assist in collaborative nonviolent activity. At another level, international sport volunteers practically involved in SDP programmes engage, experience and learn in a number of different ways (Mojab and Dobson, 2008). Should such voluntarism be welcomed based on the assumption that such contribution is good without understanding fully the impact of engaging 'irrelevant or interfering groups'? (Cochrane and Dunn, 2002, p. ix).

Such involvement, therefore, raises a number of important issues that this chapter will explore. First, it considers whether international volunteers act as modernizing agents for development organizations, socialized to the norms and aspirations of international aid organizations or, as cultural mediators, able and skilled in improving local relations albeit through a globalized perspective (Brown, 2009). Second, there are questions regarding the proximity to such new social and physical experiences and how these impact upon the cultural and social prestige of volunteering (Hustinx and Lammertyn, 2003). This also brings into question the role of volunteers and/or the capacity of sport to understand important societal issues such as peace and conflict. Finally, and raised later in this chapter, there is still relatively little known about volunteers learning interdependently within a variety of practices, including SDP, organizational culture, conflictual contexts, international volunteer interactions, or establishing and experiencing temporary communities (Darnell, 2011; Gawerc, 2015). The importance, we would contend, is to understand any nascent relationship between SDP as a peace building vehicle and learning through the involvement of international volunteers.

After introducing how sport is often framed through the interconnected ideas of development and peace (SDP), this chapter will focus on how volunteers experience peacebuilding and sport. Drawing upon the authors' combined qualitative research and work with SDP programmes, volunteer insights provide a new field of progressive social movement in understanding and learning about peace, which it itself a highly contested concept (Harvey *et al.*, 2014). This learning will then highlight how volunteers are often less concerned with the politics of peace, while actively seeking to improve the social and communal circumstances of those with whom they volunteer. The question of internationality raises the key issues of learning for volunteers and the ideology of neutrality as volunteers assume informal educational roles. This will also point to those elements of SDP activities which are yet to be fully translated, 'outlining some of the qualities such individuals should be seeking to develop in order to engage in a more transformative education process through sport' (Spaaij and Jeanes, 2013, p. 442). Reviewing global sport processes from an international volunteer's perspective will, therefore, help to consider fully sport's role as a peace inspiring and building force (Craig and Craig, 2012).

Sport for development and peace (SDP)

Despite the burgeoning of SDP programmes positively focusing upon social change promoted by numerous sporting organizations (international, national and corporate), contemporary SDP literature has raised legitimate concerns regarding, for instance: the hegemony of westernized representations of sport (Giulianotti, 2012); a lack of understanding regarding effective pedagogical approaches (Spaaij and Schulenkorf, 2014); the challenges to accurately assess SDP impact (Sugden, 2014); and the political commandeering of 'sport for good' without theoretical or adequate empirical underpinning (Young and Okada, 2015). Out of this work, both by sociologists and those interested in peace building, a revisionist analysis of the functioning of SDP has started to emerge (Coalter, 2012; Craig, 2016). Broadly speaking, it can be said to maintain a rational action approach whilst superimposing an organizational framework that embeds social justice, equality and an understanding concerning global relations of power and oppression. This awareness reflects a growing understanding of mitigating factors, such as contextual complexity, the sending community's capacity leverage (McCartney, 2006; Sherraden *et al.*, 2008), unintended consequence of tacit interaction and democratic decision-making (Ogonor, 2003).

Although considerable research exists generally in relation to social, communal and political develoment through sport, those seeking to achieve outcomes of 'peace' are relatively few – most present peace as an outcome or component of development (Giulianotti, 2012). Peace is presented, in the functionalist explanations of new social factors, as a linear concept in description or aspirational outcome. As a linear description, peace is often defined on a continuum from contexts of belligerent conflict, through repression, subjugation and ongoing tensions to levels of normality or tranquility (Parker, 2013). As an aspirational outcome, peace is described as dependent upon whether cessation of conflict exists or not, thus allowing peace-building processes to continue. Alternatively, it is whether conflict is ongoing and any peace process has yet to occur. As evidence from contexts such as Northern Ireland, Israel/Palestine and South Africa, such processes are often dependent upon the historical, societal and conflictual precedents. SDP programmes can proceed in both instances. That said, interventions, however well-intentioned, need to avoid unintended mimesis of social control or pacification, especially if invited in by particular parties or organizations. This means there is a clear requirement of SDP organizations and their sponsors to critically examine whether they have sufficient expertise to function and develop sustainable and contextual social change.

Seeking to introduce sport within conflictual contexts is, however, not a new phenomenon. From at least the eighth century BC, the ancient truce and Olympic Games helped bind three Greek states together. As Bach (2013, p. 2) notes: 'the *ekecheiria* ensured a halt to hostilities, allowing athletes and spectators to travel safely to Olympia and home again'. As part of the modern Olympic Games revival at the end of the nineteenth century, Pierre de Coubertin's modernist and cosmopolitan vision included international understanding and, therefore, the development of peace. However, it was not until political and social conditions became favourable that the Olympic Truce could be revived. By 1992 'political events conspired to provide a space and a role for the Olympic Movement' (Briggs *et al.*, 2004, p. 29). For example, when Yugoslavs and Serbians wanted to compete in Barcelona in 1992, it was the International Olympic

Committee (IOC) mediating with the UN which allowed athletes to compete under the Olympic flag. Since this time the notion of 'peace' inherent within Olympism has become an ever more visible area for the Olympic movement with its developing partnership with the UN and allied organizations (e.g. UNICEF) – leading to the formation of the International Olympic Truce Foundation (IOTF) (Loland, 1995). The IOC's idealism is echoed in the aspirational rhetoric of many SDP organizations and activities. As Briggs *et al.* (2004, p. 17) note: 'behind the tough realities of international relations, an ideal can still move hearts and minds and, in small ways, help to spur individuals to take action in the pursuit of peace'.

Like many other peace-building approaches, SDP activities, initiatives and programmes are eclectic, organic and actively analytical (McGlynn *et al.*, 2009), thus making unclear what sporting activities and programmes will best assist peace-building processes. Giulianotti (2012) and Young and Okada (2015) provide a comprehensive overview of SDP's contribution, recognizing the difficulties in seeking a grand narrative to understand peace, indeed for many SDP initiatives the primary focus is based upon a developmental approach. Darnell (2010) suggests that initial waves of developmentalist interventions with SDP programmes adopted a 'foreign aid' contact hypothesis approach (Craig and Craig, 2012). Sport development enthusiasts and advocates emphasize such contact, however, such an approach often reinforced or supported corruption and economic inefficiency in its neo-liberal interventionist position or failed to sensitize staff and volunteers to the relevance of dialogues and activities congruent to the contexts of community conflict (Delanty, 2003). In conflictual societies this lack of understanding often starts from a naive acceptance without recognizing 'the signals of peace' (Boulding, 1995) or the psychological, sociocultural, political and experimental parameters that allow single community or cross-community contact (Spaaij and Schulenkorf, 2014). These sentiments also reflect the research and evaluation of the increasing number of sporting activities defined as SDP, whose attributes and capacities influence and shape the impact of such social contact through events, programmes and activities (Kidd, 2011). Initially and naively unwavering in their assumptions that sport provides a 'field of play' that can be independent of the surrounding social conditions and their enthusiastic commitment to use 'sport for good' SDP has emerged into a more reflexive, theory-informed, collective approach, a new horizon to entwine sport and peace (Sugden, 2014).

The unfolding story of SDP programmes linked to a progressive rationalization where sport for good represents an idea of freedom (of expression, choice, etc.), is aligned to other rationalizations which may be more economically driven (a feature of a utilitarian/modernist agenda), seeking to create a pluralistic global community based on a homogenized praxis

(Harber, 2000). In this position, sporting donors view inherent sporting values and lusory attitudes (Suits, 1979) as able to instil positive outcomes universalized in cognitive and instrumental terms as a basis for social and cultural progress (McNamee, 1998). Peace is therefore presented in generic terms (as progressive and developmental or modernizing), with sport providing an efficient and globalized vehicle for SDP programmes or interventions. The difficulty within this construct is that peace building is non-linear with multiple stakeholders, requiring collaborative processes and informal learning (Craig and Craig, 2012).

The assumed alignment between peace building, development and sport, provides a number of important ideological junctures. First, culturally, sport becomes elevated to the moral high ground as part of political liberationist project against a view of conflict being the social inhibitor on modernization. Faith exists in the power of this rational, highly westernized operation of reason and emancipation. As Berman notes (1982, p. 86), 'modern people have the power to create a better world than the world they have lost'. Sport has widespread appeal as a social development tool; it is well developed in the global north, waiting, patiently and financially, to be inserted into conflict-ridden places in the world. SDP is part of the solution to help reduce human suffering and give meaning to principles of equality and justice as well as overcome ideologies of suppression, pacification and domination. It is fairly evident that most SDP programmes are therefore concerned with peace building as an element of such development. Second, in respect to the prioritization of development this partially obscures rather than focuses upon conflictual elements existing within contested societies. Such elements present as direct expressions of violence as well as subtle and polite forms of avoidance and contestation requiring collaborative and analytical SDP programmes. SDP needs to hold such particularly violent and obvious expressions of conflict as a signifier of negative peace, and to acknowledge that SDP programmes need to understand the needs and fears of adversarial groups. It may be impossible to implement due to the scale of such conflict or that sport is used co-operatively to generate reassurance, confidence and a willingness to accommodate cessation of violence. This complexity raises important questions regarding how those volunteers who are delivering SDP programmes are aware of the challenges and are adequately trained and supported in their delivery of peace building.

Volunteer reflections

In this section we discuss how volunteers encounter and experience sport as a peace-building tool. To highlight such volunteer contributions, qualitative accounts discussed in this chapter are based on research with international sport volunteers engaged in SDP and practical peace-building training programmes (Craig and Craig, 2012). Such accounts were collected as part of the author's doctoral thesis and ongoing SDP work with international volunteers based in Northern Ireland and include an outline of SDP volunteer biopic (see Table 9.1). Volunteer transcripts were coded for anonymity (for instance R1, R2, R3, etc.). Volunteers who participated in this study originated from Bosnia and Herzegovina, Canada, El Salvador, Germany, Holland, Ireland, Scotland, South Africa, Spain, Sweden and United States.

SDP aspirations raise the question of recognizing what is peace. Is it simply the absence of violence or hostilities as expressed in some accounts, such as the ancient Olympic Truce? This notion of peace is often referred to as 'negative peace', signifying the absence or cessation of direct violence or war (Wilson, 1999). In contrast, is it the presence of desirable qualities that contribute to equality, justice and well-being, a form of 'positive peace' where structural, institutional and communal violence can be challenged, often through political mechanisms, processes and initiatives (Aghazamani and Hunt, 2015)? This is not to suggest that tensions, oppression or segregation do not exist in both perspectives. However, the conditions of a positive climate include opportunities for progressive, impactful and sustainable interventions. Peace building can therefore be seen as a process; a willingness to move beyond some form of violence or experience of oppression and where there is a need to systematically reconcile differences and historical antagonisms as well as having positive conditions to permit some movement (Darnell, 2012). For example, a national reconciliation policy was established in East Timor, a Truth and Reconciliation process in South Africa and an amalgamation of the above within Northern Ireland, which included a significant role fulfilled by the civil society. Parallel to such conditions either in response to governmental inactivity or active community initiatives, third sector activity can also establish peace-building opportunities. In each case, building peace included reconciliation between victims and perpetrators, dealing with societal and

Table 9.1 Research participants

Anonymity code	Volunteer nationality	Gender	Age	Location
R2	Bosnian	F	24	Northern Ireland
R3	Northern Irish	F	17	Northern Ireland
R4	Northern Irish	M	20	Northern Ireland
R5	Swedish	F	46	Sweden
R6	El Salvador	F	21	Northern Ireland
R8	Swedish	M	19	Northern Ireland
R9	Bosnian	M	27	Northern Ireland
R11	American	F	23	Ireland
R16	South African	M	24	Northern Ireland

individual trauma as well as the socio-political needs to acknowledge the difficulties, realities and possibilities that reconciliation may offer. As President of Timor-Leste, Xanana Gusmão (2003, p. 18), states, peace building is

> not the mere absence of conflict, nor merely an agreement between countries to avoid war – it must derive from the peace of mind within each human being, from the solidarity between individuals and from the tolerance within society until it reaches the level of mutual respect between countries.

Volunteers recognize their responsibilities, abilities and limitations within this process:

> I feel sometimes uncomfortable with the whole peace and reconciliation thing kind of not wanting to be flippant or talk about peace and niceness because I feel very sensitive about being seen as here to solve other people's problems. I felt quite embarrassed by that possibility.
>
> (R8)

Criticism of SDP exists precisely because of the issues highlighted above. As Sugden (2014) notes, SDP activity was often based on a naive and unshakeable belief that sport has some intrinsic good. A growing consensus suggests that sport programmes, rich in activity focus but limited in educational, social or political understanding, restrict success. Increasingly, activity focused programmes are being replaced by processes, relationships and outcome-focused experiences (Coalter, 2012). Furthermore, SDP programmes often locate volunteers into a system of planning and practice assuming that richness in programmes is more valuable than volunteer skill, knowledge or understanding, the preference is in activity rather than local and international expertise. In respect to this, international volunteers often highlighted some of the challenges facing local facilitators:

> I remember being in a games workshop and I was the facilitator. There were three other teachers in there but they let me do it. I guess it was safer for them to some extent.
>
> (R3)

The conjured optimism is that international volunteers provide a rich, relational and diverse resource less problematic to be accepted into new communities or societies. There is, however, limited pedagogical research into the value of sport volunteers as informal educators engaged in critical, reflexive educational mobilisation despite their obvious engagement (Spaaij and Jeanes, 2013), as explained:

On one occasion I remember I was playing table tennis with someone who had been recruited into a paramilitary organization and talking to him, I got an insight into how you would get involved into that.

(R8)

In short, sport volunteers deliver to recipients, themselves subjugated by the very organizations that seek social change rather than considering what pedagogical philosophies best suit the social or conflictual needs. In short, it ignores the 'border pedagogies' that Giroux (1992) alludes to with educators affirming local meanings whilst simultaneously interrogating the oppressive interests, ideologies and social practices. Unintended dialogues and experiences place the international volunteer, allowing them to learn about vulnerability when it comes to sharing about conflict. As one Bosnian volunteer notes:

to understand any kind of conflict you must then learn about peace building and it is not something you learn in school ... at least not in Bosnia.

(R2)

Their views, involvement and their learning, especially within the area of peace building, is often seen as coming with the territory, when exposed to trauma, tragedies and suffering. There is something profoundly difficult in working in the proximity to the suffering of others (Bar-on, 1996). There is also the difficulty of understanding the nature and characteristics of conflict and contested contexts from an international voluntary perspective without understanding practitioner development (Huzejrovic, 2003).

International sport volunteer research, it may be suggested, has therefore sought to focus upon development and social change at three levels: the macro or social; the meso or organizational; and the micro or the individual and their immediate relationships (Hylton, 2013). At the macro level, the complex relationship between sport and social change places volunteers as human resources key to the sustainability and diffusion of understanding (Giulianotti, 2012). It is also deeply connected to the social reality of the extant social, economic and political conditions existing within the specific country or region. At the meso level, it is the effectiveness of organizations and their projects that is of most interest. Organizations providing and promoting SDP programmes are constantly seeking to identify models of good practice without a sufficiently analytical framework (Sugden, 2014). Coalter (2012) points to the systems of social relationships – the collective interactions, professional/voluntary roles and informal contacts directly involved in SDP activities. He suggests that SDP programmes provide sites for contact and socialization, grounded within a local context and dealing specific local issues (Spaaij and Jeanes, 2013).

If you are not provided with enough information, it makes difficult to build a right approach and communication as well. It means then that you need to play by ear but then you know that it can be risky because it's all about people and their lives.

(R2)

When drawing upon international volunteer accounts from episodic sporting activities within peace-building projects, understanding focuses considerable attention on organizational and political imperatives rather than individual learning (Giulianotti, 2012). Volunteer accounts suggest a move from a utilitarian functionalist project to a more relational and transformative approach, as one volunteer notes:

there is a lot of peace building that goes on behind the scenes just informal discussion, casual conversation, just passing a ball to someone.

(R8)

In the next section the focus will be on international sport volunteers learning about peace building, drawing on some of the detailed ethnographic insights from international volunteers. This is not as complex as initially imagined, as Foley (1999) and Davis Smith et al. (2005) suggest, volunteering in its many guises sustains civic engagement, promotes positive participation and reflects conditions of learning both planned and incidental. Finally, and associated to these tasks, is whether international sport volunteers who learn about and engage in peace building inform a larger picture of SDP participation.

Sport volunteering for peace: an international value

Whilst acknowledging an unprecedented expansion both in volunteers and organizations which contribute to global affairs, international understanding, well-being and peace building there is increasing concern over the role of volunteers in peace building (Sherraden et al., 2008). The international community is well aware of the potential power of sport volunteers to support important societal facets and promote important ideological practices (Kearney and Osborne, 2003). What is less frequently explored is the actual experience and learning of international sport volunteers engaged in SDP programmes. There are exceptions, such as McGlynn et al. (2009), who consider the role of facilitators, educators and volunteers in the active practices of peace building, and Spaaij and Jeanes (2013), whose Frierean pedagogical interpretation considers cultural constructions to understand SDP as a transformative educational process for learners. In other post-conflictual contexts, research on established projects such as *Football 4*

Peace and *Peace Players* provide some attention to the importance of volunteer coaches (Sugden, 2014). Collectively, these authors note the dearth of an analysis based on sport volunteer experiences and, more specifically, how relatively few studies consider directly international volunteer learning within SDP initiatives and activities despite an increased attention to learning and coaching (Avis *et al.*, 2010). This is not surprising. SDP programmes focus, rightly, upon the recipients, facilitating visible outcomes and developing meaningful approaches while tacitly implying that international volunteers have an a priori capacity to inspire and help build peace. Though not always an integral element of programmes and volunteer preparation it is evident that reflecting upon their own background and context provides a lens to understand valuable pedagogical practices, comparing and transforming their own experiences and learning in new environments, cultures and contexts.

For NGOs and INGOs, such as Amnesty International or the Red Cross, etc., international volunteers provide an opportunity to engage citizens in international community building, harness a semi-skilled workforce replete with enthusiasm and talent, as well as reaffirming organizational reputation. This utilization favours a human capital concept, allowing organizations to identify ability and characteristics fit for purpose through a screening and investment perspective. In return, there is a vesting of trust as a mutual organizational tripartite bond between volunteer, organization and hosting country (Giddens, 1990).

Exemplifying this, Yazawa's (2003) focus upon volunteer exchange programmes between Japan and Korea, Gnecco de Ruiz's (2003) examination of displaced families in Colombia, as well as Coy and Woehrle's (2000) critical assessment of understanding the impact of peacebuilding volunteers suggest, collectively, the importance of grassroots dialogue and action. However, Williamson *et al.* (2000, p. 52) suggest the difficulties identifying such initiatives through dialogue where local volunteers 'fear identification' and 'may tend to mute critical comments or are genuinely anxious to support anything that seems likely to promote alternatives'. Engagement and integration into SDP activity is sometimes based on a Maffesolian idea of emotional commonality and shared participation, where volunteers provide physical, emotional and cognitive capacity. Cochrane and Dunn's (2002) study of the evolution and impact of ten peace/conflict resolution voluntary and community organizations in Northern Ireland suggest that relatively little is known about the contribution of such NGOs to the social and political fabric of contested societies. Although focused at an organizational level, they recognize that much voluntary activity within this field is often indiscernible.

Collectively, and at a general policy level, Barnett Donaghy (2004) suggests that four important factors distinguish voluntary involvement in contested societies from elsewhere. First, research has focused too broadly at a generic level, thus negating the important and distinctive social circumstances of conflict and peace building. Second, there is often advanced public discourse around social inclusion and discrimination in contested societies although this may not be obvious, easily integrated or valued openly. This is despite the important political role of the voluntary sector in certain societies, especially during civil unrest, in filling the democratic and policy void (Williamson et al., 2000). As Kaldor (2006, p. 86) notes, 'an active civil society tends to counterbalance the distrust of politicians, the alienation from political institutions, and the sense of apathy and futility'. Third, there is a willingness of government(s) to support initiatives to counter the obvious void, and fourth, there exists an expertise, freedom, access and mobilization readily apparent in voluntary and community groups (McKie, 2005). There is, however, the issue of international volunteer awareness pertaining to communal and societal frontiers in contested societies. As one volunteer notes:

> I didn't really have a specific idea about why I wanted to get involved in peace building as such it was really my own focus upon my own personal and professional development so the peace building stuff took quite a while to dawn on me exactly how that worked and how I contributed.
>
> (R6)

Such contemporary studies broadly support the view that much of the international voluntary activity and policy 'is premised on the belief that many people wish to make a difference to daily community life', despite real experiences of violence which restrict the choice on how, where and when people volunteer (Morrow and Wilson, 1995, p. 77).

Whilst recognizing the increasing number of SDP groups engaged in peace initiatives there is less understanding of volunteer practices and impact (Giulianotti, 2012; Sugden, 2014). 'There is a corporate responsibility for areas like business, the churches, the trades unions and the voluntary sector to question whether they are doing enough ... examining their own role in creating a new society here' (Ringland, 2008, p. 18). Such voluntary organizations working behind the scenes, embedded in local issues, seek to deal constructively at both community and personal level with conflict, however, do not champion peace building as it may suggest particular alliances and therefore linked incongruously with a certain legacy or future partisan configuration. There is also ambivalence towards individual volunteer accounts despite such meaningful engagement. Nevertheless, the progressivism of volunteer involvement has been formed by a confluence of ideas from a variety of sources, some concerned with the potential of international volunteers, the notion of educational empowerment (Friere,

1974), the identification of peace education (McGlynn *et al.*, 2009). Such progressivism occurs on a number of conceptual and practical levels and will now be considered.

International volunteer learning

Within SDP organizations the notion of benefiting or learning as international SDP volunteers is assumed to be understood, albeit mostly tacitly. It is rarely visible in research terms and there are two immediate reasons for this. As previously noted, people rarely volunteer with clarity of their own learning needs or goals (Darvill *et al.*, 1988). Learning is seen as being meaningful to the participant(s), the volunteer providing the resources, where competences are trained for delivery rather than shared purpose. Educationally, John Dewey and later Kolb's (1984) conceptualisation of experiential learning emphasises the importance of learning as a holistic activity. This does not, however, account for the ability to think beyond the constraints of culture – based on the translation of learning that international volunteers encounter:

> Every day you can learn something new about these particular matters, there's no formula for peace building or reconciliation, so it is about attitude, beliefs, feelings, experience, background. And because I'm from the region which was involved in conflict, I felt that I need to learn as much as I can about these matters and to try to bring back that experience and knowledge.
>
> (R2)

Moreover, and connected to the above example, McGivney (2001) suggests that volunteers (through incidental learning activities) gain a personal learning starting point often without realizing it (they often learn without considering they are learning), perceived through necessity rather than as dispensable learning.

> I wouldn't normally describe myself in relation to peace building. Just somebody who works in the voluntary sector and promotes social justice but not really a peace building volunteer.
>
> (R11)

What is less clear, however, is how can volunteer learning be understood if it is tacit, unintentional and embedded in socially situated action: a by-product of volunteering rather than within formal educational structures? This is a common theme raised by other researchers focusing upon lifelong learning, adult and informal learning (Jeffs and Smith, 1999). Commissioned to explore the relationship between adult learning, the statutory and voluntary sector, Tusting and Barton (2003) suggest that volunteering can provide important educational experiences and learning that can transfer to other life experiences.

McGlynn *et al.* (2009) explore informal learning generally whilst reflecting upon those involved in voluntary activity, social struggle and political action. Their main interest is the learning dimension of emancipatory social struggle. They draw upon a wide-ranging number of cases to illuminate the learning that occurs as people struggle to make sense of what is happening to them when they challenge oppression. Although volunteer learning in SDP programmes is treated as a uniform element of voluntary activity, this brings into debate the relationship between volunteering as a social movement and volunteering as a site of learning. As already highlighted, this learning tends to be informal and incidental, reflecting the importance of socially situated learning (Lave and Wenger, 1991). In contested or conflictual situations, Spinner-Halev (2003) suggests that conflictual complexity challenges educational understanding in order to incorporate important political and reconciliatory goals. A similar point is raised by Daniels (2003) in her study about female community leadership training in an African settlement. She suggests that narrowly defined learning methodologies are found wanting and her work explores the relationship between informal learning, conflict resolution and social action. Her conclusion is simple, everyday learning is negotiated, ambiguous, complex and contested – something that can transform and disrupt lives. Kovan and Dirkx (2003) address the role of transformative learning, focusing on people participating in social movements. They suggest that there is little understanding of the learning process and, second, factors beyond an individual's scope influence learning and participation.

> one young man in particular said he would be shot if anyone knew he was even meeting Catholics. He had lied to his family about where he was going. This discussion happened at the beginning of the programme and allowed others to appreciate the risk that he had taken.
>
> (R5)

Such research collectively raises the question of what is understood by volunteers-as-learners on at least three fronts:

- First, the volunteer-as-learner is something yet to be fully explored as Darvill *et al.* (1988) suggest and echoed by Spinner-Halev (2003) in relation to the Israeli–Palestinian context. They also raise the obvious general questions of what and how do volunteers learn? Reflecting upon work-based contexts, Eraut (2000, p. 15) suggests: 'not only is implicit learning difficult to detect without prolonged observation, but reactive learning and some deliberate learning are unlikely to be consciously recalled unless there was an unusually dramatic outcome'.

- Second, seeking to learn as a volunteer can appear to cast aspersions on the very philanthropic nature of volunteering (Foley, 1999). Is proposing volunteering as learning an oxymoron? An attractive educational discourse immersed in political and societal values.
- Third, international volunteer learning is problematic, especially when hosting and sending countries' learning practices are embedded in the action and activity of temporary, unique or exceptional communities and subsequently difficult to translate or evaluate (Darvill et al., 1988). Are international volunteers asked to empty themselves of their former culture since the capacity to be present in cultural conflicts requires new positioning, enunciation and understanding?
- Fourth and finally, confusion about how to understand volunteer learning often results in an umbrella of frameworks being used as the point of departure, such as 'lifelong learning' (Ogonor, 2003), active citizenship (Dekker, 2002) and 'informal learning' (McGivney, 2001).

There is no doubt about the importance of learning how to resolve conflicts and problems in a nonviolent manner. For international SDP volunteers who are often asked to model a peaceful pedagogy, it is unclear how this is understood or learnt. Gratton et al. (2004) provide an assessment of the strategic role of volunteering as perceived by government together with the challenges at an organizational level. Their focus upon cross-community mixing suggests that the voluntary sector has mitigated some of the worst aspects of community conflict in Northern Ireland. In conclusion, however, they suggest that still relatively little is known in relation to voluntary and community contribution to peace building. The following international SDP volunteer accounts, however, point to several emergent themes concerning learning about peace building.

Contact theory

Volunteers through their responses point towards the importance and limitations of contact between communities, especially when it is not sustainable, evolutionary or consolidatory. Contact theory is described and used within the area of conflict resolution and peace building (Lederach, 1997). Based on the work of Gordon Allport (1954), contact theory's starting premise is, to some extent, increased individual contact with those from opposing groups will challenge existing prejudices and stereotypes. Volunteer experiences, however, suggest that this is not that straightforward:

> One youth club had a court that you could play basketball and all kinds of stuff so it was trying to bring people together.
>
> (R4)

However, according to another volunteer:

> We did have some joint sports day events to try and bring the different schools together but it was just more competition to see who was better.
> (R3)

Volunteers also question how sustainable and co-operative the sporting practices are:

> Discussion was quite heated with open conflict about why they should accept each other and how difficult it would be for them on their return to their respective communities.
> (R5)

Volunteers are not justifying integrated or segregated sport, merely considering sporting contact and everyday living. Their concerns suggest that such sporting experiences may serve to reinforce the binaries of 'us and them'. Friere's (1974) focus is upon dialogue and conviviality as times, places and processes for learning rather than anti-dialogical confrontation. Volunteers talk of sharing, reflection and translation, describing how sporting experiences can be used to describe different sporting structures, events and competitions (McCartney, 2006). This sharing was concerned with facilitation of knowledge, understanding and skills emerged from genuineness, prizing and empathy:

> to allow people to share their own stories and through the listening to those stories you get an understanding and that's what I found volunteering.
> (R4)

Trust within SDP

A reoccurring theme emerges in the above volunteer comments revealed through the desired or unintended goal of shared experiences: establishing a climate where mutual bonds can frame the past in a way that develops confidence to withstand future traumas. Emerging from this picture is the role of the volunteer, but the conception is instrumental, using sport to bring people together, as highlighted by R11:

> It can be very overtly talking about what is peace, what is reconciliation. How can we bring two different communities, conflictual communities or groups together well that's clearly peace building.... How we live our lives, how we talk to other people that's a much larger picture of peace.
> (R11)

Despite the cultivation of trust to create, maintain, further as well as evaluate the quality of social and communal relations, trust remains intangible (Van Maele *et al.*, 2014). Proponents of social capital theory argue that trust and trust building has lasting benefits between individuals and communities (Putnam, 1997). Spaaij and Schulenkorf (2014) apply the metaphor of 'safe space' to SDP projects and events to highlight the duality of trust, its centrality in leverage within social systems and the intangible multi-dimensional notion of emotional and psychological safety. This dimension is often described generically as a desired goal of social interaction, without which trust decays. Giddens (1990) and White (1996, p. 57) suggests that within a democratic society, people need to trust 'that the institutions within which they are living are informed by goodwill towards all members of society'. Spaaij and Schulenkorf (2014) describe the establishment of trust as professionalized friendliness and McNamee (1998) adds that trust cannot be demanded nor is it separate from sport in society. In SDP programmes, volunteers comment on the quality of trust sought as being fundamental and intangible:

> You need to have trust to work with people and also know you are supported by others, volunteers may not get to know the person long enough to establish a real supporting relationship. It is not a straightforward process and you can't simply do an activity or play a game and then people trust each other.
>
> (R5)

The duality surrounding the concept of trust is referred to in a number of SDP programmes, although it may be argued that what is often called trust is in fact reliance. Reliance, in such instances, emerges as the interdependence of organizational functioning to realize collective goals rather than the climate in which to value a participant's contribution (Van Maele *et al.*, 2014). In SDP programmes, implications for understanding trust are raised by international volunteers. First, as an expression of relational and social bond, not as an outcome of people thrust together bound by sporting activities and getting on. The 'getting on' assumes that the pluralistic activity of sport is shared, it has an interactional-situational field (Bourdieu, 1984) through its public understanding, constitutive rules and lusory attitudes. These dimensions reduce uncertainty thus increasing trust. Co-operation is voluntarily agreed and trust reduces the possibility of one group controlling the other. It also substantiates the credentials of the stranger (Giddens, 1990). In doing so, it assists in what Spaaij and Schulenkorf (2014) call the cultivation of safe space – physically, figuratively and psycho-social. One volunteer describes their experience of describing societal conflict:

and they were asking me about my experience of war in Bosnia. And I was telling them. I tell them that I was 13 years old and I was just a kid and that nowadays I am missing my childhood so bad, playing games, you know, all that and six or seven of them were sitting in this smoking area where we were having this chat and actually they were saying I am missing my childhood as well.

(R9)

The establishment of trust in this example is courted by the contrasting effects of war experiences not within the formal activities of an SDP programme structure but through informal opportunities. In contrast to Spaaij and Schulenkorf (2014), effort in establishing relational contracts between SDP volunteers and participants, often translated culturally, provides the preconditions for the building of safe spaces. In this sense, safe spaces are described through contractual understandings and relational trust. This also acknowledges the complex task settings in which SDP volunteers engage which goes hand-in-hand with volunteer/participant interdependance. International volunteers come into the social and cultural contexts largely depending on the structure of sport and organization, the construct of peace building and the interaction of culturally different groups where post-conflictual settings may leave participants culturally vulnerable to their own multi-faceted sense of national and regional identity without secure egress points.

This notion of project development is aptly concluded by Spaaij and Schulenkorf (2014), when they argue that 'safe space is best facilitated in SDP projects with a conflict resolution objective, different from how this is done in sports events or projects'. A safe space should not, therefore, be viewed as a managed product to be framed around the particpant and volunteers, but rather a transformative expression of values and a communicative process which reveals problematic aspects in understanding trust.

Volunteers as international educators

Learning opportunities are raised repeatedly by volunteers facilitating SDP programmes. Regardless of an inability to identify critical pedagogical practices, philosophical underpinnings or curriculum expectations, their accounts describe an experiential, empowering and dialogical value to sporting activity. In short, their critical learning experiences are with and for learners. Spaaij and Jeanes (2013) note the liberating educational process of dialogue with participants, constructing societal knowledge that illuminates and grows interdependently (Maney et al., 2006). Learning is shared, gaining critical distance from conditions of oppression to seek change. This is echoed by one volunteer:

It was exciting and hugely emotional. I was helping out about with children and adults in wheelchairs. I got to see the basketball and a lot more, helped with the lunches, with access, everything. Basketball is really violent. I could spend all morning just talking about it. It made me realize that I could do so much with my life.

(R16)

Volunteers do not describe an ability to define and analyse their own educational performance – investigating their own aspirations, interests and skills. Such learning is integrated through actualized practices, transformative activities and mindfulness to the social and personal context (Martin and Williamson, 2002). Such development may involve watching, reframing, coaching or supporting, at other moments, facilitating, negotiating and prompting. This constant refocusing is both developmental and dispositional. Understanding the physical literacy and agency that such engagement involves demonstrates a commitment to transformative learning. As volunteers note:

Sometimes a group can be working on issues when one person says something and the group then gets split, changes direction, gets annoyed or stops. As a volunteer I have to help. Sometimes it means keeping the group together, sometimes to help a group see another point of view or feelings. Sometimes I do nothing but watch.

(R2)

Volunteers may see their approach as different from the organizational aspirations. The organization would seek to develop programmatic activities and events that would be regarded as valuable. In contrast, the volunteer would seek to create a climate in which the participant would feel safe to learn about the other, to ask difficult questions, be curious about the stranger. Such learning requires a range of approaches, negotiating beforehand, attending actively and altering creatively. It is not about rudderless activity or game, it is enriched programmes enriched by purposeful dialogue determined by focused and engaging opportunities.

International volunteers returning to their host country are equally vulnerable to impact of peace-building learning, in danger of being seen as resources imbued with new skills on cross-cultural interaction and conflict resolution skills, an increase in human capital, possibly leading to economic and social development (Sherraden et al., 2008). Through this lens, volunteer learning is seen as a tool for public service rather than self-development or nuanced understandings of global issues. Modernizers' assumptions of this are three-fold. Exposure to inequalities and oppression will lead to individual civic action to help challenge and narrow the inequalities gap. That international volunteers have the social or

206 M. Bartle and P. Craig

educational capacity to perform such function is questionable although in contrast to traditional development models relying upon technical competences, international volunteers may provide new informal opportunities and understanding. Second, balancing the internal competition for a livelihood with the opportunities to use such experiences may be subsumed by the privileges already held. This may leave international volunteers revitalized, with a sense of educational purpose through intercultural and social engagement not merely as a process that fulfils a neo-liberal educational function, but as a transformative structure that has history, relations and continuity.

Conclusion

SDP's social construction project often fails to mobilize the population in the interests of liberation for several reasons. First, such sporting activities become an exceptional experience. Its boundaries, rules and necessary voluntary obligation does not easily transfer to more complex social everyday contexts. In short, it is easier to label this sporting experience *as exceptional*, rather than extrapolate new beliefs and attitudes to life in general as a result of such experiences or activities. Whatever happened was unique to the sporting activity or environment. As such, the experience becomes silenced as the project departs, fuelled by a retrograde notion that others are equally and relationally distant. Second, international sport volunteers cannot easily enter into debate over conflict without understanding the wider theoretical and practical issues associated with conflict resolution or dialogical methodologies (Lederach, 1997). The assumption is almost exclusively based on a contact hypothesis creating forms of mutual understanding and tolerance of diversity often without a priori knowledge of the potential of sporting contact to create meaningful outcomes (Goldring, 2004). Volunteers are invited into new countries, contexts and conflicts as if this was a power-neutral intercultural experience to impart skills and enthusiasm in exchange for global or relational knowledge. Viewed from this perspective it is a determined effort to see a global and holistic pluralism. Volunteers, however, describe meaningful learning through sporting practices, narrative configurations of social justice and equality whilst interrogating the interests and perspectives of excluded or marginalized groups.

International sport volunteers engaged in peace building also highlight the limitations of assessment tools, failing to include all stakeholders beyond project outcomes and objectives. This chapter has suggested that broadening learning aims, to include volunteer experience, will capture the richness of SDP for all involved, including international volunteers whose lives involve establishing temporary communities, arriving and leaving interculturally and the importance of contextualized learning. Sending and hosting communities provide mechanisms to boost or inhibit learning, however, peace building transmutes beyond the limitations of contact (Craig, 2010). The more holistic the SDP programme the more favourable the learning potential for the volunteer. How well international volunteers learn will depend on many factors but they rely particularly on being afforded an understanding programmatic structures alongside benign and tacit cultural practices of fear, communal tension and distrust (Brown, 2009). Post-conflictual societies often lack future planning structures, therefore programmes which seek to develop peaceful and sustainable outcomes, the expectation of return often appears incongruent with local communities – which are challenged, constrained and preoccupied with more immediate vistas (Wilson, 1999). There are programmes which understand and centralize volunteer learning, so that skill acquisition includes notions of safe spaces, developing trusting relationships and cross-cultural contracts to ensure SDP is both practically and theoretically driven (Parker, 2013).

Constructed in ways informed by these critical insights, SDP programmes, projects and activities can encourage participatory peace, freedom and justice if such analysis and practice embed conflict and change theory (Lederach, 1997). Sport, however, has resulted from a rather unseemly commercialized development to compound the challenges in understanding the role of international volunteers (Craig and Craig, 2012). International volunteers are not neutral organizational confederates; they reveal the limitations of a contact model of shared experiences. Their reflections suggest new ways of understanding conflict, in the passing of a ball, explaining rules, hearing stories and in some cases developing visions of reconciliation that embody sporting values informally, interdependently and sustainably.

References

Aghazamani, Y. and Hunt, C.A. (2015). Beyond historical adversaries: Exploring new grounds for peace through tourism between Iran and the US. *Tourism Culture & Communication* 15(1): 59–64.

Allport, G. (1954). *The nature of prejudice*. Reading, MA: Addison-Wesley.

Avis, J., Fisher, R. and Thomson, R. (2010). *Teaching in lifelong learning*. Maidenhead: Open University Press.

Bach, T. (2013) *68th Session of the UN General Assembly: Statement on the occasion of the adoption of the resolution. 'Building a peaceful and better world through sport and the Olympic Ideal'*. New York: IOC.

Bar-on, D. (1996). Attempting to overcome the intergenerational transmission of trauma. In R.J. Apfel and B. Simon (eds) *Minefields in their hearts: The mental health of children in war and communal violence*. New Haven: Yale University Press (pp. 165–187).

Barnett Donaghy, T. (2004). Mainstreaming Northern Ireland's participative-democratic approach. *Policy and Politics* 32(1): 49–62.

Berman, M. (1982). *All that is solid melts into air: The experience of modernity*. New York: Simon & Schuster.

Boulding, E. (1995). The dialectics of peace. In E. Boulding and K.E. Boulding (eds) *The future: Images and processes*. Thousand Oaks: Sage (pp. 196–204).

Bourdieu, P. (1984). *Distinction: A social critique of the judgement of taste*. London: Routledge.

Briggs, R., McCarthy, H. and Zorbas, A. (2004). *16 days: The role of the Olympic Truce in the toolkit for peace*. IOTC.

Brown, L. (2009). International education: A force for peace and cross-cultural understanding? *Journal of Peace Education* 6(2): 209–224.

Coalter, F. (2012). 'There is loads of relationships here': Developing a programme theory for sport-for-change programmes. *International Review for the Sociology of Sport* 48(5): 594–612.

Cochrane, F. and Dunn, S (2002). *People power? The role of the voluntary and community sector in the Northern Ireland conflict*. Cork: Cork University Press.

Coy, P. and Woehrle, L.M. (eds). (2000). *Social conflict and collective identities*. Oxford: Rowman & Littlefield.

Craig, C. (2010). *Dialogue for peaceful change training manual*. Belfast: TIDES Training.

Craig, P. (2016). *Sport sociology*. London: SAGE.

Craig, P. and Craig, C. (2012). *Sport and conflict resolution: Challenging the mythology and methodology of current policy and practice*. Bedford, Unpublished Conference Paper.

Daniels, D. (2003). Learning about community leadership: Fusing methodology and pedagogy to learn about the lives of settlement women. *Journal of Adult Education* 52(3): 189–206.

Darnell, S.C. (2010). Power, politics and 'sport for development and peace': Investigating the utility of sport for international development. *Sociology of Sport Journal* 27: 54–75.

Darnell, S.C. (2011). Identity and learning in international volunteerism: Sport for development and peace internships. *Development in Practice* 21(7): 974–986.

Darnell, S.C. (2012). *Sport for development and peace: A critical sociology*. London: Bloomsbury Academic.

Darvill, G., Perkins, E. and Unell, J. (1988). *Learning from volunteering: An exploratory study*. Leicester: NIACE.

Davis Smith, J., Ellis, A., Howlett, S. and O'Brien, J. (2005). *Volunteering for all? Exploring the links between volunteering and social exclusion*. London: Institute for Volunteering Research.

Dekker, P. (2002). On the prospects of volunteering in civil society. *Voluntary Action* 4(3): 31–48.

Delanty, G. (2003). *Community*. London: Routledge.

Eraut, M. (2000). Non-formal learning, implicit learning and tacit knowledge in professional work. In F. Coffield (ed.) *The necessity of informal learning*. Bristol: Policy Press (pp. 113–136).

Foley, G. (1999). *Learning in social action: A contribution to understanding informal education*. Leicester: NIACE.

Freire, P. (1974). *Pedagogy of the oppressed*. Harmondsworth: Penguin.

Gawerc, M.I. (2015). Persistent peacebuilders: Sustaining commitment during violent conflict. *International Journal of Peace Studies* 20(1): 35–50.

Giddens, A. (1990). *The consequences of modernity*. Cambridge: Polity.

Giroux, H. (1992). *Border crossings*. London: Routledge.

Giulianotti, R. (2012). The sport for development and peace sector: An analysis of its emergence, key institutions, and social possibilities. *The Brown Journal of World Affairs* 18(11): 279–294.

Gnecco de Ruiz, M.T. (2003). How volunteers are helping internally displaced families in Colombia. *Voluntary Action* 5(2): 111–116.

Goldring, B. (2004). Conflict resolution: Towards a better understanding. *Child Care in Practice* 10(3): 291–293.

Gratton, C., Nichols, G., Shibli, S. and Taylor, P. (2004). *Valuing volunteers in UK sport*. London: Sports Council.

Gusmão, X. (2003). Reaching out for reconciliation and peace in Timor-Leste. *Voluntary Action* 5(2): 15–23.

Harber, C. (2000). Schools, democracy and violence in South Africa. In A. Osler (ed.) *Citizenship and democracy in schools: Diversity, identity, and quality*. Stoke-on-Trent: Trentham Books.

Harvey, J., Horne, J., Safai, P., Darnell, S. and O'Neil, S.C. (2014). *Sport and social movements: From the local to the global*. London: Bloomsbury.

Hustinx, L. and Lammertyn, F. (2003). Collective and reflexive styles of volunteering: A sociological modernisation perspective. *International Journal of Voluntary and Non-Profit Organisations* 14(2): 167–183.

Huzejrovic, V. (2003). Youth volunteering in Bosnia & Herzegovina. *Voluntary Action* 5(2): 83–86.

Hylton, K. (ed.) (2013). *Sport development: Policy, process and practice*. London: Routledge.

Jeffs, T. and Smith, M. (1999). *Informal education: Conversation, democracy and learning*. London: YMCA George Williams College.

Kaldor, M. (2006). *New and old wars*. Cambridge: Polity Press.

Kearney, J. and Osborne, W. (2003). Time changes lives – trust changes everything: Volunteer work for conflict resolution and reconciliation in Northern Ireland. *Voluntary Action* 5(2): 45–51.

Kidd, B. (2011). Cautions, questions and opportunities in sport for development and peace. *Third World Quarterly* 32(3): 603–609.

Kolb, D.A. (1984). *Experiential learning: Experience as the source of learning and development*. Englewood Cliffs: Prentice Hall.

Kovan, J.T. and Dirkx, J.M. (2003). 'Being called awake': The role of transformative learning in the lives of environmental activists. *Adult Education Quarterly* 53(2): 99–118.

Lave, J. and Wenger, E. (1991). *Situated learning: Legitimate peripheral participation*. Cambridge: Cambridge University Press.

Lederach, J.P. (1997). *Building peace: Sustainable reconciliation in divided societies*. Washington, DC: United States Institute of Peace Press.

Loland, S. (1995). Coubertin's ideology of Olympism from the perspective of the history of ideas. *Olympika* 4: 49–78.

McCartney, C. (2006). *Engaging armed groups in peace processes: Reflections for practice and policy from Columbia and the Philippines.* London: Conciliation Resources.

McGivney, V. (2001). Informal learning: A neglected species. *Journal of Adult and Continuing Education* 7(2): 101–109.

McGlynn, C., Zembylas, M., Bekerman, Z. and Gallacher, T. (2009). *Peace education in conflict and post-conflict societies.* London: Palgrave Macmillan.

McKie, L. (2005). *Families, violence and social change.* Buckingham: Open University Press.

McNamee, M. (1998). Celebrating trust: Virtues and rules in the ethical conduct of sports coaches. In M. McNamee and S.J. Parry (eds) *Ethics and sport.* London: E & F N Spon (pp. 161–179).

Maney, G.M., Ibrahim, I., Higgins, G.I. and Herzog, H. (2006). The past's promise: Lessons from peace processes in Northern Ireland and the Middle East. *Journal of Peace Research* 43(2): 181–200.

Martin, S. and Williamson, B. (2002). Included in exclusion: Learning, civil society and widening participation. *Journal of Access and Credit Studies* 4(1): 51–62.

Mojab, S. and Dobson, B. (2008). Women war and learning. *International Journal of Lifelong Education* 27(2): 119–127.

Morrow, D. and Wilson, D. (1995). Voluntary action towards sustainable peace. In A. Williamson (ed.) *Beyond violence: The role of voluntary and community action in building a sustainable peace in Northern Ireland.* Belfast: University of Ulster/Community Relations Council (pp. 47–59).

Ogonor, B.O. (2003). The impact of training on the conflict resolution ability of rural women in the Niger Delta, Nigeria. *International Journal of Lifelong Education* 22(2): 172–181.

Parker, C.A. (2013). Peacebuilding education: Using conflict for democratic and inclusive learning opportunities for diverse students. *International Journal of Peace Studies* 18(2): 5–26.

Putnam, R.D. (1997). *Bowling alone.* New York: Simon & Schuster.

Ringland, T. (2008). What are the chances? Can a shared future be born from an imperfect political deal? *Corrymeela News* 8(1): 23–27.

Sherraden, M.S., Lough, B.J. and McBride, A.M. (2008). Effects of international volunteering and service: Individual and institutional predictors. *Voluntas* 19(4): 395–421.

Spaaij, R. and Jeanes, R. (2013). Education for social change? A Frierean critique of sport for development and peace. *Physical Education and Sport Pedagogy* 18(4): 442–457.

Spaaij, R. and Schulenkorf, N. (2014). Cultivating safe space: Lessons for sport-for-development projects and events. *Journal of Sport Management* 28: 633–645.

Spinner-Halev, J. (2003). Education, reconciliation and nested identities. *Theory and Research in Education* 1(1): 51–72.

Sugden, J. (2014). Assessing the sociology of sport: On the capacities and limits of using sport to promote social change. *International Review for the Sociology of Sport* 50(4–5): 606–611.

Suits, B. (1979). What is a game? In E. Gerber and W. Morgan (eds) *Sport and the body.* Philadelphia: Lea and Febiger (pp. 11–17).

Tusting, K. and Barton, D. (2003). *Models of adult learning: A literature review.* Lancaster: NRDC.

Van Maele, D., Houtte, P. and Forsyth, M. (2014). *Trust and school life: The role of trust for learning*. Dordrecht: Springer.

White, P. (1996). *Civic virtues and public schooling: Educating citizens for a democratic society*. New York: Teachers College Press.

Williamson, A., Scott, D. and Halfpenny, P. (2000). Rebuilding civil society in Northern Ireland: The community and voluntary sector's contribution to the European Union's Peace and Reconciliation District Partnership Programme. *Policy and Politics* 28(1): 49–66.

Wilson, R. (1999). *Beyond either/or the politics of 'and' in ethno-nationalist conflicts*. Belfast: Democratic Dialogue.

Yazawa, Y. (2003). A volunteer exchange programme between Korea and Japan. *Voluntary Action* 5(2): 107–111.

Young, K. and Okada, C. (2015). *Sport, social development and peace*. Bingley: Emerald Group.

Chapter 10

The motives and social capital gains of sport for development and peace volunteers in Cameroon

A comparative analysis of international and national volunteers

Joanne Clarke and Paul Salisbury

Introduction

The popularity of using sport as a tool for international development has escalated in recent years, with 166 registered organizations globally rising to over 700 in less than a decade (International Platform for Sport and Development, 2016; Kidd, 2008), thereby increasing the opportunities for unique international sports volunteering experiences. Fuelled by the volun-tourism phenomenon of combining volunteering with international travel, sports enthusiasts too are travelling the world to 'make a difference'. Moreover, the United Nations commitment to achieving the Millennium Development Goals and more recently the Sustainable Development Goals, the international community has begun to gain 'consciousness of the full magnitude of sport's potential as a tool in achieving development goals' (Beutler, 2008, p. 359). As such, sport has been recognized for its *potential* contribution to a variety of international development agendas in global south countries, including education, health improvements, gender relations and peace (Beutler, 2008; Darnell and Hayhurst, 2012; Levermore and Beacom, 2009; Lindsey and Grattan, 2012; United Nations, 2016).

The growth of institutions, corporations and International Non-Governmental Organizations (INGOs) using sport as a tool for social mobility in developing countries has placed the Sport for Development and Peace (SDP) sector within broader debates of northern hegemony (Giulian-otti, 2004; Hayhurst, 2009; Kidd, 2008). Critical analyses of the SDP sector has suggested that such INGO programmes operate within hege-monic relations in which privileged groups (i.e. the international organiza-tion) maintain a position of benefit and leverage over others (i.e. national organizations in the global south) through social and cultural negotiations.

This chapter is based upon the context of Sport INGOs' tendency to use volunteer-based delivery models within Sub-Saharan Africa (SSA), which has been described as a *prime location* for SDP activities (Levermore and Beacom, 2009). Using a combination of post-colonial and social capital theory the chapter draws on the suggestion by Darnell and Hayhurst

(2012) to illustrate the perspectives, motivations and personal gains of the SDP sector's front line, its volunteers, as a topic for critical inquiry. In doing so, it compares the motives of international volunteers from a global north country (UK) and national volunteers from a global south nation (Cameroon) who work together on the same programme.

In order to understand the context of international and national sports volunteers, the chapter comprises the following sections. Beginning with an outline of the academic context and analytical frameworks of post-colonial and social capital theory, we then move onto an introduction of the research context and methodology. Next, drawing on empirical data we highlight the key similarities and differences of international sports volunteers from Cricket Without Boundaries (CWB) and national sports volunteers from Cameroon Cricket Federation (CCF) who have volunteered on a two-week project in Cameroon. Finally, we reflect on the data within the context of the theoretical frameworks introduced earlier. By highlighting our chosen case study it is our intention that our work provokes debate and reflection by volunteer-led organizations operating within an international collaboration.

Historical background and the contemporary context of international sports volunteering

International volunteering is not a new concept in the global north; with its history deeply linked to that of the evolution of the international development agenda. The establishment post-Second World War of the Bretton Woods institutions (now the World Bank group) saw regulation of nation states' economic and political systems which prompted the increased presence of global north NGOs in developing countries. At this time economic and political growth was viewed as *the* process to overcome issues of poverty and underdevelopment (Alacevich, 2007), a framework which provided the mentality for the arrival of the first volunteer organizations.

The first instances of international volunteering within Africa, according to Manji and O'Coill (2002), involved missionary societies and voluntary organizations assuming a purpose beyond simply providing welfare services, acting as a means of controlling the native population. Therefore during this period the work of international voluntary organizations concerned themselves more with the 'apparent failings of Africans' (Manji and O'Coill, 2002, p. 5) and correcting their 'uncivilized' nature rather than seeking to redress the socio-economic circumstances that they faced. A major critique of early international volunteering came from Ivan Illich, an Austrian philosopher, in an address to the volunteers of the Conference on InterAmerican Student Projects (CIASP) where he used his speech to focus on inappropriate and offensive paternalism, which he saw as inherent within CIASP's work in Mexico where he told volunteers, 'To hell with

good intentions ... you will not help anybody by your good intentions'
(Illich, 1968, p. 1). He continued with his speech, condemning the narrow
perspectives and lack of cultural understanding amongst the untrained
volunteers.

A key distinction between international sports volunteering today and
its earlier equivalent comes from links with the tourism industry. The last
few decades have brought travel and volunteering possibilities that simply
didn't exist previously, prompted by the expansion in cheap global travel,
shifting demographics and identities, and changed work and learning patterns (Randel et al., 2005). In addition, modern society, according to Callanan and Thomas (2005), has become restless, jaded and increasingly
guilt-conscious due to the increased media exposure of global inequalities,
international initiatives and goodwill activities.

The recruitment message from CWB (2015) used to entice prospective
volunteers highlights the opportunity to assist with such inequalities:

> In volunteering for two weeks the difference you can make is surpris-
> ingly big. We are looking for volunteers from all backgrounds to have
> a life changing experience, while transforming the lives of others. We
> are looking for general sports enthusiasts, qualified or unqualified and
> it is not essential to have any knowledge of Cricket or HIV/Aids but a
> willingness to work hard and get involved.

Over the past decade, this kind of rhetoric has become increasingly popular
in global north societies. The concept of sending international volunteers
to developing countries in a spirit of altruistic compassion to help others
has turned into a tourism activity for people wanting to 'make a difference'. This practice, primarily known as voluntourism, is identified by
Wearing (2001, p. 1) as a process that 'applies to those tourists who, for
various reasons, volunteer in an organised way to undertake holidays that
might involve aiding or alleviating the material poverty of some groups in
society'. In contrast to the global north discourse that promotes voluntourism, the volunteering sector in Cameroon is relatively new. In 2015, the
Minister of Youth Affairs and Civic Education, made the announcement
that volunteering in Cameroon would soon be increased with the launch of
a national volunteering strategy. Following the theme, 'The world is
moving. Are you? Volunteer!', the minister aligned the new volunteer
strategy with Vision 2035, Cameroon's aim to be an emerging country by
2035 with specific objectives around economic growth, poverty reduction
and improve social services (London School of Economics, 2016). The
minister proposed that the youth of the nation should get involved in volunteering to boost the socio-economic development of communities, promotion of solidarity and humanitarian activities and the preservation of
world peace. The new strategy gives strong encouragement, particularly to

Cameroonian youths, to utilize volunteer opportunities to develop a range of skills that will provide personal, communities and wider society gains (Ndukong, 2015).

Sport and international development: an analytical framework

Just over a decade ago, the United Nations declared 2005 to be its 'International Year for Sport and Physical Education', subsequently there has been a proliferation in the use of sport as a tool for initiating social change. Levermore and Beacom (2009, p. 1) suggest:

> Projects involving sport have included attempts to educate young people to appreciate health concerns (such as the dangers of HIV and malaria), engender respect for local communities, discourage antisocial behaviour, increase gender awareness, as well as assist with the rehabilitation of people with disabilities and the reconciliation of communities in conflict.

Reflecting on the growth of the western-dominated SDP sector, preceded by the emergence of international development and western colonialism, a multitude of structures and practices have played a significant role in shaping the contours of the world that we know today. Post-colonial theory, according to Prasad (2003), recognizes the need to investigate such complex and deeply fraught dynamics of colonialism and the ongoing significance of how the colonial encounter has affected people living in the west and the non-west. Post-colonial theory has developed through the works of political critics, such as Said (1978) and Bhabha (1994), who in various ways have sought to uncover the agency and resistance of people subjugated by both colonialism and its contemporary appearances. Of particular concern to post-colonial studies is the way that the global south is portrayed in a negative, derogatory and stereotypical manner and attempts to recover the local, indigenous understandings in order to disrupt entrenched systems of (northern) knowledge contemporary voices of the colonially marginalized (Mwaanga and Banda, 2014).

CWB, a UK based sports INGO, initiated a collaboration with CCF, the recognized cricket governing body for Cameroon, in 2012, having previously created collaborations with national cricket federations in the former British colonies of Botswana, Kenya, Rwanda and Uganda. The nature of such international collaborations inherently positions the INGO and its international volunteers in a delicate position amidst dominant discourses of western hegemony and neo-colonial critics. Razack (1998) has suggested that contact and collaborations between the global north and the global south organizations is often fraught with messages of southern cultural inferiority and northern domination socially and economically. To explore the post-colonial discourse we also draw on dependency theory and its intent to explore the unequal power relations that have developed as a result of colonialism. In short, dependency theory contends that economic events in history have encouraged developing countries to depend on the support of more developed nations (Sugden and Tomlinson, 2002). Within SDP this may be evidenced by a dependence on material goods such as sports equipment and health supplies and through a reliance on human and financial resources such as international volunteers' knowledge and delivery budgets. Consequently the SDP sector has been critiqued for producing and reinforcing wider power discourses of initiating a 'northern led' and 'top down approach' to development (Darnell and Hayhurst, 2012). In practice, we used post-colonial theory as a lens to explore the extent to which historical colonial positions of power are played out in a contemporary collaborative SDP programme in Cameroon. Examples of evidence, consistent with post-colonial theory, may include international volunteers being positioned by themselves or by Cameroonian national volunteers in the role of 'teacher' and 'giver', with the national volunteers being positioned as 'pupil' and 'receiver' of knowledge, goods and global northern ideologies. We took note of previous studies which have evidenced that global north workers are positioned as the benevolent, educated development individual and the southern worker (specifically the African continent) as the poverty-stricken and disease-ridden child in need of salvation (Nicholls *et al.*, 2011), reflecting and legitimizing relations of power whereby the northern development paradigms dominate SDP policy and practice (Mwaanga, 2014). This exchange and dominant structure has been evidenced within SDP volunteering, in which the majority of people involved in the planning and delivery of SDP initiatives tend to be western institutions, volunteers, academics, sports students, all of whom typically share western ideologies and practices (Mwaanga and Banda, 2014). Whilst there is evidence to suggest that national sports volunteers, sometimes referred to as 'peer leaders', volunteer alongside international volunteers within SDP initiatives (UK Sport, 2013), there is still a recognized gap and desire for literature which articulates and explores the experiences and motives of such individuals (Hayhurst, 2009). Of the few studies that have directly sought the views of local participants (Fokwang, 2009; Guest, 2009; Kay, 2009; Lindsey and Grattan, 2012; Spaaij, 2009; Schulenkorf, 2010), they tend to be framed in the context of examining how sports initiatives and policies are delivered, with no previous focus being given to local volunteer motives and personal gains.

In addition to post-colonial theory, we draw on social capital theory as a framework to analyse volunteer motivations. Despite a growing number of organizations in the SDP sector and assertion that INGOs rely on volunteers (Lacey and Ilcan, 2006), there is actually little known about the motives of sport volunteers working within the SDP movement – whether international or national in focus. Clary *et al.* (1998) have suggested six key functions as to why people volunteer:

1   developing and enhancing one's career (*career*);
2   enhancing and enriching personal development (*esteem*);
3   conforming to the norms of, or establishing norms for, significant others (*social*);
4   escaping from negative feelings (*protective*);
5   learning new skills and practising underutilized abilities (*understanding*); and
6   expressing values related to altruistic beliefs (*value*).

These functions enabled us to think of motives as being altruistic and for the purposes of self-gain, for example enhancing one's career through learning new skills. Volunteering according to Nichols and Shepherd (2006) has never had a purity of purpose and has always been and will always be a balance between altruistic motives of helping others and volunteering for self-interest. Motivations therefore should be seen as a complex mix which differs between people, their priorities and circumstances and which are likely to change over time. We are interested in the notion that volunteers stand out socially from non-volunteers in having more extensive social networks and being affiliated with more secondary organizations (Lofland, 1996), in short, they possess more social capital. Therefore, we aimed to explore how and why international and national volunteers made new and built on existing contacts, networks and friendships for purposes of social gain and career development.

At the root of power discourses within SDP is the debate about whether change is brought about or constrained by forces beyond people's control (social structures such as gender, class, ethnicity, religion) or through individual and collective action (agency). Lindsey and Grattan (2012) have argued that SDP volunteers in Zambia had the capacity for acting freely by exerting their own agency in pursuing SDP programmes on their own terms and in their own context. On the other hand Darnell and Hayhurst (2012) argued that local agency of SDP volunteers in developing countries occurs amidst a western hegemonic backdrop often promoted by global north institutions as a way to constrain and control the actions of individuals in developing countries. Broader international development research has criticized international volunteers for ignoring, and being ignorant of, the bigger picture of western dominance and the colonial past of the destinations which they visit, with western volunteers often having little knowledge or experience of the work they are undertaking (Brown and Hall, 2008). Similarly, Perold *et al.* (2012) have recommended that international volunteers need to challenge their own personal notions of development, which typically perceive the north as coming to 'save Africa'. Our study is positioned within this context and debate and drew on post-colonial and social capital theory, a 'lens' to explore the motives and subsequent personal gains (social capital) of international volunteers from the global north and national volunteers from the global south.

The research context

Participants for this study had experience of sports volunteering in Cameroon, Central West Africa, a sporting nation often referred to as Africa in Miniature (Amin, 2014). Boasting a triple colonial legacy, having been colonized by Germany, France and Britain, Cameroon, like many former colonies in Africa, has faced a difficult political, cultural and social set of circumstances following independence and reunification (Clarke and Ojo, 2016). Modern-day Cameroon has over 200 ethnic groups that retain ethnic identities and affiliations, which are also fused with elements of French (Francophone) and English (Anglophone) cultures that have survived the colonial period (Angwafo, 2014). Cameroon comprises of ten regions, eight of which are Francophone dominated with the remaining two regions being Anglophone.

Sport is predominantly government-led in Cameroon, although there are a growing number of international organizations, typically from the global north, that deliver sport in Cameroon (Clarke and Ojo, 2016). The participants who took part in our research ($n=23$) come from the UK and Cameroon, were aged between 22 and 56 and volunteer as part of an ongoing international collaboration between CWB and CCF who have worked on joint SDP initiatives in Cameroon since 2012. Both organizations are volunteer-led at all levels: governance, operations and delivery. The two organizations work together to achieve three main goals of CWB:

1   To spread cricket through coaching children and teaching adults how to coach.
2   To link cricket to HIV/AIDS awareness and incorporate these messages into coaching sessions.
3   To bring together and empower local communities through cricket.

The collaboration involved organizing and delivering two-week sports coaching and education projects in Cameroon, typically twice a year. Volunteers were recruited from the UK to travel to Cameroon by CWB via a number of means including local cricket/sports clubs, previous volunteers and through social media. Each project is typically made up of six to eight UK volunteers, who are a mix of coaches and non-coaches (Cricket Without Boundaries, 2015). UK volunteers are joined in Cameroon by four to six local volunteers. Often, the volunteers from Cameroon are players from the national cricket team who co-deliver educative messages around HIV/AIDS awareness to school teachers and children in targeted communities.

Methodology

The experiences and insights of both international and national sports volunteers are essential in providing a fresh and valuable contribution to the research field of SDP. Our study therefore recognized this and attempted to address such a balance within its methodology. Utilizing a post-colonial lens has enabled us to be more sensitive to broader notions of power and inequality in combination with social capital theory which prioritizes motivations and the opportunities for personal gain. It is widely acknowledged that qualitative research is not value-free and that researchers should be explicit about the values, identity and biases that underpin their study and reflect on the possible implications of their own position in relation to participants, and the potential impact this has on the research (Janesick, 1999; Smith, 2003). In addition to researching in the SDP sector, the first author has worked with CWB in a voluntary capacity for five years and therefore we felt it important to consider this position with respect to issues as suggested by Rose (1997), which include: insider/outsider status, education, class, race, gender and cultural background in order to understand the dynamics of researching across cultures. Of the 23 participants, 11 were recruited from CWB and 12 from CCF through purposeful and snowball sampling techniques. Our initial contact was made with potential participants through the first author who was working directly with the two organizations as part of their PhD research. We were very aware of the negative power relationships that can potentially affect our research as white middle-class individuals from the global north, particularly interviewing national volunteers in Cameroon. In an attempt to minimize obligation to take part in the research we informally discussed the research with both organizations and asked who would be interested in taking part to reduce pressure on potential participants. In Cameroon, a local research assistant who was known to CCF was recruited to assist with the research study. The decision was made to adopt semi-structured interviews following careful consideration; as the focus was on the individual motives and personal gains of sports volunteering other options such as focus groups were not deemed to be as suitable. Some volunteers disclosed some sensitive information about their circumstances and motivations and so disclosing this in front of their peers would not have been appropriate. We offered the option for volunteers to speak to us in English or in French, depending on their preferred language. In instances where French was the preferred language our research assistant also doubled up as an interpreter. Of the 23 interviews, 15 were conducted in English and eight in French.

The interviews lasted between 35 and 100 minutes, each were transcribed verbatim. An inductive and manual coding approach was used to initially analyse the transcripts and identify the emergent key themes. Themes were compared between the international and national volunteers to identify which were most prominent before re-analysing the data to identify and explore sub-themes (Creswell, 2012). Our chapter is organized around key themes that emerged from the comparative data set, focusing on:

1   the individual motivations to volunteer; and
2   to what extent volunteering has led to personal gains (social capital).

Findings

Motivations to volunteer and social capital gains

Typically the act of volunteering is linked with notions of doing good and altruism, typified as 'the willingness and ability of citizens to give their time, out of a sense of solidarity and without expectation of monetary reward' (UN Volunteers, 2005, p. 6). However, modern-day volunteer tourists are evidently motivated by dual purposes (Forsythe, 2011), which include reciprocal forms of engagement, with a desire for social capital personal gains as well as the spirit of benevolence. The initial part of our interviews focused on the motivations of sports volunteers. Superficially, both international and national volunteers showed similarities in their overarching motive to use cricket as a tool to deliver HIV/AIDS awareness messages in the Central West African nation of Cameroon. However the analysis also revealed a complex set of underlying motivations which fundamentally differ between international and national volunteers.

International volunteers: a desire to 'help' Africa through sport

The overwhelming motive for international volunteers was to make a positive contribution in Africa. For some respondents, their motivation was described as wanting 'to help' individuals in the communities and schools they visited. Terms such as *help, support, assist, develop* were all used to indicate the intentions of international volunteers when working with local communities. Two volunteers describe their initial motivations for volunteering:

> Well I didn't think in my head I am going to go out and make a difference, but I think that as westerners, you can almost have that sense of I am going to do something good. I am going to try to help these people.
>
> (Rebecca, international volunteer, aged 38)

It was nothing to do with cricket at all, it was for other reasons. I wanted to go out there and experience the country and I wanted to help children, if I could.

(Sarah, international volunteer, aged 32)

Post-colonial theory enables us to analyse how 'Africa' is depicted to the western world through the eyes of international sports volunteers. For example, at the end of the above quote by Rebecca, her language choice positions herself as the do-gooder, travelling to 'help' Africans who are dependent on her acts of western aid. A number of international volunteers shared similar insight which aligned with dependency theory, consistent with the work of Perold *et al.* (2012) who suggested that although the relationships between African countries and their former colonial masters are no longer characterized by formal dependence, a dependency relationship continues to exist.

A number of international sports volunteers shared how they received a warm welcome by the CCF and the schools in which they worked. The term 'mzungu' was commonly reported as being used by some Cameroonians during their volunteer experience to describe their white race, as one volunteer described:

We were often called mzungu, usually by school children or by local people in the communities we visited during our breaks or time off. The children and adults seemed to find it funny to call after us to get our attention. We were told it meant 'white man', so I guess what they were saying was harmless.

(Alan, international volunteer, aged 42)

Whilst such terms were discussed as being friendly and informal gestures from the perspective of the western volunteer, the term itself is rooted in the history of colonial and post-colonial relations between Africa and the global north. The term mzungu has a tendency to be interpreted from one of two perspectives (Baaz, 2005). The traditional colonial understanding of mzungu produces images of an untouchable superior wealthy and trustworthy white master. Conversely, the term mzungu can show a more endearing and empowering side of westerners, often staying with, working and learning alongside locals. Despite positive intentions being reported by volunteers, the nature of a western organization sending volunteers to deliver programmes in local African communities would appear to reinforce the notion of superiority (largely through the knowledge exchange of cricket coaching and HIV/AIDs awareness messages).

International volunteers were especially motivated to combine travel and sports coaching in a different way to a more a traditional UK sports club setting, as indicated here by a volunteer:

> The initial thing that drew me in was the fact that it was cricket coach-
> ing, having never been abroad before I thought that this might be a
> good chance to go on a type of holiday as well on my own.
>
> (Simon, international volunteer, aged 24)

In a similar way that international volunteers seek experiences that make a difference by combining volunteering with travel (Wearing, 2001), the SDP sector is now providing an alternative medium for sports enthusiasts to have a piece of the 'voluntourism' pie.

Also, international sports volunteers relished the opportunity to introduce a new sport in Cameroon, as one volunteer articulated:

> This is a place where we would genuinely be turning up with a cricket
> bat and people had no idea what a cricket bat was, to then 12 months
> later 12 schools playing a cricket festival and then Ashu a local
> teacher, and now coach, recording a video saying what nice things we
> had done for his children.
>
> (Robert, international volunteer, aged 42)

It was outlined how the project was able to introduce cricket to schools that had never seen or heard of the sport before, as Patrick, an international sports volunteer aged 22, explained:

> When you enter an institution and say that you would like to intro-
> duce cricket they will tell you 'what is that?'. Cricket and they will
> liken it to a cricket, the insect. People will say 'that it is an insect, how
> can you play that?'

Patrick provides an example whereby as an international volunteer he positioned himself as the 'giver' and the local school children as the 'receivers'. Consistent with dependency and post-colonial theory, inter-
national volunteers shared that in some cases they would work in a school to introduce the game of cricket, which without them would have left children believing that cricket was only an insect and not also a sport. It has been widely observed that the discourse of cricket and colonialism has a long history (Odendaal, 1988) and in particular the use of cricket as a way to advocate British imperialist ideology (Nauright, 2005). There is an argument that Sub-Saharan Africa has undergone a total and passive acceptance of the British modern sports and in doing so western standards can be seen as a second nature and are used to symbolize the uniformity of western hegemony (Dejonghe, 2001). We do not suggest that the international sports volunteers intended to reinforce a dependency mentality during their volunteer experience; however, the connotations of cricket do conjure up hegemonic images of the British Empire, a game originally

played predominantly by white settlers. Whilst the study centres on motivations and personal gains through volunteering, it remains unclear how the international volunteers perceive the bigger picture of using cricket (with all of its associated connotations) as a delivery tool in a former British colony. One could assume that volunteers have bought into the concept by the fact that they have chosen to volunteer for the INGO, delivering its aims and committing to raise funds to do so. Whether in fact the international volunteers were unaware or chose to ignore the historical implications and context of the sport they use as a delivery tool is unclear. What was clear was the awareness articulated by the Cameroonian national volunteers who made continued references to cricket's history as being an 'Englishman's' game, cricket's colonial influences and how these set of circumstances affect their own mindset as volunteers in modern-day Cameroon.

National volunteer motives: popularizing cricket and learning from the 'experts'

National sports volunteers shared a collective motivation to grow the relatively new sport which has been in existence in Cameroon since 2005 (International Cricket Council, 2016). Many of the national volunteers working alongside CWB also doubled as national cricket players or coaches and as such shared motives to spread the popularity of the game to secure its future in a country dominated by football (Nkwi and Vidacs, 1997). Qualifying as an affiliate member of the International Cricket Council, funding and exposure of cricket in Cameroon is relatively low, so therefore volunteers voiced a motivation to popularize the sport by other means. Drawing on the publicity of the international partnership with CWB was cited as a common motive to expose the game of cricket:

> Their presence (of CWB) in schools makes a lot of noise, people are wondering why they go to schools and what is the cricket all about. The media talks about it, they talk about it in the press. It makes and brings it about in the mind of every other person. It elevates the level of publicity of the game considering the fact that they are white and that conception of white skin it pulls, it rather pulls people, because when you hear about maybe a white something, the whites somewhere, it is still in the minds of people that it attracts, so if a white is here it means it is important it means it has value.
>
> (Junior, national volunteer, aged 25)

Reflecting on this statement, 55 years after Cameroon gained its independence from France and Great Britain, the national volunteers illustrate the mindset of modern-day Cameroon. The paternal relationship between the global south and the global north is very much apparent, as Junior suggests: that the conception of white skin pulls and attracts because it has greater value than black skin. This appears to reinforce neo-colonial constructs that continue to propel the view and influence of its former colonizer, in this instance by sending white, British sports volunteers, maintaining local control of socio-cultural values and colonial attitudes of power.

Further discussion with national volunteers illustrated an underlying motive to learn from the international volunteers with frequent references made to their white skin and their contested supposed 'expert status'. Christian, a national volunteer (aged 38), who spoke of his role in recruiting other national volunteers, mentioned: 'they become more motivated when they see experts, the white colour, the white skin'. Similarly, when coaching in schools, a national volunteer spoke of the 'pull' of the white skin for the school children:

> Let's say the training could have been taught by us blacks, we are not sure how they would react. But seeing the whites the students are very happy I don't know if only the black would have come they would not be very happy. But for now it is the whites who have come and so we are happy with that.
>
> (Patrick, national volunteer, aged 22)

Drawing on Darnell's work (2007), we do not to suggest that the global north is always white, either socially or ethnically, but rather that whiteness as a position of dominance is linked with these examples as a position of the northern expert in development. In describing the roles of the two organizations from which volunteers derive, one national volunteer suggests that:

> Cricket Without Boundaries is like the teacher coming to teach the student, so whatever they say we listen and take to what they have to say because one knows more than the other in this aspect of the discipline, they are coming to teach so we just have to learn.
>
> (Thierry, national volunteer, aged 23)

The Cameroonians' response is limited to that of gratitude, which positions the international NGO and its volunteers as generous and deserving of their 'expertise status' and is therefore a key motive to volunteer. Notions of 'whiteness' and superiority are (re)confirmed by national volunteers, as Darnell (2007) has previously suggested, positioning international volunteers as benevolent experts.

Several national volunteers discussed receiving sports equipment and resources as being a key motive to volunteer:

It is an advantage for Cameroon Cricket to work with the English NGO because first of all they have the materials (equipment), everything is available, when they come they are able to give it out to schools and institutions where they are going to sensitize, something which we can't do.

(Samuel, national volunteer, aged 37)

The international partnership is reliant on specialized equipment such as plastic Kwik Cricket equipment being donated by global north countries. This set-up therefore positions the national sports volunteers as mere thankful recipients, passive to the INGO at the hope and motivation of being awarded free equipment. The second part of our interviews focused on personal gains through their SDP volunteering experiences. The analysis uncovered subtle differences on how national and international volunteers used their involvement within the international partnership to gain stocks of social capital.

International volunteers: new friendships and professional gain

The opportunity to forge friendships was a clear motivating factor for international volunteers. The term *friendship* and *family* was used by volunteers when describing their relationship and bond with other international volunteers and national volunteers in Cameroon:

I am in the charity family. You know everyone talks to each other most weeks and you know that's nice.

(Alan, international volunteer, aged 42)

This supports the notion that friendships are the new families (Watters, 2004). Friends, according to Watters, can be understood as urban tribes who meet to learn and acquire new shared skills and experiences. International volunteers discussed the intense schedule for the two-week volunteering project in Cameroon, citing camaraderie and friendship as central motives:

Personally, I feel that volunteering has broadened my personal horizons. If you volunteer, you meet new people and make new connections from different backgrounds. We all have a common interest, in that we've done that experience and so have other volunteers from Cameroon. I made some good friends whilst we were there on the trip, for example I am still in contact with them through social media.

(Luke, international volunteer, aged 27)

Contrary to discourses which suggest a power imbalance between national volunteers, 'the locals', and international volunteers, 'the tourists' (Urry and Larsen, 2011), there were genuine feelings from international volunteers that friendships formed with Cameroonian national volunteers are two-way, equal and ongoing. Post-colonial theory provides a useful lens to draw on the work of Said (1978) who contended that in the global north, colonial discourses continue to dominate representations of the global south, focusing on the ways in which Europe produced colonial order to exert power over the colonized. Unlike the national volunteers, the international sports volunteers did not appear to show any level of awareness to the sensitive post-colonial context in which they volunteered, perhaps because it was so well embedded. Similar to Perold et al.'s (2012) findings the international sports volunteers operating in Cameroon actively reinforce the colonial legacy either by way of ignorance or a lack of knowledge of the bigger picture of western dominance and the colonial past of the country which they volunteered in.

International sports volunteers showed very high levels of awareness when it came to the possibility of developing social capital through volunteering. Moreover, international volunteers demonstrated extensive social networks in the UK and in Cameroon as a result of their volunteering, which created a breeding ground for both bonding and particularly bridging social capital. Seemingly, social capital is used for personal gain, particularly by international volunteers to advance their careers. When asked about how volunteering impacts on either his personal or professional life, Simon responded:

> There are three key things for me [for remaining involved as a volunteer]; getting experience at board level [at the organization] is absolutely key, soaking up the expertise of other volunteers within the charity of professionals, and then having that network of both friends on a personal level, but also contacts in different industry and walks of life.
>
> (Simon, international volunteer, aged 34)

Likewise, Sarah recognized the skills that she acquired through her role have enabled her to find a new job:

> Because of my involvement, I've now got another piece of work, as I work for another NGO and my cricket experience definitely helped me get that job. The experience from the sport for development sector, along with my organizational skills which I need for my new job, have very much been honed by volunteering. And I am thinking, very seriously now, looking at and considering what my next move might be, either internally or within the international development movement.
>
> (Sarah, international volunteer, aged 32)

These quotes by Simon and Sarah show similar insight to Clary *et al.*'s (1998) argument concerning motivational functions – in that international sport volunteers seek out opportunities to develop and enhance their career. These attributes further align to Putnam's notion that bridging social capital helps individuals to get ahead in life (Putnam, 1995, 2000).

National volunteers: gaining social capital and status by association

The dominant finding from national volunteers is they often focused on their ability to gain kudos and status (socially and professionally) from their association with white international volunteers. Findings indicate that, in a manner consistent with post-colonial literature, national volunteers and, more widely, Cameroonian citizens perceive international volunteers as being of higher economic status than themselves, as having special skills, and often as a superior race, as an interview with one volunteer explained:

> We look at whites like the superior being. We regard you people as a superior being. We learn that if you want to look at the historical way, you see how the whites, us blacks were being controlled by the whites. So blacks have always regarded the whites as a superior being and more to that, we have been colonized by whites which means that you people are superior.
>
> (Patrice, national volunteer, aged 27)

The researcher conducting the interview (aware of their own positionality) had not previously met this participant and their affiliation to CWB was not known by the participant. Despite this, the participant drew the researcher into the discussion through continual references such as 'you people, you whites', an association made purely on race and 'whiteness' grounds, evidence of post-colonialism and dependency theory. This example by a national sports volunteer reaffirms the position of international volunteers in relation to patriarchal power hierarchies by drawing on Cameroon's colonial history.

National volunteers recognized the western hegemonic system in which they operate and used this to create stocks of bridging capital by creating links with people outside of their immediate circles (i.e. international volunteers help broaden their personal opportunities and personal gains within Cameroon). An example of this is Claude, a national volunteer whose children attend a school visited by CWB. He discussed how the head teacher has allowed special financial payment arrangements for him due to his association with the INGO:

I was the one, even though I am a parent, because I brought CWB to them. My children can go for the whole year without me paying my fees. The head teacher has confidence in me. So I can pay at the end of the year. Not as other parents do, they will be putting pressure on them. The school always asks when are they coming again, when are we working, when are we working. You know, that enthusiasm is always there, always there.

(Claude, national volunteer, aged 26)

Similarly, bridging social capital is used as an exchange for professional gains for national sports volunteers. Samuel, a national sports volunteer and PE teacher, was rewarded by his head teacher who has also witnessed an increase in pupils attending his school as a result of the association with the INGO:

Last year my boss, the principal of this school had to congratulate me for the hard working in order to bring you people in. He told me that he really like the way I am moving as far as sport is concerned. I have really brought in some people and also sensitized. I have also brought in some new students. The population of this school I think is due to those visits. It has increased because people are coming here to learn the cricket game. They are coming to learn the cricket game, they also like the association that we have. They are liking the interaction that we have with you people.

(Samuel, national volunteer, aged 34)

Findings showed that national volunteers utilize the contacts made with international volunteers to create bridging capital, which represents 'social capital currency' (Portes, 1998). This view suggests social capital as the property of individuals, but only in relation to others in particular contexts.

Our data has shown that international sports volunteers, whilst well intentioned to 'help' and deliver aid in its broadest context, unintentionally reinforced dominant discourses of western privilege and power. National sports volunteers appeared to be more open and conscious of such discourses by accepting this dominant discourse. National sports volunteers also subsequently found themselves manipulating situations for personal gain by celebrating connections with white international volunteers. Given these complex dynamics and discourses at play, we advocate for an expansion of post-colonialism within SDP. To fully consider the effect of post-colonialism on those from the west and the non-west (Prasad, 2003) we promote that future SDP research embraces dual perspectives to include insights from the global northern organizations (and their workers/ volunteers) and any collaborators in the global south (and their workers/ volunteers).

Interwoven with post-colonialism has been social capital theory, which has enabled us to highlight ways in which international and national volunteers used their experiences for personal and professional gain. Previous studies using social capital have tended to centre the focus of the study on the social capital gain of global northern volunteers. Considering the views of both international and national volunteers has facilitated us to have a more holistic debate of structure and agency and, second, to place this debate into broader understandings of how this interplays with post-colonialism.

Conclusions

The opinions and insights outlined in this chapter illustrate the complexity and often contrasting motives of international and national sports volunteers within the SDP sector. More than a decade and a half ago, Willis (2000, p. 844) questioned whether sport in the global south 'can provide a unique opportunity to break down patriarchal structures, leading towards more equality'. Our study would suggest that INGOs operating in this sector, often through international volunteers, continue to buy into this rhetoric with aims of international collaborations built on equal contributions and knowledge exchange. However, the findings suggest a different reality in that dominant hegemonic discourses remain intact and in some cases have become intensified by international and national sports volunteers working together.

As discussed, international sports volunteers evidenced strong altruistic motivations to 'help' others via programmes which use cricket coaching as a vehicle to deliver HIV/AIDS awareness messages in Cameroon. In addition these motivations are used as a mechanism for creating stocks of social capital which is used for both personal (friendships, networks) and professional gain (developing or enhancing skills for career advancement). It is not surprising that volunteering is seen by some sport-for-development volunteers as an opportunity for self-gain; which shows synergy with Putnam's notion of 'getting ahead in life'. In comparison, national volunteers shared motivations to popularize the sport of cricket and in doing so draw on the colonial past and position themselves as the pupil and the international volunteer and INGO as 'expert' and 'teacher'. Such connotations are ironic, given that many national volunteers are also national cricket players and coaches working with an INGO that does not stipulate that volunteers necessarily need to have any experience of cricket coaching to qualify them to deliver programmes in Africa (Cricket Without Boundaries, 2015).

Evidence suggested that national volunteers utilize the broader post-colonial discourses and ideologies for their own personal gain by generating bridging social capital currency (socially and professionally) from their association with white international volunteers and the sports INGO. Drawing on previous post-colonial studies (Baaz, 2005; Darnell and Hayhurst, 2012; Gilbert and Tompkins, 1996; Lindsey and Grattan, 2012; Mwaanga and Banda, 2014; Perold *et al.*, 2012) our study questioned whose interests are served through dominant sport-for-development discourse. This research suggests that the international volunteers maintain a dominant position, evident through their motivations and social capital gains from their experiences. However, evidence also suggests that national volunteers, aware of the dominant western hegemony in which they live and volunteer, utilize levels of agency (within these constraints) for personal gain.

In summary, we maintain that only by prioritizing both international and national volunteer insights and motives can the SDP sector fully appreciate the full picture of its policies put into practice locally by its volunteer workforce and local partners. It is recommended that volunteer organizations who buy into the notion of deploying international volunteers to developing countries should take seriously the critiques of the broader international volunteer industry (Forsythe, 2011; Lyons and Wearing, 2008; Perold *et al.*, 2012; Wearing, 2001) when recruiting and training volunteers in order to identify and recreate best practices and avoid the innate paradoxes within these sectors. We suggest that SDP INGOs should look for best practice outside the existing SDP body of INGOs, institutions and corporations to the broader international development sector for support in programme design and training of international volunteers. The volunteers' accounts have assisted us in highlighting the dominant ideologies of western hegemony which still exist in the former British colony of Cameroon. Only by considering these views from both perspectives and listening to the responses with an open mind can INGOs fully evaluate their practices and subsequently strive for change.

References

Alacevich, M. (2007). The changing meaning of development: SID's first decades. *Development* 50: 50–65.

Amin, J. (2014). *African immersion: American college students in Cameroon.* Maryland: Lexington Books.

Angwafo, P. (2014). *Cameroon's predicaments.* Monkon, Bamenda, Lanngaa Research and Publishing CIG.

Baaz, M. (2005). *The paternalism of partnership: A postcolonial reading of identity in development aid.* London: Zed Publishing.

Beutler, I. (2008). Sport serving development and peace: Achieving the goals of the United Nations through sport. *Sport in Society* 11: 359–369.

Bhabha, H. (1994). *The location of culture.* London: Routledge.

Brown, F. and Hall, D. (2008). Tourism and development in the global south: The issues. *Third World Quarterly* 29: 839–849.

Callanan, M. and Thomas, S. (2005). Volunteer tourism: Deconstructing volunteer activities within a dynamic environment. In M. Novelli (ed.) *Niche tourism: Contemporary issues, trends and cases*. Oxford: Elsevier.

Clarke, J. and Ojo, J. (2016). Sport policy in Cameroon. *International Journal of Sport Policy and Politics* (online first) DOI: 10.1080/19406940.2015.1102757.

Clary, E.G., Snyder, M., Ridge, R.D., Copeland, J., Stukas, A.A., Haugen, J. and Miene, P. (1998). Understanding and assessing the motivations of volunteers: A functional approach. *Journal of Personality and Social Psychology* 74: 1516–1530.

Creswell, J.W. (2012). *Qualitative inquiry and research design: Choosing among five approaches*. London: Sage.

Cricket Without Boundaries. (2015). *Our mission*. www.withoutboundaries.com/about/our-mission.

Darnell, S. (2007). Playing with race: Right to play and the production of whiteness in development through sport. *Sport in Society* 10: 560–579.

Darnell, S. and Hayhurst, L. (2012). Hegemony, postcolonialism and sport-for-development: A response to Lindsey and Grattan. *International Journal of Sport Policy and Politics* 4: 111–124.

Dejonghe, T. (2001). The place of Sub-Sahara Africa in the worldsportsystem. *Afrika Focus* 17: 79–111.

Fokwang, J. (2009). Southern perspective on sport-in-development: A case study of football in Bamenda, Cameroon. In R. Levermore (ed.) *Sport and international development*. Basingstoke: Palgrave Macmillan (pp. 198–218).

Forsythe, R. (2011). Helping or hindering? Volunteer tourism in Ghana and its critical role in development. *Rethinking development in an age of scarcity and uncertainty*. University of York.

Gilbert, H. and Tompkins, J. (1996). *Post-colonial drama: Theory, practice, politics*. London: Routledge.

Giulianotti, R. (2004). Human rights, globalization and sentimental education: The case of sport. *Sport in Society* 7: 355–369.

Guest, A.M. (2009). The diffusion of development-through-sport: Analysing the history and practice of the Olympic Movement's grassroots outreach to Africa. *Sport in Society* 12: 1336–1352.

Hayhurst, L.M.C. (2009). The power to shape policy: Charting sport for development and peace policy discourses. *International Journal of Sport Policy* 1: 203–227.

Illich, I. (1968). *To hell with good intentions*. Cuernavaca, Mexico: InterAmerican Student Projects (CIASP).

International Cricket Council. (2016). Cameroon affiliate member. www.icc-cricket.com/about/177/icc-members/affiliate-members/cameroon.

International Platform for Sport and Development. (2016). All organisations. www.sportanddev.org/en/connect/organisations/organisations_list/.

Janesick, V.J. (1999). A journal about journal writing as a qualitative research technique: History, issues, and reflections. *Qualitative Inquiry* 5: 505–524.

Kay, T. (2009). Developing through sport: Evidencing sport impacts on young people. *Sport in Society* 12: 1177–1191.

Kidd, B. (2008). A new social movement: Sport for development and peace. *Sport in Society* 11: 370–380.

Lacey, A. and Ilcan, S. (2006). Voluntary labor, responsible citizenship, and international NGOs. *International Journal of Comparative Sociology* 47: 34–53.

Levermore, R. and Beacom, A. (2009). *Sport and international development*. New York: Palgrave Macmillan.

Lindsey, I. and Grattan, A. (2012). An 'international movement'? Decentring sport-for-development within Zambian communities. *International Journal of Sport Policy and Politics* 4: 91–110.

Lofland, J. (1996). *Social movement organizations: Guide to research on insurgent realities*. London: Transaction Publishers.

London School of Economics. (2016). *Cameroon Vision 2035*. www.lse.ac.uk/GranthamInstitute/law/cameroon-vision-2035/.

Lyons, K.D. and Wearing, S. (2008). *Journeys of discovery in volunteer tourism: International case study perspectives*. Wallingford: CABI.

Manji, F. and O'Coill, C. (2002). The missionary position: NGOs and development in Africa. *International Affairs* 78: 567–583.

Mwaanga, O. (2014). NGOs in sport for development and peace. In I. Henry and K. Ling-Meo (eds) *Routledge handbook of sport policy*. London: Routledge (pp. 83–92).

Mwaanga, O. and Banda, D. (2014). A postcolonial approach to understanding sport-based empowerment of people living with HIV/AIDS (PLWHA) in Zambia: The case of the cultural philosophy of ubuntu. *Journal of Disability & Religion* 18: 173–191.

Nauright, J. (2005). White man's burden revisited: Race, sport and reporting the Hansie Cronje cricket crisis in South Africa and beyond. *Sport History Review* 36: 61–75.

Ndukong, K.H. (2015). Cameroon: National volunteer programme envisaged. *All Africa News*.

Nicholls, S., Giles, A.R. and Sethna, C. (2011). Perpetuating the 'lack of evidence' discourse in sport for development: Privileged voices, unheard stories and subjected knowledge. *International Review for the Sociology of Sport* 46: 249–264.

Nichols, G. and Shepherd, M. (2006). Volunteering in sport: The use of ratio analysis to analyse volunteering and participation. *Managing Leisure* 11: 205–216.

Nkwi, P.N. and Vidacs, B. (1997). Football: Politics and power in Cameroon. In G. Armstrong and R. Giulianotti (eds) *Entering the field: New perspectives on world football*. Oxford: Berg (pp. 123–140).

Odendaal, A. (1988). South Africa's black Victorians: Sport and society in South Africa in nineteenth century. In J.A. Mangan (ed.) *Pleasure, profit, proselytism: British culture and sport at home and abroad 1700–1914*. London: Frank Cass (pp. 193–214).

Perold, H., Graham, L., Mavungu, E., Cronin, K., Muchemwa, L. and Lough, B. (2012). The colonial legacy of international voluntary service. *Community Development Journal* 48: 179–196.

Portes, A. (1998). Social capital: Its origins and applications in modern sociology. *Annual Review of Sociology* 24: 1–24.

Prasad, A. (2003). *Postcolonial theory and organisational analysis*. New York: Palgrave Macmillan.

Putnam, R.D. (1995). Tuning in, tuning out: The strange disappearance of social capital in America. *PS-WASHINGTON* 28: 664–664.

Putnam, R.D. (2000). *Bowling alone: The collapse and revival of American community*. New York: Simon & Schuster.

Randel, J., German, T., Cordiero, M. and Baker, L. (2005). *International volunteering: Trends, added value and social capital.* Oslo: Development Initiatives.

Razack, S.H. (1998). *Looking white people in the eye: Gender, race and culture in courtrooms and classrooms.* Toronto: University of Toronto Press.

Rose, G. (1997). Situating knowledge: Positionality: Reflexives and other tactics. *Progress in Human Geography* 21: 305–320.

Said, E. (1978). *Orientalism.* New York: Vintage Books.

Schulenkorf, N. (2010). Sports events and ethnic reconciliation: Attempting to create social change between Sinhalese, Tamil and Muslim sports people in war-torn Sri Lanka. *International Review for the Sociology of Sport* 45: 273–294.

Smith, F. (2003). Working in different cultures. In N.J. Clifford and G. Valentine (eds) *Key methods in geography.* London: Sage (pp. 157–172).

Spaaij, R. (2009). The social impact of sport: diversities, complexities and contexts. *Sport in Society* 12: 1109–1117.

Sugden, J. and Tomlinson, A. (2002). *Power games: A critical sociology of sport.* Abingdon: Routledge.

UK Sport (2013). IDEALS Zambia summary report. UK Sport website.

UN Volunteers (2005). *Developing a volunteer infrastructure: A guidance note.* Bonn: United Nations Volunteers.

United Nations. (2016). *Sport and the Sustainable Development Goals.* www.un.org/wcm/content/site/sport/home/sport/sportandsdgs.

Urry, J. and Larsen, J. (2011). *The tourist gaze 3.0.* London: Sage.

Watters, E. (2004). *Urban tribes: Are friends the new family?* New York: Bloomsbury Publishing.

Wearing, S. (2001). *Volunteer tourism: Experiences that make a difference.* Wallingford: Cabi.

Willis, O. (2000). Sport and development: The significance of Mathare Youth Sports Association. *Canadian Journal of Development Studies* 21: 825–849.

Chapter 11

Volunteer tourism and international sport volunteering

Angela M. Benson

Introduction

As discussed in the Introduction to this volume, sport is often a vehicle for engaging in development. However volunteer tourism, per se, is not 'situated' within the international development field of study, however there are clear reference points linking these two fields of study. Wearing and Grabowski (2011, p. 193) state that 'volunteer tourism as a form of international development has been posed as an alternative mechanism which has the potential to achieve different socio-cultural outcomes'. Simpson (2004) and Palacios (2010) also support this notion of volunteer tourism and international development, albeit, often with critical references as to the extent it is actually moving the international development agenda along. It can also be seen through government initiatives. For example, the International Citizen Service (ICS)[1] is an overseas volunteering programme for young adults (aged 18–25 years old) which is now in its second cycle of funding from the UK Government via the Department of International Development.

If sport is a vehicle for engaging in development it would seem a natural progression for volunteer tourism companies to use sport as the basis for part of their project portfolio. For example GVI[2] offers sports and surfing programmes in South Africa, Globalteer[3] offers volunteers opportunities to help coach children in sports in Cambodia. Jaeger and Mathisen (Chapter 1, this collection) indicate that there are volunteer tourist packages related to dogsled races now available. Consequently, this chapter explores the nature of international volunteer tourism using the context of sport projects and sport volunteers by using the case study 'Projects Abroad'.[4] Like many other volunteer tourism organizations, Projects Abroad couch their marketing in terms of development projects, worthwhileness and making a difference. This chapter will start by examining volunteer tourism, then moves on to outline details of the case before overviewing the methods. The findings section presents an analysis of the 26 volunteer stories by highlighting the details of the three key themes: sporting contexts, children and personal benefits. The chapter will finish with a short conclusion.

Volunteer tourism

Whilst both volunteering and tourism are not new concepts, the bringing together of them as 'volunteer tourism' is a relatively recent phenomenon. Volunteer tourism is also known as voluntourism, international volunteer tourism, volunteering for development and international volunteering. This chapter will use the term volunteer tourism. Volunteer tourism is often associated as being part of 'alternative tourism' (albeit a macro niche) rather than attributed to the 'sustainable tourism development' paradigm. It is clear to see in the literature generally, that volunteer tourism is rarely measured against all the three fundamental pillars of sustainability (economic, social and environmental) at the same time; however, this is also true of tourism studies.

The most cited and recognized definition of volunteer tourism is one by Wearing (2001, p. 1), who defined the activity as to: 'volunteer in an organised way to undertake holidays that might involve aiding or alleviating the material poverty of some groups in society, the restoration of certain environments or research into aspects of society or environment'. Even the author (Wearing, 2001) now agrees that this early definition is narrow in focus (see Benson, 2010; Lyons and Wearing, 2008). As the literature has expanded, so has the number of definitions (see, for example, Brown, 2005; McGehee and Santos, 2005). In addition, some of the other terms have also been defined. For example, voluntourism[5] is defined as: 'The conscious, seamlessly integrated combination of voluntary service to a destination and the best, traditional elements of travel – arts, culture, geography, history and recreation – in that destination' (voluntourism.org). The growing complexity of the international volunteer tourism marketplace alongside the continuing debate and critique of volunteer tourism makes defining international volunteer tourism all the more difficult, hence the diversity in definitions with different focuses.

The literature on volunteer tourism in the early days of research was almost exclusively on the volunteer, and whilst this has diversified to other areas, volunteers are still highly researched. Despite the growing research on volunteers there is no profile of volunteer tourists; as such we must create one from existing research. The literature notes women are generally more likely to participate in volunteer tourism than men (Brown and Morrison, 2003; McGehee, 2002; Stoddart and Rogerson, 2004). The age range seems to run from youth to senior citizens (e.g. Brown, 2005; Coghlan, 2008), and indeed my own research of interviewing 55 volunteers over three companies spanned from 16 years to 72 years (see Benson, 2010). Educations level also varies, but McGehee (2002) suggests that most volunteer tourists have earned a university degree and that many of them have international travel experience. However, what this actually tells us is little; it only demonstrates that a wide range of people engage in volunteer tourism.

One of the key areas of research has been to examine what motivates volunteer tourists to engage in volunteer tourism. As you would expect with a diverse range of people the motivations are also diverse. Wearing (2001) found that these included altruism, travel and adventure, structure of programme, right time and right place, personal growth, cultural exchange and learning and professional development. Brown (2005) and Benson and Siebert (2009) have similar findings. Although in Wearing's (2004) work, he suggested that pull factors might be ranked higher for volunteer tourists than mainstream tourists, the work by Benson and Siebert (2009) purports that from their top five motivational factors, four were in fact push factors (see also Dann, 1981). There is no doubt that altruism is a motivation that is cited as part of volunteer tourism. The other, which is now becoming more commonplace, is that of 'self-interest' – thus creating a 'give and take' disposition amongst volunteer tourists.

Whilst there are no recent figures that clearly state the size of the volunteer tourism market, there are a few older reports (see Mintel, 2008; TRAM, 2008). The numbers were relatively stable throughout the recent recession years and the growth of this sector is predicted to continue. With this growth has come a proliferation of organizations (for example, charities, private, social enterprises, brokers) entering the marketplace and as such a number of mechanisms can be seen:

1   Opportunities for volunteers have become highly segmented with offerings for volunteering at different stages of a person's life cycle (youth, mid-life, retirement and families), as highlighted above.
2   The marketplace has become more commercialized (Benson and Wearing, 2012), which is one of the key criticisms of volunteer tourism in that the commercialization of the sector has meant that the value chain between customer, company and community has become more tenuous. This is particularly pertinent if you consider the issues of commercialization and/or international development as being mutually exclusive, or are they? Some of the types of companies indicated above would say that as a social enterprise, for example, they can be commercially orientated but still have humanitarian and aid-related goals.
3   Whilst the companies traditionally have been predominantly western, the movement of volunteers has been mostly from the north to the south. More recently there has been a growth in organizations from the south making volunteer tourism offerings at lower prices, thereby setting up in direct competition to their northern counterparts. The literature on the sector and on the organizations has been very limited (see, for example, Benson and Blackman, 2011; Benson and Henderson, 2011; Coghlan, 2008; Coghlan and Noakes, 2012), although some company case studies are evident as part of studies on volunteers (similar to this chapter).

Discourses linking communities who engage with volunteer tourism projects are becoming more prevalent; however, the community voice still remains a voice that is often heard through a third party (e.g. governments, academics and companies) and appears not to be an easy voice to access. It is also a voice that is often referred to as being mute or passive with calls for more research associated with communities who are net receivers of volunteer tourists. Clifton and Benson (2006) found that volunteer tourism created a number of income-generating activities within host communities in the form of employment for local residents, accommodation for volunteers (renting or hosting), sales of food and handicrafts. English language competence facilitated these opportunities and transactions. On the other hand, Zahra and McGehee (2013) found that host communities appeared to be indifferent to financial gain and were experiencing leakages (e.g. host families buying volunteers soft drinks). Raymond and Hall (2008) suggest that their research reinforces the concept of western stereotypes who believe they are racially and culturally superior to locals. Another area that is often associated with community engagement is the 'they are poor but happy' syndrome (see Simpson, 2004) which is often a simplistic view held by volunteers and does not facilitate the development side of volunteer tourism. Volunteer tourism is linked to neoliberal times (Mostafanezhad, 2012; Vrasti, 2013) and is also criticized for being another form of neo-colonialism (see Butcher and Smith, 2015; Ward, 2007).

There is much discussion in the literature about the positive and/or negative outcomes of volunteer tourism programmes. Recently, there has been a growing level of criticism around the concept of volunteer tourism, particularly around volunteer tourism and children, which to some extent is being fuelled by the media and organizations like Tourism Concern.[6] There is no doubt that the concept of volunteer tourism has its challenges and to some extent there has been a response to this by the academic community and industry to move towards best practice initiatives. This can be seen through the special issue in WHATT[7]; the recently completed ESRC seminar series (Reconceptualising International Volunteering[8]); a number of codes of practice but a recent move by the International Standards Office (ISO) to develop a set of standards for volunteer tourism.[9] In contributing to this recent work, the next section will outline the organization in this study that offers volunteer tourism and sporting projects.

Projects Abroad

Projects Abroad is the largest volunteer tourism organization in the UK and arguably across the world. It indicates that since the organization was founded in 1992 it has sent almost 100,000 volunteers to 30 different countries on five continents. Whilst a family business until very recently, the company has expanded and runs over 129 projects worldwide with 20 staff working in the UK office and 700 trained staff, mainly locally employed, at the project destinations. There is also a network of recruitment staff working around the world. Projects Abroad recruits volunteers from across the 16–75 age spectrum but indicates that the majority of its volunteers are gap year volunteers and recent university graduates. The core values of the company are Contribution, Company, Community and Culture. Furthermore, one of the key terms used on the company website is 'worthwhile'. There is little doubt that this company has taken on board a number of the criticisms raised above and is seeking to engage both volunteers and communities in projects that matter and potentially make a difference. Dr Peter Slow, Founder and Director of Projects Abroad, states that 'Last year, we channelled into less developed countries the energy, skills and commitment of some 8,500 volunteers, not to mention over £12,000,000. This is a major achievement' (projects-abroad.co.uk).

Like many other volunteer tourism companies, the projects are generally for 2–12 weeks, although further weeks can be purchased. The price includes food, accommodation, local transport (to and from project), insurance and back-up in the form of 24-hour contacts. The accommodation is with host families, which Projects Abroad believes makes it 'unique'. The typology of projects is extensive and can be found in Table 11.1. The projects tagged with an asterisk (*) in the table are indicated as the top projects on the Projects Abroad website. It must be noted that sport is not listed. This chapter, however, is only concerned with the (international) sport volunteer projects.

Method

In this chapter a qualitative approach is used by drawing on secondary data and analysing 26 (25 individual and one couple) volunteer stories

Table 11.1 Projects Abroad volunteer projects

Agriculture and farming	Culture and community	Micro-finance
Archaeology	International development	Teaching*
Building*	Journalism	Sport
Business	Language courses	University dissertations
Care*	Law and human rights	Veterinary medicine and animal care
Conservation and environment*	Medical electives	
Creative and performing arts	Medicine and healthcare*	

Source: www.projects-abroad.co.uk/about-us/what-we-provide/.

from the Projects Abroad website. Table 11.2 indicates the countries where the sporting projects take place, the type of sport and the name of the volunteer, indicating which sport and which country they volunteered in. There were 11 female volunteers, 15 male volunteers and one couple making a total of 12 female and 16 male. Whilst not all volunteers indicated their nationalities, some of those mentioned included the United States, Canada and the UK.

NVivo 11 was used as the vehicle for working through the volunteer stories, thus allowing unstructured data to be analysed and interrogated

Table 11.2 Types of sport, country of project and volunteer stories

Sport	Country of project	Volunteer story
Athletics	Sri Lanka	No volunteer stories available
Basketball	Ghana, Toga	No volunteer stories available
Cricket	India,	No volunteer stories available
Football	Bolivia, China, Ghana, India, Romania, Peru, Togo	Ghana: Alice Wonnacott PU, Jasmine James US, John Carroll RG, Scott McQuarrie CB Peru: Tyler Stitzman RG Toga: Jesse Banks-Hudson PU
Multi-sports	Argentine, Ecuador, Ghana, Morocco, Peru	Ghana: Peter Gwilliam CB, Tanveer Ditta US Morocco: Emma Pugsley PU, James Spencer US Peru: Craig Bannerman PU, Michael Pope US, Pete Morrow PU
Rugby	Ghana, Samoa	Ghana: Alice Llelliott PU, Liam Sharpe RG, Stuart Pollock CB
School sports	Costa Rica, Ethiopia, Fiji, India Jamaica, Kenya, Mexico Mongolia, Peru, Philippines, Romania, Samoa, South Africa, Sri Lanka, Tanzania, Vietnam	Costa Rica: Elliott Poynter US Ethiopia: Erik Teig CB, Gayle Lindsay CB Jamaica: Bob and Jenny Wells CB Peru: Emily Bourn US Samoa: Alex Bouteiller PU South Africa: Melissa Kroslak RG, Sean McEwan RG
Surfing	South Africa	South Africa: Connor Quinn PU, Emma Fauquier RG
Volleyball	Bolivia	No volunteer stories available

Source: adapted from www.projects-abroad.co.uk.

Key
PU = Pre-University;   US = University Student;   RG = Recent graduate;   CB = Career Breaker/older volunteer.

for themes. One of the key limitations of the research is that these are volunteer stories from a company website and as such may only be positive portrayals.

Perceptions from volunteer stories

The volunteer stories are just that, they are a story about their volunteer trip. Whilst some write more about the sporting aspect than others, all have some reference to their sporting project. It is quite clear to see though that from these stories they are trying to convey an essence of a holistic experience. Therefore, references are made about the organization Projects Abroad; push and pull motivations; the project country; cultural aspects; host families; other activities they engaged in as part of the overall trip and what they had personally gained from the experience. As this was in essence a volunteer tourism trip, many of the findings are similar to what you might find in other volunteer tourism articles. Cultural encounters are part of the volunteer tourism experience (McIntosh and Zahra, 2007), and were emphasized by participants in this case. For example, comments on culture shock make us aware that: 'the experience was also eye opening to me and was a very big culture shock' (Emma) and 'The market stalls varied from fabric and jewellery to cow's heads – it was another big culture shock' (Alice). Furthermore, whilst there were some comments about poverty these were not excessive but all were related to projects in Africa: 'Many of them lived in poverty and had little money' (Alice L); 'where we were in the heart of poverty' (Connor); 'busy streets and noticeable poverty with street food, tin shack houses, homeless people and open raw sewage at the side of the streets' (Sean). There was only one defining quote that was directly related to the issue of 'poor but happy' syndrome (see Simpson, 2004), where one volunteer spoke about 'seeing such acute poverty contrasted with such happiness' (Alice W).

The focus of this section will now turn its attention to examine volunteer stories within sporting contexts. This is followed by a sub-section on children as all of the projects are in some way linked to children and the final theme discussed will be personal benefits to volunteers.

Sporting contexts

It is clear from the volunteer stories that there were a number of challenges in teaching sport in many of the destinations, because of a lack of necessary equipment, poor quality training facilities and large class numbers. As volunteers point out:

> the school had very limited resources and facilities, but the students were keen on PE.
>
> (Bob and Jenny)

Hillwood [primary school] is sadly severely underfunded.

(Sean)

My first lesson game me a taste of how tough it is to teach sport in an Ethiopian school – the average class size was between 40–50 children and there was a distinct lack of equipment – 1 basketball, a couple of footballs and a few skipping ropes for the whole school!

(Gayle)

[...] rugby placement and was very shocked when many of the players turned up bare footed and many were as young as 6. This was something I had not seen before, even after playing rugby for 8 years.

(Alice L)

These experiences were similar to Jesse's, who states: 'My boys would play wearing odd boots often with large holes and soles so worn down they might have better off barefoot.' Several of the volunteers brought sporting equipment with them, however, it is unclear as to if this an impromptu situation or more structured through the organization, however, the following quotes demonstrate that the new kit was greatly appreciated: 'The excitement on the kids' faces when they saw the athletic equipment I brought was incredibly gratifying' (Melissa) and 'I just had to bring hockey gear, and I am so glad I did. I have never seen such amazing and beautiful smiles as when the kids saw the equipment' (Sean).

It is also clear to see that many of the volunteers took their sport project very seriously and were often either qualified coaches themselves or engaged in sport at home to a reasonable level. The majority of these volunteers were therefore not unskilled, which is often a criticism levelled against short-term volunteer tourism projects. Sport was taken seriously with training and coaching being key elements in the volunteer stories, although it was also clear that often the volunteers were working with a Head of Sport/Head Coach and were also working alongside other volunteer coaches, although often they were given some area of responsibility or training type assignment to fully engage in:

the boys would turn up every day for a two-hour training session.

(Alice L)

[the head coach] gave me tremendous autonomy in training the kids in fitness.

(Tyler)

[...] teams training in a local park with a sheep and a cow tied up behind one of the goals.

(Michael)

Planning joint training sessions and talking over any issues [with other volunteers].

(John)

Other participants put emphasis on coaching sport, for instance:

[I] combined sports coaching with athletics training.

(Gayle)

coaching football to young Moroccan children.

(James)

Coaching is something I have a lot of experience in and is a passion of mine.

(Erik)

I could really make a difference when coaching.

(John)

Volunteer tourists also spoke about the passion people (especially kids) in the community had for sport:

I came to understand how everyone loved football!! Children loved to talk football, play football, watch football, football was everything and they all loved it ... I got to lead and teach my sport ... cricket. Children in Ghana are not too familiar with the sport of cricket. They all seemed quite confused at the onset ... seemed to enjoy it and did not want to stop playing.

(Tanveer)

The ex-footballer [Head Coach role] comes from one of the worst slum regions in Accra and he, every day, gets a bus full of keen children, aging between 5 and 12 and gives them the opportunity to get some fresh air away from the bustling, polluted city centre.

(Alice W)

One of the key themes coming out of the sporting contexts was that the volunteers were exuberant in their praise for the people (predominantly children) they were coaching. There is no doubt that they took pleasure in not only coaching but also seeing the improvement and change taking place. They highlight the level of talent and accomplishment that they see:

some of the players have unbelievable talent for their age and are a pleasure to work with.

(Elliott)

There was one child ... who I taught in 3 hours to paddle properly, turn in for a wave, and actually stand up and ride a wave.... The joy and sense of accomplishment on this boy's face was beautiful.

(Emma F)

The boy's teams demonstrated quite a deal of natural talent and competitive spirit so perhaps one day the West Indies will return to the top of world cricket once again.

(Bob and Jenny)

I could see vast improvements in the team as a whole ... I saw many of them improve as players and I knew that if they kept playing that they could become very talented rugby players.

(Alice L)

In all honesty I have never seen a fitter or more compliant group of young footballers in my life – they really became a joy to coach.

(Jesse)

Because I am an athlete by trade I was presented the unique opportunity to train with the high level academy kids every day ... the academy kids are tremendously talented.

(Tyler)

Whilst these are stories from the volunteers, we do not hear voices from children or the communities. Project Abroad has on its website a two-minute video of three children talking about their experience of volunteers who work in their school teaching sport.[10] The children name volunteers and talk about how great it is to have them teaching them specific sports at school as the local teachers do not have their level of expertise.

Working with children

Probably one of the most contentious areas linked to volunteer tourism at the present time is that of volunteers (and other tourism products) interacting with children. Whilst this chapter did not set out to have a particular focus on child-related volunteer placements, from the reading of the stories it was evident that this was an emerged recurring theme and, therefore, it would be remiss not to engage in the wider discussion. As such, initial text searches were run on 'children', 'child', 'kids', 'boys' and 'girls', which showed 25 of the 26 stories indicated links to these terms. The final volunteer story was then interrogated, showing that it was also associated with children but had used the term 'players' to refer to the children. Consequently all 26 of the volunteer stories are associated in some way with children though their sporting project. You can see from the statements above that children feature highly and they are similar in nature to the quote here:

> I cannot express in words the joy that I saw on the faces of these little children whilst playing football and having a good kick around. Every one of the children comes from a family with problems.
>
> (Alice W)

The wider debate around volunteer tourism and tourism linked to child-related projects and orphanages offers confusing and often contradictory rhetoric with expert opinions being diametrically opposed. The continuum ranges from 'it is not acceptable in any way, shape or form' to 'it is acceptable as long as certain practices and policies are in place'.

Richter and Norman (2010) in their article suggested that one of the main problems with volunteers/tourists is associated with the short-term dimensions of the encounters and the extent to which attachments are formed and broken in a continuous cycle. One participant mentioned, 'I went in not expecting to get so attached to the kids that I worked with' (Connor), although the report findings were predominantly about working in orphanages rather than with healthy children in school sport. Moreover they also outline that: 'In a recent *Time* magazine article on the topic of volunteering with children in residential care settings, two opposing views were presented.' Tricia Barnett, director (now a former director) of Tourism Concern, an industry watchdog in the United Kingdom, stated that:

> If you're going to work with children in an orphanage, [how will they] understand what you're trying to do when you don't speak their language and you don't stay long enough to form a relationship? ... what does it mean to the child?

However, Sally Brown, founder of Ambassadors for Children,[11] countered that 'If a kid can be held for a couple of days, you're able to make a small difference' (p. 224).

Two key reports on this topic are the United Nations Children Fund (2011) and the Next Generation Nepal (NGN) 2014 entitled *The paradox of orphanage volunteering: Combating child trafficking through ethical voluntourism*.[12] All of the reports indicate a number of issues around volunteers/tourists working with child-related projects and in some case offer advice and recommendations. Tourism Concern,[13] a UK campaigning organization for tourism which is ethical, has on its website an emotive picture of a young male child holding a sign saying 'I am not for sale'[14] and appears to be supportive of the principles of these reports. On the other hand, as might be expected, organizations are defensive (see Benson and

Wearing, 2012; Slowe, 2010) about their projects and the role they believe they fulfil. It is also evident that on the Project Abroad website there is a Child Protection Policy for Projects Abroad Volunteers.[15] A recent decision by Responsibletourism.com is to promote only those volunteer projects from partner organizations that commit to the promises which are outlined in the Guidelines for Partner Operators: Volunteering Directly with Vulnerable Children.[16] These include principles such as 'must be DBS checked', 'volunteers must be qualified', 'volunteer for no less than 4 weeks' and 'to work to UNICEF recommended levels'. As would be expected with this level of controversy a small but growing literature has begun to appear (see, for example, Rogerson and Slater, 2014; Reas, 2013; Proyrungroj, 2014). One of the more interesting papers is by a social worker practitioner working with volunteers in Peru (Wilson, 2015).

Personal benefits

Whilst these next sets of quotes are not necessarily directly related to sport, it is clear that the volunteer stories are predominantly positive about their volunteering experiences and that they perceived benefit from having taken part. Whilst once again, some of these quotes would not be out of place in many of the articles published on volunteer tourism (see Zahra *et al.*, 2007), in light of the growing level of criticisms regarding volunteer tourism it is a reminder that volunteer tourism involves both 'give and take' situations. Comments by participants to support this context include:

Life changing.

(Melissa)

one of those experiences which really touched me.

(Tanveer)

it was genuinely one of the best months of my life.

(Jasmine)

My life was changing every day, every hour, every second here in Cape Town and I knew it.

(Emma F)

Once I arrived back home, I was a changed man.

(Connor)

a significant moment for me, at 23 years of age, because it was my first step outside of the United States [and] it was certainly a new chapter in my life.

(Tyler)

I acquired a very impressive feature on my CV.

(Alice W)

[...] story of a sports placement with Projects Abroad. I managed to pass it off as a global perspective module for university as well, so it was a double bonus.

(Elliott)

it opened my eyes to a new world and to what life is all about.

(Sean)

I still look fondly upon my African drum that hangs in my room at home and remember all the happy memories that are associated with it.

(Alice W)

Some thoughts and reflections of the volunteers were linked to sport; the first two are volunteers who were clearly exhilarated to be able to train with world-class elite runners:

I was paired with Legesse, an athlete who can run 10 km in an impressive 31 minutes, and it was a true honour to train with this man.

(Gayle)

[...] connected me with a world-class elite runner to train with. We would meet before school and/or after school every day to run. He became my best friend while I was in Ethiopia.

(Erik)

The final two quotes in this section highlight what I believe sums up the sentiments held by the other volunteers in their stories:

The programme really gave me a good opportunity to improve both my coaching and personal skills. This was largely due to the level of responsibility I was given.... Consequently, I feel I achieved a lot during my placement.

(John)

[...] but the opportunities Projects Abroad provided encouraged me to grow as a teacher, coach, athlete and ultimately as a person.

(Erik)

As we see from the above quotes, when individuals reflect on their experiences as a volunteer, they often emphasize the lasting benefits they gain from volunteering in international settings. In the context of sport, whether training or coaching, from a critical standpoint we need to identify who gains more from the volunteer experiences. The local communities will meet different people throughout the year, and will be exposed to differing coaching and training styles, and perhaps even introduced to different sports, but the lasting impact on the person volunteering is something that they will take with them in the form of improving their skills, working in a multicultural setting and with underrepresented groups – which will arguably have a much longer lasting impact on the individual volunteers than those who will continue to live in the local communities. In the cases noted above, where the volunteers had the opportunity to train with world-class athletes, the volunteers might also have gained from the perspective of their own performance.

Concluding remarks

This chapter examined international volunteer tourism using sporting projects as the context. The concept of volunteering was outlined by demonstrating the complexity and challenges of this sector. Through using volunteer stories drawn from the largest UK volunteer tourism operator an analysis was undertaken highlighting three key themes:

1 sporting context;
2 working with children; and
3 personal benefits.

It is clear to see that in many instances the volunteers of sporting projects do not differ significantly from other volunteer tourists in terms of their general experiences. Surprise was evident in volunteer stories of their encounters of a developing country (i.e. culture shock, poverty) and in particular upon the limited sporting resources at their disposal to work with community recipients. Terms that you would expect to find linked to sport were evident and teaching, coaching and training were all part of the general rhetoric of volunteers. Volunteers were also very forthcoming about the level of talent that they saw and were pleased to be a part of improving sporting ability.

All of the volunteer stories were associated with working with children, which is currently a 'hot topic' and, as such, was discussed. In terms of the continuing debate around volunteers working with children, this chapter was not about siding with one end of the continuum or the other, but to outline that whilst much of this debate is linked to orphanages some of the issues are related more broadly. This then not only affects volunteer tourism but the broader context of international sport programmes that engage volunteers to deliver sport to children. Questions should be asked about the policies and practices to which they are adhering. To what extent are companies and volunteers having informed debates about what they should do?

The final theme examined the personal benefits to volunteers following their volunteer tourism experience. Whilst it is clear to see from the stories that some of the motivation to travel and volunteer was altruistic, it is also evident that volunteers benefited. Whilst some of these might be more closely aligned with cathartic and life-changing experiences, others are linked to CV building and/or university credits. Of course, what we do not have here is the voice of the 'other' and in order to offer a balanced view of this or any other study more than one stakeholder's voice needs to be heard.

Therefore, studies focusing on understanding how the local community and local field workers who work with organizations benefit will frame a broader understanding of the impacts of volunteer tourism. There is also the need to further consider the role of sport from a range of perspectives, because whilst sport (as noted above) was not listed as one of the top projects on the Projects Abroad website (refer back to Table 11.1), we still see from the volunteers that sport is playing an essential role in the associated projects volunteers spoke about. Sport adds another element to the volunteering journey, and sport is used a powerful tool to unite people across cultures and different backgrounds. But the challenge in all critical research is identifying who truly benefits from programmes associated with sport, volunteering and international development. This chapter outlined the voices of volunteers, and, as made evident from the data presented in this study, the Projects Abroad website includes voices of volunteers as a means of recruiting volunteers to work, train and gain new skills and experiences in international settings.

Notes

1 www.volunteerics.org/.
2 www.gvi.co.uk/volunteer-abroad/.
3 www.globalteer.org/.
4 www.projects-abroad.co.uk.
5 www.voluntourism.org/.
6 www.tourismconcern.org.uk/.
7 www.emeraldinsight.com/toc/whatt/7/2.
8 www.reconintvol.org.uk/2016/06/09/reconceptualising-international-volunteering/.
9 www.iso.org/iso/home/store/catalogue_tc/catalogue_detail.htm?csnumber=68548.
10 www.projects-abroad.co.uk/videos/?content=south-africa/sports-testimonial/.
11 Ambassadors for Children, www.ambassadorsforchildren.org/www2/.
12 www.nextgenerationnepal.org/File/The-Paradox-of-Orphanage-Volunteering.pdf.
13 www.tourismconcern.org.uk/.
14 www.tourismconcern.org.uk/campaigns/.

15 http://docs.projects-abroad.co.uk/uk/volunteer-projects/child-protection-policy/
child-protection-policy-for-volunteers.pdf.
16 www.responsibletravel.com/holidays/volunteering-with-children/travel-guide/
volunteering-with-children-our-guidelines.

References

Benson, A. (ed.). (2010). *Volunteer tourism: Theoretical frameworks and practical applications*. Abingdon: Routledge.
Benson, A. and Blackman, D. (2011). To distribute leadership or not? A lesson from the islands. *Tourism Management* 32(5): 1141–1149.
Benson, A. and Henderson, S. (2011). A strategic analysis of volunteer tourism organisations. *Service Industries Journal* 31(3): 405–424.
Benson, A. and Siebert, N. (2009). Volunteer tourism: Motivations of German participants in South Africa. *Annals of Leisure Research* 12(3–4): 295–314.
Benson, A.M. and Wearing, S. (2012). Volunteer tourism: Commodified trend or new phenomena. In O. Moufakkir and P.M. Burns (eds) *Controversies in tourism*. Wallingford: CABI (pp. 242–254).
Brown, S. (2005). Travelling with a purpose: Understanding the motives and benefits of volunteer vacationers. *Current Issues in Tourism* 8: 479–496.
Brown, S. and Morrison, A. (2003). Expanding volunteer vacation participation: An exploratory study on the mini-mission concept. *Tourism Recreation Research* 28 (3): 73–82.
Butcher, J. and Smith, P. (2015). *Volunteer tourism: The lifestyle politics of international development*. Abingdon: Routledge.
Clifton, J. and Benson, A.M. (2006). Planning for sustainable ecotourism: The case of research ecotourism in developing country destinations. Journal of Sustainable Tourism 14(3): 238–254.
Coghlan, A. (2008). Exploring the role of expedition staff in volunteer tourism. *International Journal of Tourism Research* 10(2): 183–191.
Coghlan, A. and Noakes, S. (2012). Towards an understanding of the drivers of commercialization in the volunteer tourism sector. *Tourism Recreation Research* 37(2): 123–131.
Dann, G. (1981). Tourism motivations: An appraisal. *Annals of Tourism Research* 8(2): 187–219.
Lyons, K.D. and Wearing, S. (eds). (2008). *Journeys of discovery in volunteer tourism: International case study perspective*. Wallingford: CABI.
McGehee, N. (2002). Alternative tourism and social movements. *Annals of Tourism Research* 29(1): 124–143.
McGehee, N.G. and Santos, C.A. (2005). Social change, discourse and volunteer tourism. *Annals of Tourism Research* 32(3): 760–779.
McIntosh, A.J. and Zahra, A. (2007). A cultural encounter through volunteer tourism: Towards the ideals of sustainable tourism? *Journal of Sustainable Tourism* 15(5): 541–556.
Mintel. (2008). Volunteer tourism–international – September 2008. *Mintel Reports*. www.reports.mintel.com/display/294955/?_cc=1.
Mostafanezhad, M. (2012). *Volunteer tourism: Popular humanitarianism in neoliberal times*. Abingdon: Routledge.

Palacios, C.M. (2010). Volunteer tourism, development and education in a post-colonial world: Conceiving global connections beyond aid. *Journal of Sustainable Tourism* 18(7): 861–878.

Proyrungroj, R. (2014). Orphan volunteer tourism in Thailand: Volunteer tourists' motivations and on-site experiences. *Journal of Hospitality & Tourism Research* DOI: 10.1177/1096348014525639.

Raymond, E.M. and Hall, C.M. (2008). The development of crosscultural (mis) understanding through volunteer tourism. *Journal of Sustainable Touris*m 16(5): 530–543.

Reas, P.J. (2013). 'Boy, have we got a vacation for you': Orphanage tourism in Cambodia and at the commodification and objectification of the orphaned child. *Thammasat Review* 16: 121–139.

Richter, L.M. and Norman, A. (2010). AIDS orphan tourism: A threat to young children in residential care. *Vulnerable Children and Youth Studies* 5(3): 217–229.

Rogerson, J.M. and Slater, D. (2014). Urban volunteer tourism: Orphanages in Johannesburg. *Urban Forum* 25(4): 483–499.

Simpson, K. (2004). 'Doing development': The gap year, volunteer-tourists and a popular practice of development. *Journal of International Development* 16: 681–692.

Slowe, P. (2010). Gap-year volunteers fulfil a vital role abroad. *Telegraph*. www.telegraph.co.uk/travel/hubs/gapyear/8110847/Gap-year-volunteers-fulfil-a-vital-role-abroad.html.

Stoddart, H. and Rogerson, C.M. (2004). Volunteer tourism: The case of habitat for humanity South Africa. *GeoJournal* 60(3): 311–318.

Tourism Research and Marketing (TRAM). (2008). *Volunteer tourism: A global analysis*. ATLAS Publications.

United Nations Children Fund. (2011). With the best intentions: A study of attitudes towards residential care in Cambodia. UNICEF.

Vrasti, W. (2013). *Volunteer tourism in the Global South: Giving back in neoliberal times*. Abingdon: Routledge.

Ward, L. (2007). You're better off backpacking: VSO warns about perils of 'voluntourism'. *Guardian*. www.guardian.co.uk/uk/2007/aug/14/students.charitable giving.

Wearing, S. (2001). *Volunteer tourism: Experiences that make a difference*. New York: CABI.

Wearing, S. (2004). Examining best practice in volunteer tourism. In R.A. Stebbins and M. Graham (eds) *Volunteering as leisure/leisure as volunteering: An international assessment*. Wallingford: CABI (pp. 209–224).

Wearing, S. and Grabowski, S (2011). Volunteer tourism and intercultural exchange. In A. Benson (ed.) *Volunteer tourism: Theory framework to practical applications*. Abingdon: Routledge (pp. 193–210).

Wilson, L. (2015). Finding the win-win providing supportive and enriching volunteer tourism experiences while promoting sustainable social change. *Worldwide Hospitality and Tourism Themes* 7(2): 201–207.

Zahra, A. and McGehee, N. (2013). Volunteer tourism: A host community capital perspective. *Annals of Tourism Research* 42(July): 22–45.

Zahra, A., Alison, J. and Mcintosh, A.J. (2007). Volunteer tourism: Evidence of cathartic tourist experiences. *Tourism Recreation Research* 32(1): 115–119.

Concluding comments and future directions in international sport volunteering research

Nicholas Wise and Angela M. Benson

Going forward

This book brings together a collection of chapters focusing on international sport volunteering. It starts what we hope will lead to a further expansion in the future of subsequent edited collections and a more coherent research agenda. As outlined in the Introduction, and recognized in a number of chapters, sport volunteering has a strong domestic base; but it is becoming more evident that international volunteering has seen increased popularity as a result of seemingly altruistic motives and increased mobility (Urry, 2000, 2007; Hall, 2005). There has been a recent focus in the field of event studies to focus on international experiences (see Smith *et al.*, 2014; Hannam *et al.*, 2016). By bringing together this collection of chapters we aimed to add diversity into what we consider to be the interdisciplinary nature of contemporary sports volunteering, and to span the arbitrary boundaries of the sport, events, leisure and tourism fields of study.

Going forward, this book includes a strong base of internationally informed sport volunteering studies. However, what we also recognize is that this book barely scratches the surface when examining the field of sport volunteering in an international context. This field is clearly both dynamic and diverse with a range of opportunities emerging, but we must also recognize that alongside these burgeoning opportunities is a long list of challenges emerging – thus raising a plethora of questions and issues. What is also evident is that the current literature offers few answers, although this book now goes some way to giving the field a starting point.

This collection presented a number of experiences and perspectives of international sport volunteering. Each chapter in this collection discussed international sport volunteering framed around events (Part I) or sport and development programmes (Part II). These two key themes connecting chapters show that these are currently the main areas that are being researched, and maybe to some extent demonstrate the accessibility of opportunities to undertake research. Arguably, the international focus is much clearer when we look at sport and development cases. We see participants, often from the global North, traveling to and volunteering in sport for development programmes in the global South. As this collection shows, Africa is a popular destination for sport and development programmes that predominantly attract international volunteers from Europe. The international focus in this case is explicit based on the host (the destination) population and the international volunteers who spend a predetermined (often very limited) amount of time in the host country. Looking at event and international sport volunteering and events, the distinct lines are much more blurred in terms of who is a local volunteer and who is an international volunteer. Because of this blurring, the international events chapters offer different theoretical understandings. These chapters argue volunteering is inherently linked to different dynamics positioning how we see events gaining from international exposure, and from other similar events. Some chapters focus on how international events are an opportunity for local volunteers to meet and interact with international volunteers, bound through shared interests, thereby showcasing how events create a sense of cohesion among international and local volunteers. While we do see shared interests among locals and international volunteers in the sport for development cases, we are also informed of power relations and we can frame how motivations differ among locals and internationals.

The chapters in this book present a range of different conceptual and methodological approach to shows the range of potential and future research development in this field of study. Some chapters in this collection outlined examples domestically, but there was still an international influence. Moreover, the perspectives overviewed suggest a framework for future research that can be applied to current and ongoing internationally focused sport volunteering research. As such, future research needs to build on the questions asked here in this collection and relate to new cases. While Africa is receiving much attention for its sport for development programmes, it is expected that more research focusing on programmes in parts of Asia and South America, especially, will attract attention from scholars critical of legacy initiatives following the hosting of mega sporting events. The theoretical guidance gained from the four sport for development chapters in this book will need to be expanded and challenged from a range of interdisciplinary approaches to broaden the scope of knowledge that aims to position motives and impacts of sport for development programmes in developing or emerging economy countries. Perhaps different challenges and perspectives will face the international events industry. There has been more emphasis on social and intangible benefits that destinations need to consider when bidding for and hosting events. Volunteering is seen a part of these wider discussion to encourage involvement, pride in place and a sense of community (see Getz, 2013; Minnaert, 2012; Smith, 2012; Wise and Perić, 2017). But again, the international focus needs further considered and brought more so into these discussions – because people seek to be a part of global spectacles such as the Olympic Games or Commonwealth Games, or travel to new places to experience a sport someone sincerely enjoys to connect with other members in that international community, as we have seen in the cases of Norway and Russia.

However, what is also evident is that there are many opportunities for individuals to volunteer in international settings, currently not discussed in this book. Another specific point is that engagement in research in some areas is still limited. When we conceived the idea for this book the call for chapters suggested the following topics, albeit that this was not considered to be an exhaustive list:

- Understanding the sport volunteer in an international context (who is the volunteer in regards to their behaviour, motivation, experience, gender, contribution, impact)? To what extent are they similar or different to other international volunteers (volunteers on projects such as humanitarian, conservation, medical)?
- Intercultural perspectives on international sport volunteering (a recent advert stated that 'sport is a universal language'; is this true? If so, what affect does it have on adaptation, culture confusion and cultural exchange? If not, what engagement is happening?).
- Supply side (which sectors are involved – private, public or third sector organizations? To what extent are partnerships being formed?).
- Sponsorship, funding and payment (how is international sport volunteering being funded?).
- Impact (social, economic, environmental) (is it sustainable?) upon people and places (host communities, volunteers, cities, townships – and are host communities in western cities less impacted than host communities in developing countries where international sport volunteering takes place?).
- Social development aspects (whose development, the volunteers' and/ or the participants'?).
- Legacy of volunteering in international sport volunteering – tangible and intangible (whose legacy – the country where the volunteering took place or the country the volunteers return to?) (To what extent do relationships continue after volunteers return home?) (Do episodic volunteers become long-term volunteers?).
- Management of key stakeholders (what are the issues related to the management of international sport volunteering?).
- The media is full of articles regarding the quality of volunteer tourism. Should the current academic debates and discussions around this include international sport volunteering?
- Critical reflections of self, including auto-ethnographies where the international volunteer critiques their role/position during the process of volunteering and conducting research.

And, whilst it is evident that some of the topics have been addressed within the book, there are clearly others that are still 'open' to extend the narrative of research in this area. What is clear is that we need to continue to ask questions and engage in critical discussion regarding 'international sport volunteering' in order to contribute to building a knowledge base which offers interdisciplinary insight. We must also work towards informing policies that are inclusive and establish valuable legacies in the very places where sport volunteering and international sport volunteering is most likely to play an important role in the future of leisure mobility and active participation. Therefore, we suggest that the future research agenda is initially set by addressing the gaps identified from the ideas when developing the book and by the research directions indicated by the book chapters.

References

Getz, D. (2013). *Event tourism*. Putnam Valley: Cognizant Communication Corporation.

Hall, C.M. (2005). *Tourism: Rethinking the social science of mobility*. Harlow: Pearson Education Ltd.

Hannam, K., Mostafanezhad, M. and Rickly, J. (eds). (2016). *Event mobilities: Politics, place and performance*. Abingdon: Routledge.

Minnaert, L. (2012). An Olympic legacy for all? The non-infrastructural outcomes of the Olympic Games for socially excluded groups (Atlanta 1996–Beijing 2008). *Tourism Management* 33(2): 361–370.

Smith, A. (2012). *Events and urban regeneration*. London: Routledge.

Smith, K.A., Lockstone-Binney, L., Holmes, K. and Baum, T. (eds). (2014). *Event volunteering: International perspectives on the event volunteering experience*. Abingdon: Routledge.

Urry, J. (2000). *Sociology beyond societies: Mobilities for the twenty-first century*. London: Routledge.

Urry, J. (2007). *Mobilities*. Cambridge: Polity Press.

Wise, N. and Perić, M. (2017). Sports tourism, regeneration and social impacts: New opportunities and directions for research, the case of Medulin, Croatia. In N. Bellini and C. Pasquinelli (eds) *Tourism in the city: Towards an integrative agenda on urban tourism*. Berlin: Springer Verlag (pp. 311–320).

Index

Page numbers in *italics* denote tables, those in **bold** denote figures.

Africa, sport development in 212–30; Cameroon 214–15, 218–30; Namibia 145–62; Zambia 145, 165, 166, 170–84, *174*, 217
age: and golf volunteering 109–11, *110*; and volunteer tourism 235
Allen, J.B. 26
Allport, Gordon 201
altruistic motivations 1, 43, 52–4, 105, 214, 217, 220–3, 236
Ambassadors for Children 244
Amnesty International 197
Anderson, B. 63, 68
Argentina *239*
associative-supportive motivation 137
Athens Olympic Games (2004) 49
Atlanta Olympic Games (1996) 46, 48–9
Australia: golf tournaments 98, 103, 104, *104*, 105, 106–14, *109*, *110*, *113*; levels of volunteering 1
autoethnography 64–5

Bach, T. 190
Banda, D. 175, 182
Bang, H. 99
Barcelona Olympic Games (1992) 41
Bargal, D. 127–8
Barnett, Tricia 244
Barnett Donaghy, T. 197–8
Barros, C.P. 100
Bartle, M. 26
Barton, D. 199–200
Baum, T. 5
Beacom, A. 215
Beijing Olympic Games (2008) 48

belonging, sense of 62–4, 67–9, 72–3
Berman, M. 192
Bhabha, H. 215
Bolivia *239*
Botswana 151, 215
Bradbury, S. 153
Bramham, P. 8–9
Briggs, R. 191
Brown, Sally 236, 244
Brunel University 180

Callanan, M. 214
Cambodia 234
Cameroon 214–15, 218–30
Cameroon Cricket Federation (CCF) 215, 218–29
Canada 2
Cater, C.I. 25
Chalip, L. 4
Chavis, D. 63, 68
Chelladurai, P. 99
children: cultural programmes with 40, 45, 46–57, *47*, *50*, *53*; volunteering at ski flying events 136–7; working with 243–5, 247–8
Chileshe, Clement 180
China 48, *239*
Clarke, A. 24
Clary, E.G. 217, 227
Cleveland/Akron Gay Games (2014) 77, 78, 80–94, *83*
Clifton, J. 237
Cnaan, R.A. 105
co-creation in events 21–36
Coalter, F. 162, 167, 168, 195
Cochrane, F. 197

Collins, M. 8
commercialization of volunteer tourism 236
Commonwealth Games, Glasgow (2014) 60–1, 64–73
community, sense of 4, 34–5
community engagement, volunteer tourism 237
compensation 25–6
Conference on InterAmerican Student Projects (CIASP) 213–14
contact theory 201–6
Costa Rica 239
Coy, P. 197
Coyne, B.S. 105
Coyne, E.J.S. 105
creativity-based volunteering 39–57, 47, 50, 53; defining 44–5
Cresswell, T. 63–4, 67, 72
Cricket Without Boundaries (CWB) 214, 215, 218–29
Csikszentmihalyi, M. 25
cultural awareness development, IDEALS programme 153–4
Cultural Olympiads 39–41; Sochi (2014) 46, 47, 49–56, 50, 53
cultural programmes 39–57, 47, 50, 53
Cuskelly, G. 100, 124

Daniels, D. 200
Dann, G.M.S. 99
Darcy, S. 4
Darnell, S. 188, 212–13, 217, 224
Darvill, G. 200, 201
Davis Smith, J. 196
de Coubertin, Pierre 190
Debord, G. 80, 93
demographics of volunteering: golf tournaments 108–12, 109, 110; volunteer tourism 235
Department of International Development, UK 234
dependency theory 216, 221, 222–3, 227
development see sport development
Dewey, John 199
Dirkx, J.M. 200
dogsledding races 22, 25, 27–35
Doherty, A. 124
Dunn, S. 197
Dwyer, P.C. 43

East Timor 193, 194
Easton, S. 5–6

Ecuador 239
EduSport 165, 171–84, 174
emotional phase of volunteering 126, 127, 133–4, 133
employment opportunities, student volunteers 160
employment status, and golf volunteering 110, 110, 111
Eraut, M. 200
established phase of volunteering 126, 127, 134–5, 135
Ethiopia 239
ethnicity: and golf volunteering 111
event gypsies/nomads 128, 136
event volunteerism 6–8, 125; creativity-based volunteering 39–57, 47, 50, 53; Cultural Olympiads 39–41, 46, 47, 49–56, 50, 53; dogsledding races 22, 25, 27–35; Gay Games 77, 78, 80–94, 83; Glasgow Commonwealth Games (2014) 60–1, 64–73; indirect volunteering 122–38, 131, 132, 135; ski flying events 128–38, 131, 132, 133, 135; social legacies of 77–94; transnational migrants 60–74; typology of sport events 7; value creation in 21–36; see also golf tournaments; Olympic and Paralympic Games
experienced phase of volunteering 126, 127, 133–4, 133

Fairley, S. 105–6
Federation of Gay Games (FGG) 82
FIFA (Fédération Internationale de Football Association) 151
Fiji 239
Finnmark Race, Norway 22, 25, 27–35
flow 25
Foley, G. 196
Football 4 Peace project 196–7
Football for Hope Project 151
Frank Fredericks Foundation 149, 150
Fredericks, Frank 150
Freire, P. 202
Friendship Force International (FFI) 46

Gallarza, M.G. 6
Galz and Goals project, Namibia 149–50
García, I. 63
Gay Games 77, 78, 80–94, 83
gender: and golf volunteering 108–9, 110, 111; and volunteer tourism 235

Georgeou, N. 147
Ghana *239*
Giddens, A. 79–80, 93, 203
Gilbert, D. 83
Giroux, H. *195*
Giulianotti, R. 191
Glasgow Commonwealth Games
    (2014) 60–1, 64–73
Globalteer 234
Gnecco de Ruiz, M.T. 197
Goldblatt, J. 104, *104*, 111
Golf Tournament Attendee Push–Pull
    Factors Model 98, 99–101, **100**, 114
golf tournaments 98–116; volunteer
    demographics 108–12, *109*, *110*;
    volunteer motivation 99–101, **100**,
    101, 102, 103–6, *104*, 112–15, *113*,
    115
Golf Volunteer Engagement Strategy
    (GoVolES) framework 98, 101–2,
    101, 112–13, 114–15
Grabowski, S. 234
Grattan, A. 217
Gratton, C. 201
Greece 49, 190
Gruneau, R. 91
Gursoy, D. 86–7
Gusmão, Xanana 194
GVI 234

Haanpää, M. 21
Haldane, David Andrew 4
Hall, C.M. 69, 237
Hamm, S. 99
Handy, F. 147–8
Harris, J. 64
Haski-Leventhal, D. 127–8
Hayhurst, L. 212–13, 217
health education programmes 149–50,
    169, 171–2, 175, 181–2, 219, 220,
    229
Hewitt, L.N. 111
HIV/AIDS education 149–50, 169,
    171–2, 175, 181–2, 219, 220, 229
Holmes, K. 168
Houlihan, B. 8, 9, 148
Hustinx, L. 124
Hwang, S. 109–10
Hylton, K. 8–9

IDEALS *see* International Development
    through Excellence and Leadership in
    Sport (IDEALS)

Iditarod, Alaska 22, 25, 27–35
Illich, Ivan 213–14
India *239*
indirect volunteering 122–38, *131*, *132*,
    135
input-oriented volunteers 43; *see also*
    altruistic motivations
Institute for Cultural Programs, St.
    Petersburg 49–51, **50**
International Citizen Service (ICS) 234
International Development through
    Excellence and Leadership in Sport
    (IDEALS) 165, 166, 167; Namibia
    145–62; Zambia 145, 165, 166,
    170–84, *174*
International Golf Volunteer
    Engagement Strategy (iGoVolES) 98,
    115–16, **115**
International Inspiration (IN) 145
International Olympic Committee
    (IOC) 41, 190–1
International Olympic Truce
    Foundation (IOTF) 191
International Paint Pals (IPP) 40, 45,
    46–57, **47**, **50**, **53**
international sport volunteering,
    literature review 5–6
inverse integration 82

Jackson, E.N. 103–4
Jamaica *239*
Jeanes, R. 189, 196, 204
Jenner, J.R. 105
Jepson, J. 24
Jones, A. 147
Jurowski, C. 99

Kaldor, M. 198
Kay, T. 153
Keipert, S. 100
Kendall, K. 86–7
Kenya 215, *239*
Kidd, B. 148
Kiviniemi, M.T. 124
Kolb, D.A. 199
Kovan, J.T. 200
Kristiansen, E. 4

Ladies Professional Golf Association
    (LPGA) 111
leadership skills development, IDEALS
    programmes 152–3, 159–60, 165,
    166, 167, 171–3

learning *see* volunteer learning
Lee, H. 99–100
legacies, social: defining 166–7; of sport development programmes 165–84; of sport events 77–94
leisure model of volunteering 44
Levermore, R. 215
LGBTQI sports events 77, 78, 80–94, 83
Li, S. 86, 91
life-cycle of volunteers approach 126–7, **126**
Lindsey, I. 217
Liverpool John Moores University (LJMU), IDEALS Namibia programme 145–62
Lockstone, L. 5
London Olympic Games (2012) 2, 145, 165
Longino, Linden 45, 46, 51, 54, 55
Lough, B. 153
love of sport motivation 99, 112, *113*, 129
Lund, K.A. 35
Lyu, S.O. 99–100

McCabe, S. 86, 91
McGehee, N. 235, 237
McGivney, V. 199
McGloin, C. 147
McGlynn, C. 196, 200
MacLean, J. 99
McMillan, D. 63, 68
McNamee, M. 203
Mair, J. 79
Manji, F. 213
Marston, C. 111
Marta, E. 124
Matheson, C.M. 104, *104*, 111
Messner, M. 82
Mexico 213–14, *239*
Mexico City Olympic Games (1968) 40–1
migrants, transnational 60–74
Millennium Development Goals (MDGs) 169–70, 212
Minnaert, L. 87, 90
Moital, I. 102
Mongolia *239*
Moon, K.S. 102
Morgan, H. 161
Morocco *239*
motivations for volunteering 1–2, 61–2;

altruistic 1, 43, 52–4, 105, 214, 217, 220–3, 236; cultural programmes 42–3, 52–6, 53; dogsledding races 29–32; Gay Games 89; golf tournaments 99–101, **100**, **101**, 102, 103–6, *104*, 112–15, *113*, **115**; indirect volunteering 130–5, *132*, *133*, *135*, 136, 137; love of sport 99, 112, *113*, 129; personal benefits 26, 29–32, 43, 62, **100**, 104, *104*, 105, 130–5, *132*, *133*, *135*, 147–8, 217, 226–7, 236, 245–7; push–pull factors 99–101, **100**, **101**, 102, 103–6, *104*, 112–15, *113*, **115**, 236; satisfaction 6, 43, 53; ski flying events 130–5, *132*, *133*, *135*, 136, 137; skill development 29–30, 89, 132, *132*, 217, 226–7; social benefits 30, 54–5, 62, 217, 225–6; sport development 147–8, 214, 216–18, 220–9; student volunteers 147–8; transnational migrants 66–7; and value creation 24, 29–32; volunteer tourism 236, 245–7
Museum of Greek Children's Art, Athens 49
Mwaanga, O. 169–70

Namibia, IDEALS programme 145–62
Namibia Football Association (NFA) 149–50
neo-colonialism 237
New Zealand 103
newcomer phase of volunteering **126**, 127, 132–3, *132*
Next Generation Nepal (NGN) 244
Nichols, G. 5, 124, 217
nomads, event 128, 136
nomination phase of volunteering **126**, 127, 130–2, *132*
Nordvall, A. 22
Norman, A. 244
Northern Ireland 193, *193*, 197, 201
Norway: Finnmark Race 22, 25, 27–35; indirect volunteering 122, 123, 128–38, *131*, *132*, *133*, *135*

O'Coill, C. 213
Okada, C. 191
Olympic and Paralympic Games: ancient Greece 190; Athens (2004) 49; Atlanta (1996) 46, 48–9; Barcelona (1992) 41; Beijing (2008)

48; conflictual contexts 190–1;
Cultural Olympiads 39–41, 46, 47,
49–56, 50, 53; London (2012) 2,
145, 165; Mexico City (1968) 40–1;
Sochi (2014) 46, 47, 49–56, 50, 53;
Vancouver (2010) 2
Olympic Truce 190–1
Omoto, A.M. 137
output-oriented volunteers 43; see also
personal benefit motivations

Page, S. 69
Palacios, C.M. 234
Parent, M.M. 128, 136
peace building see sport for
development and peace (SDP)
programmes
Peace Players project 196–7
Pearce, J. 124
Perold, H. 217–18, 226
personal benefit motivations 26, 29–32,
43, 62, 100, 104, 104, 105, 130–5,
132, 133, 135, 147–8, 217, 226–7,
236, 245–7
Perth International golf tournament
(2014), Australia 98, 106–14, 109,
110, 113
Peru 239
Philippines 239
Physically Active Youth (PAY) 149,
150–1
place, sense of 62–4
post-colonial theory 215–16, 219, 221,
222, 226, 227, 228–9
Powell, L. 153
Prasad, A. 215
Preuss, H. 80, 91, 92, 93, 166
Priest, E. 102
Professional Golf Association (PGA)
98, 102–3, 105, 106, 107, 111, 115
Projects Abroad 234, 237–47, 238,
239, 248
push–pull factors 99–101, 100, 101,
102, 103–6, 104, 112–15, 113, 115,
236
Putnam, R.D. 227

Raymond, E.M. 237
Razack, S.H. 215–16
Red Cross 197
Responsibletourism.com 245
retirement, and golf volunteering
109–11, 110

retirement phase of volunteering 126,
127, 135
Richter, L.M. 244
Ringland, T. 198
Ringuet-Riot et al. 124
Romania 239
Rose, G. 63
routine-based volunteering 44
Russia, Sochi Olympic Games (2014)
46, 47, 49–56, 50, 53
Rwanda 215

Sabatier, P.A. 162
safe space 203–4
Said, E. 215, 226
Samoa 239
satisfaction of volunteering 6, 43, 53
Schlesinger, T. 137
Schulenkorf, N. 203, 204
SCORE 149, 151–2
Scotland, Glasgow Commonwealth
Games (2014) 60–1, 64–73
self-interest motivations see personal
benefit motivations
sense of belonging 62–4, 67–9, 72–3
sense of community 4, 34–5
sense of place 62–4
Shaw, S. 8
Shepherd, M. 217
Sherraden, M. 167
Siebert, N. 236
Simpson, K. 234
ski flying events 128–38, 131, 132, 133,
135
skill development, as motivation 29–30,
89, 132, 132, 217, 226–7
skill-based volunteering 44–5
Slow, Peter 238
Smith, K. 105
Smith-Swan, S. 128, 136
Snyder, M. 137
Sochi Institute of Fashion, Business and
Law (SIMBiP) 49, 50
Sochi Olympic Games (2014) 46, 47,
49–56, 50, 53
social aspects of volunteering 30, 54–5,
62, 217, 225–6
social capital 4, 26, 133, 161, 203,
216–17, 218, 219, 227–9; see also
personal benefit motivations
social legacies: defining 166–7; of sport
development programmes 165–84; of
sport events 77–94

South Africa 151, 193, 234, *239*
Spaaij, R. 189, 196, 203, 204
Spain 41
Special Olympics Namibia (SON) 149, 151
Spinner-Halev, J. 200
sport clubs, indirect volunteering 122–38, *131*, *132*, *135*
sport development 8–10, 212–30; defining 148; HIV/AIDS education 149–50, 169, 171–2, 175, 181–2, 219, 220, 229; IDEALS Namibia programme 145–62; IDEALS Zambia programme 145, 165, 166, 170–84, *174*; motivations for volunteering 214, 216–18, 220–9; social legacies of 165–84; sport for development and peace (SDP) programmes 188–207, *193*; volunteer tourist packages 234–48, *238*, *239*
sport events 6–8; creativity-based volunteering 39–57, *47*, *50*, *53*; Cultural Olympiads 39–41, 46, 47, 49–56, *50*, *53*; dogsledding races 22, 25, 27–35; Gay Games 77, 78, 80–94, *83*; Glasgow Commonwealth Games (2014) 60–1, 64–73; indirect volunteering 122–38, *131*, *132*, *135*; ski flying 128–38, *131*, *132*, *133*, *135*; ski flying events 128–38, *131*, *132*, *133*, *135*; social legacies of 77–94; transnational migrants 60–74; typology of 7; value creation in 21–36; *see also* golf tournaments; Olympic and Paralympic Games
sport for development and peace (SDP) programmes 188–207, *193*
Sport in Action (SIA) 165, 171–84, *174*
sport volunteering: economic value of 4; levels of 2; literature review 2–5
Sri Lanka *239*
Stebbins, R. 25–6
Stevenson, D. 83
straight volunteers, at Gay Games 87–8
Strigas, A.D. 103–4
student volunteers: IDEALS Namibia programme 145–62; IDEALS Zambia programme 165, 166, 170–84, *174*
Sugden, J. 194
Sustainable Development Goals (SDGs) 170, 212
Symons, C. 84–5

Taks, M. 166, 167
Tanzania 145, 151, *239*
Team Leader role, IDEALS Namibia programme 159–60
Thoits, P.A. 111
Thomas, S. 214
Timor-Leste 193, 194
Togo *239*
Tolman, E.C. 99
tourism *see* volunteer tourism
Tourism Concern 237, 244
tourism motivation theory 99
transgressive potential of volunteering 77–94
transnational migrants 60–74
Treuren, G.J. 124, 137
trust, in SDP programmes 202–4
Tusting, K. 199–200

Uganda 215
UK Sport *see* International Development through Excellence and Leadership in Sport (IDEALS)
UNICEF 149–50, 191, 244, 245
United Kingdom: economic value of sport volunteering 4; Glasgow Commonwealth Games (2014) 60–1, 64–73; levels of volunteering 1, 2, *3*; London Olympic Games (2012) 2, 145, 165
United Nations 48, 191, 215; Millennium Development Goals (MDGs) 169–70, 212; Sustainable Development Goals (SDGs) 170, 212
United Nations Sport for Development and Peace International Working Group (UNSDPWG) 169
United States: Atlanta Olympic Games (1996) 46, 48–9; Cleveland/Akron Gay Games (2014) 77, 78, 80–94, *83*; golf tournaments 102–3, 104, *104*; Iditarod, Alaska 22, 25, 27–35; levels of volunteering 1, 2
Uysal, M. 99

value creation in events 21–36
Vancouver Olympic Games (2010) 2
veterinarians 25, 26, 28, 29, 31
Vietnam *239*
Vikersund, Norway 128–38, *131*, *132*, *133*, *135*
volunteer cube model 123, 125–8, **126**, 130–5, *132*, *133*, *135*, 136–7

volunteer learning 8, 199–201, 204–6;
    cultural awareness development
    153–4; leadership skills development
    152–3, 159–60, 165, 166, 167,
    171–3; skill development 29–30, 89,
    132, *132*, 217, 226–7
volunteer stages and transitions model
    (VSTM) **126**, 127–8
volunteer tourism 5, 214;
    commercialization of 236; defining
    235; Gay Games 82–3, 85–7; golf
    tournaments 99–101, **100**, 107, 112;
    packages 27, 234–48, *238, 239*;
    value creation in events 21–36;
    working with children 243–5, 247–8
volunteering: defining 25–6, 166; levels
    of 1
volunteers, categorizing 123–4; *see also*
    volunteer cube model

Waddell, Tom 82
Wallace Group universities, UK
    171–84, *174*
Watanabe, Y. 100

Wearing, S. 9, 214, 234, 235, 236
'what is in it for me?' motivation *see*
    personal benefit motivations
White, P. 203
Whitford, M. 79
Williamson, A. 197
Willis, O. 229
Wilson, J. 62, 124, 126–7
Wilson, L. 105, 109
Woehrle, L.M. 197
Wollebæk, D. 26
Won, D. 109–10
World Bank 168, 213

Yazawa, Y. 197
Young, K. 191

Zahra, A. 237
Zambia 217; IDEALS programme 145,
    165, 166, 170–84, *174*
Zambian National Sport Development
    Conference 175
Zàtori, A. 24, 36

For Product Safety Concerns and Information please contact our EU
representative GPSR@taylorandfrancis.com
Taylor & Francis Verlag GmbH, Kaufingerstraße 24, 80331 München, Germany